T0312008

Television in the Streaming Era

This groundbreaking study explores transformations in the TV industry under the impact of globalizing forces and digital technologies. Chalaby investigates the making of a digital value chain and the distinct value-adding segments that form the new video ecosystem. He provides a full account of the industry's global shift from the development of TV formats and transnational networks to the emergence of tech giants and streaming platforms. The author takes a deep dive into the infrastructure (communication satellites, subsea cable networks, data centres) and technology (cloud computing, streaming software) underpinning this ecosystem through the prism of global value chain theory. The book combines empirical data garnered during twenty years of researching the industry and offers unique insights from television and tech executives.

Jean K. Chalaby was born in Geneva and studied at the University of Lausanne before undertaking his PhD at the London School of Economics. He joined the Department of Sociology at City, University of London, in 2000, where he is currently Professor of International Communication. He is the author of several books and multiple articles published in world-leading journals of media and communication.

Television in the Streaming Era
The Global Shift

Jean K. Chalaby

City, University of London

CAMBRIDGE
UNIVERSITY PRESS

CAMBRIDGE
UNIVERSITY PRESS

Shaftesbury Road, Cambridge CB2 8EA, United Kingdom

One Liberty Plaza, 20th Floor, New York, NY 10006, USA

477 Williamstown Road, Port Melbourne, VIC 3207, Australia

314–321, 3rd Floor, Plot 3, Splendor Forum, Jasola District Centre, New Delhi – 110025, India

103 Penang Road, #05–06/07, Visioncrest Commercial, Singapore 238467

Cambridge University Press is part of Cambridge University Press & Assessment, a department of the University of Cambridge.

We share the University's mission to contribute to society through the pursuit of education, learning and research at the highest international levels of excellence.

www.cambridge.org
Information on this title: www.cambridge.org/9781009199315

DOI: 10.1017/9781009199285

First published 2023

A catalogue record for this publication is available from the British Library.

Library of Congress Cataloging-in-Publication Data
Names: Chalaby, Jean K., author.
Title: Television in the streaming era : the global shift / Jean Chalaby.
Description: Cambridge, United Kingdom ; New York, NY : Cambridge University Press, 2022. | Includes bibliographical references and index.
Identifiers: LCCN 2022022816 (print) | LCCN 2022022817 (ebook) | ISBN 9781009199315 (hardback) | ISBN 9781009199261 (paperback) | ISBN 9781009199285 (epub)
Subjects: LCSH: Streaming video. | Internet television. | Television broadcasting. | BISAC: BUSINESS & ECONOMICS / International / General
Classification: LCC HD9697.V542 C43 2022 (print) | LCC HD9697.V542 (ebook) | DDC 006.7/876–dc23/eng/20220524
LC record available at https://lccn.loc.gov/2022022816
LC ebook record available at https://lccn.loc.gov/2022022817

ISBN 978-1-009-19931-5 Hardback
ISBN 978-1-009-19926-1 Paperback

To Felicity, Lucy, and Jemima, my in-house streaming experts

Contents

List of Figures	*page* ix
List of Tables	xi
Acknowledgements	xiii
List of Abbreviations	xv
Introduction	1
1 Global Communication and the GVC Framework	10
2 The Making of a Digital GVC	24
3 The Rise of Networks	36
4 The Rise of Platforms	56
5 Technology Designed for Scale	74
6 Infrastructure Built at Scale	93
7 Content Production	102
8 Media Delivery	120
9 Digital Disruption, Firm Behaviour, and Industry Structure	143
10 The Transnational Media Firm	158
11 Formulating GVC-Oriented Policies	175
Conclusion	189
Personal Communications and Interviews by the Author	193
Notes	195
References	199
Index	225

Figures

2.1 The making of a global value chain   *page* 33

2.2 The television GVC   35

9.1 Structure of the UK independent production sector, by turnover   150
bracket, 2021

10.1 The local/global organisational matrix of the transnational media firm   174

Tables

2.1 Telecom operators' major acquisitions in the media and entertainment sector, 2013–19   *page* 27

3.1 Korean TV exports, 2016–18 (in US$ millions)   39

3.2 Values and shares of creative goods exports, 2002–15 (in US$ millions)   41

3.3 World's top 20 travelling TV formats, 2020   46

3.4 US TV network brands established in the EU, ranked by number of localised services, 2017   52

3.5 European TV network brands established in the EU, ranked by number of localised services, 2017   53

4.1 Type of platform by streaming business model   66

4.2 Leading international SVoD platforms, by number of subscribers, November 2021   68

4.3 Leading international AVoD platforms, by advertising revenue, 2021   70

4.4 Leading international video-sharing platforms, by number of monthly users, November 2021   71

4.5 Leading international niche streaming platforms, 2021   73

5.1 Leading European video neighbourhoods, 2021   78

5.2 Streaming services launched in the mid-2000s, by launch date   83

5.3 Key CDN providers, by launch date   87

6.1 Cable rates from Britain to selected countries (per word), 1890 vs 1902   96

6.2 Median prices per month at 10 Gbit/s, selected subsea cable routes, 2015 vs 2019   96

6.3 Global application traffic share, 2021   100

6.4 Global mobile application traffic share, 2021   100

7.1 Top ten global TV studios, by estimated size and revenue, 2020   109

8.1 Media delivery: past and present 126

8.2 Outsourcing by British broadcasters in media delivery 127

8.3 Ericsson's key acquisitions in the media delivery chain 132

8.4 Communications satellite operators with global capabilities, 2021 135

8.5 Intelsat's customer set, 2019–20 136

8.6 Global CDNs for the media and entertainment sector, 2021 138

9.1 Lead firms' revenue and market capitalisation, 2019–21 149

9.2 Tech giants active in media delivery or streaming, by annual revenue, 2020 155

9.3 Facebook's and Google's advertising revenue, 2017–20 155

10.1 International audience for India's five top YouTube channels, by geographical location, October 2021 164

10.2 Ten wealthiest football clubs' YouTube presence (key metrics), October 2021 166

10.3 US sports leagues' YouTube presence (key metrics, main channel), October 2021 167

10.4 Typical organisational configurations of firms in the TV GVC 169

11.1 Development impact of GVCs: selected highlights 181

Acknowledgements

This book is the culmination of several years of research and would not have seen the light of day without support from friends and colleagues. I am thankful to all the interviewees for their time and cooperation (see full list of interviewees at the end of the book). Their insights into the TV industry have been invaluable. I would like to express my deep gratitude to the series editors, the anonymous reviewers, and colleagues in the GVC network for their kind support, comments, and feedback. I would like to thank Duke University Press; the European Audiovisual Observatory; K7 Media; Pact, Oliver & Ohlbaum; and Sandvine for granting me permission to include licensed material. I am also grateful to Jane, my wife, for the first edit of the manuscript, and the entire production team at Cambridge University Press.

Abbreviations

AI/ML	artificial intelligence and machine learning
AVoD	advertising video on demand
AWS	Amazon Web Services
BVoD	broadcaster video on demand
CDN	content delivery network
DBS	direct broadcast satellite
DTH	direct to home
EAO	European Audiovisual Observatory
ECS	European Communications Satellite
EU	European Union
FVoD	free video on demand
Gbit/s	gigabytes per second
GCC	global commodity chain
GPN	global production network
GVC	global value chain
HAS	HTTP adaptive streaming
HTTP	hypertext transfer protocol
IBC	International Broadcasting Convention
IETF	Internet Engineering Task Force
IP	internet protocol
IP	intellectual property (Chapter 11 only)
IPTV	internet protocol television
ISP	internet service provider
ITU	International Telecommunication Union
OCWG	Open Cables Working Group
PoP	point of presence
SMPTE	Society of Motion Picture and Television Engineers
SVoD	subscription video on demand
TNC	transnational corporation
TVoD	transactional video on demand
vMVPD	virtual multichannel video programming distributor
VoD	video on demand

Introduction

Two shifts are transforming television: digitisation and globalisation. Internet-based video delivery, the uptake of cloud computing in the industry, mobile video consumption, and the rise of streaming platforms, are all phenomena connected to the process of *digitisation*. Internet protocol (IP)–based video transport is powering the transition from broadcasting to streaming, thereby changing the way content is distributed and accessed. The use of cloud computing is growing fast because it delivers an unprecedented amount of computing power and capacity to media firms at a fraction of the infrastructure costs (Chapters 3, 4, and 8). Video is increasingly accessed via mobile devices, and streaming is among the most popular activities for mobile users (Chapter 6). The digital shift is evolving business models. Platforms dominate television's streaming age the way networks prevailed in the broadcasting era (Chapters 3 and 4). Media conglomerates are edging towards a direct-to-consumer (DCT) business model, revolutionising the way content rights are distributed and monetised (Chapters 3 and 9).

The second shift is *globalisation*, which combines with the first to change the scope and architecture of the TV industry. Broadcasting was a national industry that progressively internationalised, streaming is essentially a global industry that is progressively localising. The scale of tech firms and streaming platforms operating in television is unprecedented (Chapters 3 and 9). Streaming is accelerating the global integration of the industry, whose structure is underpinned by transnational production networks. They involve interdependent lead firms and suppliers that collaborate across industry segments and national borders (Chapters 7 and 8).

This research analyses the processes at the heart of this dual revolution, it examines its wider implications and addresses the following question: how is the scope and structure of the TV industry changing as it enters the digital economy? Which new forces prevail in TV production, distribution, and consumption? The book answers by applying the global value chain (GVC) framework and extending it to the study of *digital value chains*. It underscores the historicity of GVCs and their embeddedness in global capitalism, and analyses their transformation as they enter the digital realm.

This research contributes to media and communication studies' understanding of globalisation. We are accustomed to thinking *about* media globalisation. We know that a global media system exists, we know about its major constituents (technology, regulations, businesses), we speculate about the implications of this system for culture and democracy (e.g. Herman and McChesney, 1997; McChesney and Schiller, 2003; Nordenstreng and Schiller, 1979; Thussu, 2019; Winseck and Jin, 2012), but progress needs to be made in our understanding of its inner mechanisms. Shifting the analysis to the global TV industry as a whole, this research aims to think media globalisation *through*. How does it work from the inside? Which dynamics are brought into play, and how do they reshape the media industries?

Television is changing and our understanding of the term needs to be defined (Johnson, 2019). It is notoriously complex to fathom as it encompasses multiple functions. Television is, according to Jason Mittel, altogether 'a commercial industry, a democratic institution, a textual form, a site of cultural representation, a part of everyday life, and a technological medium' (Mittel, 2009: 2). For this research, the most pressing task is to define the new technological and industrial contours of the medium.

A first distinction must be drawn between the TV industry and video ecosystem (Chapter 6), which overlap but are not synonymous. Today, video is streamed and published by organisations whose core competence does not lie within the industry. Social media entertainment does not equate television (Cunningham and Craig, 2019). Platforms such as Facebook, Instagram, and Twitter participate in the video ecosystem at large but do not play an active role in the TV industry. By way of contrast, *video-centric* platforms such as Facebook Watch, TikTok, Twitch, and YouTube, which commission programming and/or pay content creators, are relevant (Chapter 4).

In particular, YouTube sits squarely at the heart of contemporary televisual culture. As Burgess and Green write: 'YouTube is now mainstream media' (Burgess and Green, 2018: 55). In many countries, young people spend more time on the platform than watching linear television (Chapter 9). YouTube's advertising revenue stood at US$19.8 billion in 2020 (Table 9.3), and broadcasters are acutely aware of the presence of the streamer in the advertising market (Greenaway, interview 2019). But broadcasters are also engaging with the platform at multiple levels, to extend viewers' engagement, reach younger audiences, and raise the awareness of their content brands (Frot-Coutaz, 2019).[1]

The distinction between video and television is bound to be subject to debate at times of fast-evolving business models and pivoting platforms.

In addition, television itself is expanding in size and scope. Today, it embraces several access modes, transmission paths, and financing models. In terms of access, content can either be scheduled and watched on a *linear* channel, or stacked up on a platform and consumed *on demand*. With respect to delivery, there are five options:

- terrestrial transmission: the TV signal is broadcast terrestrially over the airwaves on a specific frequency from an antenna to a tuner;
- satellite transmission: the signal is transmitted from a satellite via a dish to a tuner or set-top box;
- cable transmission: cable delivery uses a regional headend and a closed cable network to transmit the signal to viewers' homes;
- internet protocol television (IPTV) uses a closed internet network operated by a single internet service provider (ISP) to deliver video to a set-top-box;
- over-the-top (OTT) delivers content (scheduled, live, or on demand) over the open Internet and across an open delivery chain, using multiple ISPs to reach multiple devices (Ingold, 2020).

The first three delivery mechanisms are known as broadcasting, and the last two are referred to as streaming. Television encompasses both delivery modes, and many content providers integrate conventional transmission delivery mechanisms (terrestrial, cable, and satellite) with OTT, adopting a hybrid solution to video delivery (Ingold, 2020).

The business models of linear television have remained unchallenged for several decades: free-to-air stations are financed via advertising or a public licence and pay-to-view channels can be accessed via transactional or subscription payments. These can be complemented by additional financial streams, such as carriage fees for cable and satellite channels on pay-TV platforms.

Four payment models prevail in the video on demand (VoD) universe. With subscription video on demand (SVoD), members pay a monthly fee for access to the full catalogue of a streaming platform. Transactional video on demand (TVoD) involves a financial transaction for each request, and advertising video on demand (AVoD) implies an ad-based funding model. Video sharing (e.g. YouTube, essentially financed through advertising), and broadcaster video on demand (BVoD), which covers the platforms of commercial broadcasters, fall under the AVoD payment model but differ in terms of platform logic (Chapter 4). The streaming services of European public service broadcasters fall into the free video on demand (FVoD) category, albeit users need to hold a TV licence which they have either paid for or received for free as part of a means-tested regime. Many platforms adopt a hybrid payment model and use tiered pricing to offer different levels of package (Chapter 4). OTT (delivery) and VoD (mode of access) are often confused, but VoD can be delivered via various transmission mechanisms, including OTT, IPTV, and cable and satellite (Ingold, 2020).

The contours of the TV industry as it enters the digital economy become clearer: it has expanded from broadcasting to streaming, encompassing new delivery modes and payment models. The connection points between 'old' and 'new' television are multiple. New platforms and old networks differ in many respects, but they also hire staff from a similar talent pool, and share many suppliers from content producers to cloud services (Chapters 3, 4, 7, and 8).

This book is divided into eleven chapters, the first eight working in pairs. Chapter 1 explains why and how the GVC framework can make a contribution to media and communication studies. International communication, the discipline's subject area dealing with cross-border media scholarship, stands at a crossroads because its concepts were fashioned when a clear line of demarcation between the local and the global prevailed. This line has blurred, rendering some aspects of the discipline obsolete. The chapter argues that the GVC framework can help lay the epistemological foundations of a forward-looking paradigm that is altogether holistic, multidisciplinary, and cosmopolitan. In the global era, the global cannot be an adjunct to a pre-existing theory but must be inherent to its epistemology. With the GVC framework, the global TV industry can be holistically analysed as a single systemic entity. The first part of the chapter highlights existing theoretical issues within international communication, and the second explains how the GVC framework can contribute to solve them.

Chapter 2 applies the GVC framework in order to progress our understanding of the global TV system. Among the drivers that are changing the TV industry, three stand out: digitisation, consolidation, and vertical disintegration (also known as de-verticalisation and segmentation). While the first two trends have long been identified as driving forces, the same cannot be said about the third. The phenomenon of vertical disintegration is less known and associated with the formation of GVCs. The chapter will expand on its prevalence in television and explain its role in globalising the industry. The final section provides an introductory outline of the TV GVC and its segments.

The formation of a TV GVC was decades in the making. At the core of the historical process lies the industry's global shift, which began into the last two decades of the twentieth century (the end of the broadcasting age) and accelerated in the new millennium (towards the streaming era). Documenting this shift is the purpose of Chapters 3 and 4, which adopt a bird's-eye view and concentrate on those aspects of the shift that are most apparent. They do not consider its dynamics and underlying structure, restricting the analysis to the market-facing activities of lead firms and the industry's consumer brands.

Chapter 3 focuses on the broadcasting age and broadcasters in the streaming era, providing an overview of the growth of cross-border trade in finished programmes (e.g. drama) and TV formats (adapted shows such as reality TV), and the formation of transnational TV networks. In contradistinction to the broadcasting age, the streaming era is characterised by the emergence of platforms.

Chapter 4 surveys the streaming landscape and focuses on the distinctive feature of the TV industry in the digital era: the rise of platforms. It contextualises the advent of streaming by raising the following question: is it an evolution or revolution in the history of screen entertainment? This chapter highlights the importance of scale, before introducing the concept of the platform to explain how it is achieved. A full account of the diversity of streaming platforms follows, which distinguishes three main types (internal, multi-sided and transaction), defined by the structure of their ecosystems and the ways in which participants are involved. Each form is expressed by a different business model (SVoD, AVoD, and video sharing).

Chapter 5 examines the array of technologies that is transforming the global TV system. The first part is devoted to communications satellites, which fulfil multiple distribution functions for all kinds of rights holders; the second turns to internet distribution. It covers the origins of video streaming before explaining how it works and why it is dethroning broadcasting and downloading as the most popular way of accessing content. The chapter examines the role of video-coding formats, content delivery networks (CDNs), and cloud computing in video distribution. It concludes by highlighting the role of standards and standard-setting organisations, arguing that their international evolution mirrors that of the TV industry, and emphasising the crucial role they play in digital value chains, over which no one in particular has oversight.

Chapter 6 turns its attention to the underlying infrastructure that constitutes the material foundation of the global TV system. Technology is the application of science and knowledge to accomplish a task inside a domain, while infrastructure consists of the *material elements* that actualise it: it is the buildings, cables, servers, switches, and routers needed to transport data packets from point A to point B; it is the firms, machinery, engineers, and technicians who design, build, update, and repair these material components. This chapter examines the cloud infrastructure that sustains streaming, focusing on two key components: undersea cable networks and data centres. The final section describes the contours of the video ecosystem that technology and infrastructure have created, and within which television operates today.

Chapters 7 and 8 provide an in-depth analysis of the value-adding segments of TV GVC. This chain is composed of two distinct but related production networks: the first corresponds to the programme-making phase. It is a phase dominated by artistic intent and creation, right from the birth of the concept to post-production, where colour grading, sound mixing, and editing are taking place. The segments are: facilities (support and services to TV content producers), content production (content creation), and distribution (Chapter 7). Media delivery begins when the final production master has been approved and the programme is ready to be distributed to audiences via various channels and platforms. The focus shifts from art to science, and the protection of the quality and integrity of the original tape. Media delivery is governed by the search for efficiencies through automation and technology. The segments are: publication, transmission, and reception (Chapter 8). Schematically, the aggregation segment, where broadcasters such as the BBC and streamers such as Netflix operate, lies in between content production and media delivery, connecting the two production networks. Aggregators act as the chain's *lead firms*; they commission content from TV producers and outsource media delivery tasks to specialist firms. The latter two are part of the chain's multiple *suppliers*.

Chapter 7 traces the route content follows from creation to final production master. It provides an in-depth analysis of each segment of the programme-making phase and includes aggregation. It examines firm behaviour and explains why the search for scale plays such a determining role in the strategies of firms. It highlights three key trends that characterise the chain's programme-making production network: internationalisation, consolidation, and vertical integration, emphasising that they occur in the wider context of industry segmentation. The chapter looks back at the formation of ten global TV studios (or TV production majors) and defines the role and nature of content aggregation in the TV GVC.

Chapter 8 covers the evolution of media delivery. It argues that broadcasters had been in charge of the full transmission process once, a task once deemed core to their business. Today, media delivery is externalised to the market and devolved to a network of suppliers that collaborate along the value chain. While some suppliers work solely for the media and entertainment sector, some are no ordinary firm – they are tech giants that have developed deep global capabilities and can leverage an unprecedented infrastructure to deliver content to and from (almost) any location in the world. They gain further leverage by being cross-sectoral, serving clients across multiple industries. The chapter identifies these *global* (or *transnational first-tier*) *suppliers* and analyses their key features.

Chapter 9 pursues the analysis of the global TV industry, examining the behaviour of various types of corporate actors, and their linkages, in the context of a fast-changing GVC. The restructuring of the TV industry around trans-national production networks has created two types of companies (lead firms and suppliers), and two classes of suppliers (sector-specific and multisectoral). Using Schumpeter's notion of creative destruction, the first section reflects on the impact of the digital revolution on lead firms and sector-specific suppliers. The second section focuses on the *relationships* between the different sets of actors and examines the modes of governance that prevail in the TV GVC. The thrust of corporate strategies, it argues, is strongly influenced by businesses' positions in the GVC, and *power asymmetries* between lead firms and suppliers are leading them to divergent approaches to integration. The final section demonstrates how the rise of the global suppliers (the tech giants) in the TV industry is furthering the global integration of the sector, and facilitating industry co-evolution through the formation of a supply base that is shared across several industries.

Media globalisation entails two entwined phenomena: global-scale integration and transnationalisation. Industry integration occurs because both lead firms and suppliers are searching for growth and economies of scale *within their respective segments but across markets*. This is compounded by the emergence of tech giants with deep global capabilities. The outcome is an industry structure made of international networks populated by transnationally capable and interdependent firms.

Chapter 10 delves into the transnational dimension of the global TV system (see definition shortly). As media globalisation has progressed, transnational media have evolved, and this chapter contends that a new generation has emerged. The status quo of the later part of the twentieth century that consisted of cross-border TV networks and formats (Chapter 3) evolved with the rise of streaming platforms (Chapter 4). During the first generation, the transnational remained a *professional practice* out of viewers reach. These media are transnational because they are professionally adapted for local audiences as they cross borders. With the arrival of the second generation, the transnational has become *an everyday mode of media consumption and interaction*. Online entertainment services have altered the status of the transnational within TV culture, and what was once at the margins now sits at the core.

The chapter's second purpose is to examine the key organisational characteristics of the transnational media firm. It compares and contrasts four types of organisational configuration (multinational, global, international, and transnational), and analyses the latter in depth. It connects organisational theory to the GVC framework, demonstrating how the nature of a firm's activities and position in the value chain play a determining role in the type of organisational structure it is most likely to adopt.

Chapter 11 considers policy issues pertaining to the global TV system. The global shift thesis does not make the assumption that the world is flat, as journalists state sometimes (Friedman, 2006). GVC theorists describe the world's economic geography as 'spiky' because industrial policies and trade performances vary greatly from one country to another (Baldwin, 2013: 16; Dicken, 2015: 8; Florida, 2005). The global TV system is equally uneven. Geographies matter and markets differ in terms of taste and consumption. Media regulations also vary, determining the degree of countries' participation in the TV GVC. Global television is underpinned by values that are prevalent among open societies and market economies. Using the case study of China, the chapter shows that countries that do not share these values restrict the access of the global TV industry to their territory. By way of contrast, a range of policies is at the disposal of those governments that wish to enhance the participation of local firms in the TV GVC. Using as evidence the public policies of countries that have recently done so, the chapter details the three key aspects of an upgrading strategy.

Research for this book is in line with GVC methodology, which is designed to generate in-depth knowledge of an industry. For this purpose, it relies on primary and secondary sources. Primary sources cover personal interviews with the author, which are of two sorts. The first is the recorded interview, which can be cited once permission is received. The book relies on interview recordings conducted over a ten-year period. Some interviewees were met with on several occasions, engendering trust that enhanced the exchange of information. The second, rarer, type of interview occurs under the cloak of secrecy. Some senior executives working in the largest entertainment conglomerates agreed to talk on condition of absolute anonymity. These interviews remain undisclosed and no mention of them is ever made.

Secondary data are gathered from multiple sources, including industry reports, trade publications, conferences, and webinars. The researcher needs to be aware of the perspective from which the reports are written. Consultancy firms and suppliers circulate reports for a reason, and the robustness of the methodology and the reliability of the data vary greatly among them.

Finally, the use of three terms needs to be clarified, bearing in mind they may occasionally be employed loosely for stylistic purposes. 'International' designates an entity or phenomenon that spreads across national borders. MipCom and MipTV in Cannes are international trade fairs that bring together TV executives from more than 100 territories. The 'transnational' denotes the crossing of national borders while acknowledging their continued relevance. A distinction is made between 'global processes [that] are largely decentered from specific national territories and take place in a global space' and 'transnational process [that] are anchored and transcend one or more nation-states' (Kearney in Mikos, 2020: 75). For example, an audience gathered for a sports or political event of worldwide significance may be deemed global, while an audience of migrants who watch a TV channel from country A while in country B, is transnational (e.g. Aksoy and Robins, 2000; Georgiou, 2012).

In addition, the transnational is a *process* that designates the imbrication of several dimensions within one artefact or phenomenon. For instance, a TV network is international when it crosses borders unchanged and is transnational when it absorbs elements from different geographies as it does so. A TV format is called transnational because it combines a structure that is immutable with local elements that vary from one territory to another. Taking these elements into consideration, *an artefact or phenomenon is transnational when it transcends borders while being affected by them and is imbricated in multiple spatial dimensions.*

As used in this research, 'global' is a sociological, not a geographical notion. As Gary Gereffi explains: '"Internationalization" refers to the geographic spread of economic activities across national boundaries', while globalisation 'implies the functional integration and coordination of internationally dispersed activities' (Gereffi, 1999: 41). 'Global' denotes *integration and interdependence on an international scale*. GVCs are deemed global because of their systems of governance that coordinate firms and activities across borders. The reach of GVCs varies, but it is never global in the geographical sense of the word. Similarly, the TV industry is global because it works as a unitary trading system that encompasses multiple cultures and territories, even though some countries have no or very little involvement in it.

The use of the concept justifies the scope of the study. Following a geographical understanding of the term, books on global television purport to offer an international overview of media systems from around the world (e.g. Cooper-Chen, 2005; Curran and Park, 2000; Elasmar, 2003; Shimpach, 2020; Sigismondi, 2020; Smith, 1998). These edited collections play a crucial role in the necessary de-Westernisation and decolonisation of media studies.[2] The purpose of this book is to investigate a globally integrated system that is dominated by Western-based firms. The focus is on the firms, brands, and nations that lead and/or participate in this industry, while it is acknowledged that this system rests on a set of values that are not universally shared (Chapter 11).[3]

1

Global Communication and the GVC Framework

International communication is the area of media studies devoted to cross-border media scholarship. This research argues that the sub-discipline stands at a cross-roads because its concepts were fashioned when a clear line of demarcation between the local and the global prevailed. This line has blurred and the distinction is no longer extant, questioning the purposefulness of existing approaches. The solution I propose is for the discipline to shift to global value chain (GVC) analysis. Adopting such a network-oriented theoretical framework brings two benefits. It offers a holistic view and an integrated analysis of the whole system, eschewing a piecemeal approach that fails to give a full account of an industry that is shaped by all its components (e.g. lead firms as well as suppliers) and the relationships between them.

All industries present features that make them distinct, but all are grappling with issues, such as entry into the digital economy, which are cross-sectoral. The tools of GVC analysis facilitate the contextualisation of television in global capitalism and enable us to analyse its response to wider trends, such as the impact of digital platforms, the explosive growth of outsourcing, and the restructuring influence of GVCs.

This chapter explains why and how I intend to apply the GVC framework in media and communication, and how it can help us understand media globalisation. Chapter 2 applies the framework to television.

International Communication: The Key Paradigms

Born in the aftermath of the Second World War, international communication went through a succession of paradigms. All have strengths and weaknesses, and all reflect the political times they were born in.

The first doctrine, known as free flow of communication, was formulated at UNESCO, the United Nations' (UN) organisation for education, science, and culture, in the aftermath of the Second World War. At the organisation's second general conference in Mexico City in 1947, delegates from thirty-six member states reasoned that a free flow of communication would create a better understanding among nations and help secure peace and security. They agreed to 'remove existing obstacles to the free flow of ideas by word and image' (Valderrama, 1941: 41). As good as these intentions were, the looming Cold War would take the discipline in an altogether different direction and help shape the next two paradigms.

'Modernisation theory' arose when the Cold War's two superpowers vied for hegemony across various corners of the world. The made-in-USA theoretical framework postulated that media act as agents of change by raising aspirations and creating a positive climate for development (Lerner, 1958; Schramm, 1964). The paradigm had numerous shortcomings, not least its ethnocentrism and propensity to presume that Western civilisation was the pinnacle of development (Thussu, 2019: 42–5). Nonetheless, it is within this framework that seminal large-scale research on cross-border media flows was conducted, which produced the first data set that highlighted the inequalities of the world media system (Schramm, 1964: 90–113).

Modernisation theory was challenged by the cultural imperialism thesis that emerged in Latin America in the 1960s and that dominated the discipline for years to come. It fit in the dependency model that questioned the benefit of development imposed by the West. The theory of the 'development of under-development' held that developing countries (the periphery) were made dependent on industrialised nations (the core) in trade and technology (Fejes, 1981; Salinas and Paldán, 1974). Scholars focused on the imbalance of the communication flow and argued that news and entertainment products travelled from the West to the Global South without counterflow: whilst Anglo-American agencies dominated the global news trade and Hollywood movies travelled widely, cultural products from the developing world rarely – if at all – reached the West. They further argued that the global dominance of Western media created a cultural hegemony that threatened local cultures. Media conglomerates were the missionaries of capitalism, and their content was aimed at converting developing countries into a market economy and their audiences into consumers of global brands (Dorfman and Mattelart, 1975; Herman and McChesney, 1997; Mattelart, 1979; Schiller, 1992). A group of scholars who met in Mexico in 1991 summarised the cultural imperialism position as follows: 'We deplore the cultural pollution and loss of tradition which have led to global rootlessness, leaving humans, through the intensity of mass-marketing, vulnerable to the pressures of economic and political totalitarianism' (Schiller, 1992: 38).

It is from this premise that grievances about Western hegemony in the international communication system arose in the Non-Aligned Movement of the 1970s. Such concerns were structured into a diplomatic position that was subsequently articulated in the UN system. In 1978, UNESCO issued a declaration and the UN General Assembly adopted an official resolution calling for a 'New World Information and Communication Order' (NWICO). The commission set up by UNESCO in 1977 was chaired by Irish statesman Sean MacBride, and involved Hubert Beuve-Méry (the distinguished journalist and founding editor of France's newspaper of reference, *Le Monde*) and Columbia's Gabriel García Márquez. Its landmark report, 'Many Voices One World', made eighty-two recommendations that addressed disparities of the international communication order (MacBride, 1980; Nordenstreng, 1984; Chapter 11).

Whilst ideologically standing poles apart, modernisation theory and cultural imperialism have more in common than at first appears. Both perspectives approached international communication from a national perspective: the former sought to harness media for national development, while the latter was preoccupied with the defence of cultural sovereignty. During the Cold War, international relations were structured by an antagonism between nation states, and the prevalence of a national dimension influenced the epistemology of international communication scholarship. The discipline was suffused with methodological nationalism and all its operating concepts (e.g. national development, cultural sovereignty) were shaped by the politics of the nation state. The institutions that commissioned international communication studies, such as UNESCO, were themselves the theatre of conflicting national interests heightened by the Cold War. Governments and their rivalries shaped the terms of the debate, and it was impossible to think of international communication beyond the horizon of the nation state.

Like elsewhere in the social sciences, international communication took a postmodern turn in the late twentieth century (Susen, 2015). Mirroring other disciplines, the field eschewed a holistic and structural perspective and leant towards a relativist and interpretative path (Susen, 2015: 40–83). Focus shifted from the investigation of the economic and political structures underpinning the world media system to the study of globalisation as a cultural and subjective experience. The assumptions of the previous paradigm were dismantled one by one. The cultural imperialism thesis takes for granted the dominance of the West, argues John Tomlinson, and fails to recognise the shifting 'distribution of power' engendered by the decentring nature of globalising processes (Tomlinson, 1997: 185). The old views are too simplistic to give account of the new 'global cultural economy', which is a 'complex, overlapping [and] disjunctive order', added Arjun Appadurai (Appadurai, 1990). Néstor García Canclini set forth that the 'one-directional schema of imperialist domination' fails to provide an explanation for contemporary cultural processes provoked by phenomena such as migration

(García Canclini, 1995: 230). Sinclair, Jacka, and Cunningham concurred that the one-way flow of communication was an inaccurate depiction of reality and cultural imperialism did not take into account the emergence of geo-linguistic regions, and the growing popularity of regional content within them (Sinclair et al., 1996).

In the process, the discipline lost theoretical coherence but freed itself from the prison-house of the nation state and shed light on new trends. Where the old thesis never questioned the sanctity of national culture, the new approach focused on cultural diversity (Tomlinson, 1991: 73). Against a reified notion of culture, scholars emphasised the in-betweenness and ambivalence of cultures. Banerjee observed that a contrast had emerged between the former paradigm that emphasised cultural 'domination and hegemony' and the new research agenda that concentrates on 'interconnection and diversity' (Banerjee, 2002: 519). For Jan Nederve Pieterse, hybridity is a common feature of cultures, and 'hybridization as a process is as old as history' (Nederveen Pieterse, 2001: 222). Globalisation is simply accelerating it, producing 'fusion cultures that combine new technologies and existing social practices and cultural values' (Nederveen Pieterse, 2001: 222).

Concepts such as adaptation, deterritorialisation, and transnationalisation helped shift attention towards the interconnection and interdependence of cultures. Fears about cultural homogenisation were ill-founded because cultural products mutate and adapt as they move between cultures (Tomlinson, 1997: 181–2). García Canclini defined deterritorialisation as 'the loss of the "natural" relation of culture to geographical and social territories' (García Canclini, 1995: 229). Cultural practices are no longer fixed by geography but travel and combine with other practices to create new cultural experiences in other locales. Morley and Robins defined the transnationalisation of culture as 'a process in which the "vertical" organization of people within national communities is ... being supplanted by their organization into "horizontal" communities – people are connected electronically rather that by geographical proximity' (Morley and Robins, 1995: 61). The new research agenda made migrants' cultural practices more visible, shedding further light on the diversity and complexity of contemporary cultures. Robins and Aksoy approached migrants as transnational viewers, experts at drawing from different cultural repertoires in order to create a new knowledge experience for themselves (Aksoy and Robins 2000; Robins and Aksoy, 2005).

The great merit of the new discourses of globalisation is the deconstruction of the national dimension – once the cornerstone of all preceding paradigms. In the process, the discipline has become theoretically heteroclite and it would be vain to look for a governing paradigm. The waning of international communication as a cohesive discipline is partly explained by its postmodern turn. However, it may also reflect the evolution of cross-border media: when the local and global are closely entwined does a discipline that focuses on the international still make sense? The discipline is at a crossroads, and the investigation of the macrostructures of the media industries necessitates a renewed epistemological and theoretical thrust.

A Discipline at a Crossroads: From International to Global Communication

International communication developed as a field of study when a clear line of demarcation existed between the national and the international. Markets and broadcasters operated discreetly on a nationwide basis with no deep interaction across frontiers. The national was the prevailing dimension and the international was everything foreign. Entertainment conglomerates were expanding, but the bulk of their activities remained confined to their domestic market (Flew, 2013: 24). As the global shift progressed, the national and the international began to merge and the boundaries between the two became blurred (Chapters 1 and 2). Contemporary media trends, from TV formats to YouTube, are typically transnational. In sum, as borders become less relevant, so has international communication: its tools and concepts are rarely called upon to shed light on global media phenomena such as streaming platforms, social media entertainment, or esports (e.g. Burgess and Green, 2018; Cunningham and Craig, 2019; Lobato, 2019; Rogers, 2019).

While our understanding of contemporary cultural trends has progressed, our knowledge of the economic and political dimensions of media globalisation remains sketchy. I once fashioned the notion of a 'cosmopolitan mode of production', arguing that transnational TV networks contributed to the global integration of industries such as music, fashion, or finance (Chalaby, 2009: 230–1). However, my earlier approach could not explain how media globalisation works and why the TV industry operates as a global system. I came to the conclusion that advances in this field of research would necessitate a new perspective provided by the GVC framework. It forms the core of the *global communication approach*, which rests on three principles.

First, the global communication approach is interdisciplinary in scope, combining insights from various disciplines. Because of the growing interdependence of economies, most studies in media management and media economics (including research on media ownership, concentration, and financialisation) are relevant in an international context independently of the geography they focus on. When these studies factor in the industry's transnational scope, it increases their applicability to global communication research (e.g. Aris and Bughin, 2009; Chan-Olmsted and Wirth, 2006; Doyle, 2013; Holt and Perren, 2009; Küng, 2017;

Picard and Wildman, 2015; Vogel, 2020; Winseck and Jin, 2012). A growing body of work, subsumed under the labels of production studies and creative labour studies, focuses on the tensions between agency and social conditions, asymmetric forms of power and control, and class and gender identities in the global media industries (e.g. Banks et al., 2016; Christopherson, 2012; Curtin and Sanson, 2016). This scholarship is not automatically associated with the discipline of international communication but needs to be incorporated into the global communication approach.

Second, the concepts of global communication must embody the epistemological qualities to shed light on the historicity of the processes at play. Globalisation has multiple ramifications, but its engine is economic and is driven by capitalism. Capitalism is a historical mode of production: it replaced earlier economic models, went through multiple phases since inception, and its survival has long been questioned (Braudel, 1992a; Schumpeter, 1947). Global communication scholars must comprehend globalisation as a historical process for two reasons: globalisation is part of a multisecular evolution that began with the inception of an international division of labour several centuries ago, and it is connected to a historical mode of production. It is this connection that defines the features of economic globalisation, and must therefore remain an integral part of the analysis.

Finally, global communication is a cosmopolitan approach; it avoids all forms of nation-centrism and breaks away from the prison-house of the national perspective. Ulrich Beck argued that methodological nationalism fails to grasp the complexity of globalisation, which 'not only alters the interconnectedness of nation states and national societies but the internal quality of the social' (Beck 2000: 87). He called for his own discipline, sociology, to move towards 'methodological cosmopolitanism', which is the German sociologist's attempt to 'build a frame of reference to analyse the new social conflicts, dynamics, and structures of Second Modernity' (Beck 2002: 18).

Global communication embraces this agenda. Some scholars attempt to adapt theoretical frameworks developed in national settings to the study of media globalisation and add the prefix 'global' in front of 'media industries' or 'creative industries'. By way of contrast, the GVC perspective is explicitly designed around the study of transnational production networks. Its epistemology is devoid of nation-centrism and is dedicated to the understanding of economies and industries in a global setting.

This agenda is underscored by the unit of analysis: the *global* TV industry is examined holistically as a single systemic entity. All its interconnected elements are interdependent and therefore considered part of the same system. By focusing exclusively on lead firms, the media literature ignores suppliers. Likewise, while consolidation through various forms of integration has attracted a great amount of interest, de-verticalisation, which is as significant a phenomenon, is largely ignored. The remainder of this chapter lays out the theoretical foundations of this project.

The GVC Framework

The conceptual lineage of the GVC theoretical framework can be traced back to Fernand Braudel, a second-generation scholar of the Annales School (Burke, 2015). Braudel's work rests on distinctive principles, many of which were shared among members of the Annales. His research was grounded on strong empirical foundations and was based on *l'observation concrète*. While the French historian acknowledged the contribution of theoretical models, only a thorough empirical analysis reveals trends and patterns previously unnoticed. He contended that after a rigorous inquiry of the economic data and statistics of pre-industrial Europe, he noticed the absence of connection between the period and the grand theories that claimed to understand it (Braudel, 1992a: 23).

His approach was holistic, both in terms of time span and geography. Following a philosophy known as *la longue durée*, he shunned *l'histoire événementielle* that focused on famed events of short duration. Rather, he followed cyclical movements that spanned decades or centuries, such as the long-term evolution of trade flows and price fluctuations (Braudel, 1958). Weaving these threads with descriptions of the everyday lives of common people, his work composed the tapestry of an epoch. Braudel constructed geographical spaces within which people travelled and commodities were exchanged, that were coherent in terms of culture, society, and economy, but which were not congruent with nation states. He fashioned the concept of the 'world-economy' to describe 'civilizations' spanning territories and centuries.[1] World-economies are limited in size and time, even when they momentarily span whole empires. The method was applied first in his 1949 monograph on the sixteenth-century Mediterranean,[2] which was approached as a singular cultural and commercial space (Braudel, 1996). It was replicated full scale in his study of the capitalist world-economy between the fifteenth and eighteenth centuries (Braudel, 1992a, 1992b, 1992c).

Braudel's perspective constitutes the foundation of Immanuel Wallerstein's world-systems theory. His magnum opus retraces the origins of capitalism and its transformation into the modern world-system (Wallerstein, 1974, 1980, 1989). Capitalism started as a European world-economy, and its geographical expansion transformed it into a world-system characterised by 'a single division of labor and multiple cultural systems' (Wallerstein, 1974: 390).

The notion of 'commodity chain' was introduced to support this research agenda. Establishing the world-system as the new unit of analysis, Hopkins and Wallerstein were arguing against the classic position of international trade scholars, who saw markets and trade develop locally first and then internationally. They rejected both the sequential development and the distinction between local and international, positing that 'all . . . transactions are part of, and constrained by, something one can call a "world" market', within which production processes are transnational (Hopkins and Wallerstein, 1977: 128). They elaborated:

> Instead, we start with a radically different presumption. Let us conceive of something we shall call, for want of a better conventional term, 'commodity chains'. What we mean by such chains is the following: take an ultimate consumable item and trace back the set of inputs that culminated in this item – the prior transformations, the raw materials, the transportation mechanisms, the labor input into each of the material processes, the food inputs into the labor. This linked set of processes we call a commodity chain. If the ultimate consumable were, say, clothing, the chain would include the manufacture of the cloth, the yarn, etc., the cultivation of the cotton, as well as the reproduction of the labor forces involved in these productive activities. (Hopkins and Wallerstein, 1977: 128)

Wallerstein subsequently mentioned commodity chains twice, underscoring their transnational nature and connection to capital accumulation (Wallerstein, [1979] 1984: 2–4; Wallerstein, 1983: 15–17, 31), before devoting a study to the subject. Aiming to demonstrate that the modern world-economy developed quickly, Hopkins and Wallerstein sought to demonstrate that capital and production networks (commodity chains) were crossing boundaries by the sixteenth century, and that a world-scale division of labour is traceable to this era (Hopkins and Wallerstein, 1986: 159).

By the early 1990s, commodity chains had become a field of inquiry and the first volume dedicated to the subject was a collection of papers presented at the 16th Annual Conference on the Political Economy of the World-System (Gereffi and Korzeniewicz, 1994). The small community of scholars forged its own agenda.

The research setting shifted from historical to contemporary. While commodity chains were part of an argument about the development of the modern world-economy, the focal point became present-day capitalism. The new research agenda maintained an interest in the context within which chains operate but laid more emphasis on industries than the economy at large. This change was reflected in a streamlined definition of *global* commodity chains (GCCs), as they were now called (Bair, 2005: 155–7).

Furthermore, GCCs replaced the modern world-system as the unit of analysis. While this presents a disjuncture, GCCs inherited two key characteristics from the previous paradigm. As Hopkins and Wallerstein stated: 'If there is one thing which distinguishes a world-system perspective from any other, it is its insistence that the unit of analysis is a *world*-system defined in terms of *economic* processes and links' (Hopkins and Wallerstein, 1977: 137). Links and processes remained at the core of the new research agenda, GCCs now being defined as 'sets of interorganizational networks clustered around one commodity or product, linking households, enterprises, and states to one another within the world-economy' (Gereffi et al., 1994: 2).

The new approach remained holistic and the unit of analysis global. As noted by Bair, the 'global' in GCC 'is not meant to designate the geographical scope of the commodity chain' (Bair, 2005: 172), but is a reference to the cross-border integration of production processes within a chain. Following Wallerstein, Gary Gereffi drew a similar and crucial distinction between the international and the global: 'While "internationalization" refers simply to the geographical spread of economic activities, "globalization" implies a degree of functional integration between these dispersed activities' (Gereffi, 1994: 96).

GCCs were attributed four dimensions: *input–output structure* (the shape of its connecting production and distribution processes), *governance structure* (below), *territoriality* (spatial dispersion), and *institutional framework*, which refers to the impact that policy institutions and regulatory systems have on commodity chains (Bair, 2009: 9; Gereffi, 1994: 96–7; Gereffi, 1995: 113; Sturgeon, 2009: 130–1). Governance structure focused on coordination of economic activities and power relations among economic agents within chains. Producer-driven chains, according to Gereffi, included those chains in which large manufacturers remain in control of production and distribution networks and processes, while buyer-driven GCCs prevail in industries that are labour-intensive and controlled by large retailers and branded manufacturers that offshore production to networks of small and predominantly Asian suppliers, the fashion industry being a case in point (Gereffi, 1999: 41–2).

The next epistemological break occurred in the early 2000s. Scholars with decades of collective experience in the observation of manufacturing processes, industrial relations, and international production networks gathered together many times – most memorably at the Rockefeller Foundation Bellagio Center – to expand the scope and applicability of the GCC framework. The dichotomy between producer-driven and buyer-driven chains was ditched in favour of five archetypical modes of governance that better reflected the types of chain coordination encountered across different industrial sectors. With the same objective of being more inclusive, the term 'commodity' was swapped for 'value'. The new endeavour was more interdisciplinary in character and involved social scientists from an array of disciplines (Bair, 2005, 2009; Lee, 2010; Sturgeon, 2009).[3]

GVCs are analysed through six dimensions. *Input–output structure* (1) refers to the structure of the production process and the successive value-added stages through which a product or service flows from inception to consumption. Segments vary from one industry to another but typically involve research and design, assembling and/or production, sales and marketing, and recycling (Gereffi and Fernandez-Stark, 2016: 8).

GVCs are transnational networks of production that involve geographically dispersed firms. The analysis of the *geographical scope* (2) aims to map the trade flows within the chain and charting the supply and demand of components among the firms and territories that are involved in GVCs. In practice, most GVCs, such as automotive, consumer electronics and, indeed, television, are dominated by a relatively small set of exporters.[4]

Incorporating findings from a large set of empirical studies, five types of *governance* (3) were proposed. The typology is based on a wider range of indicators than the former dichotomy, taking into account the complexity of transactions, the ability to codify them, and capabilities in the supply base. The five chain architectures reflect diverse types of transactions and connections among participating firms (Gereffi et al., 2001: 4; Gereffi et al., 2005: 89–90). In particular, lead firms yield a certain amount of influence over their suppliers, if only because their purchasing power gives them a naturally dominant position within the chain. However, the types of governance display varying degrees of power asymmetry:

- *Market* governance is based on price and prevails when transactions are simple and necessitate little cooperation between buyers and suppliers.
- *Modular* chains are based on an architecture characterised by a high level of product codification and standardisation, enhancing the chain's interoperability and simplifying transactions among firms even when trading complex or bespoke products or services. GVCs in the consumer electronics industry are a case in point as the specifications of electronic components are fully codified and standardised, enabling buyers or assemblers to easily communicate their needs, evaluate and compare components, and keep highly competent suppliers at arm's length.
- *Relational* governance occurs when knowledge and product specifications cannot be easily codified, leading to frequent interactions and possibly complex transactions between participating firms. This causes mutual dependence between lead firms and suppliers, and relationships are based on trust and reputation. Such governance is frequent in chains operating in industry clusters, as spatial proximity lowers the cost of frequent

interactions, facilitates the exchange of knowledge and the building of long-lasting relationships.

- *Captive* governance denotes a high level of power asymmetry between lead firms and their suppliers. The former operate in segments with high entry barriers and can dictate conditions to suppliers smaller in size with a lower level of competence, which operate in the chain's least profitable segments, and are tasked with a very specific role such as the supply of raw products or materials. This type of coordination is on display when Western-based multinationals operate networks of suppliers scattered in low-cost countries (a procurement strategy known as low-cost country sourcing). It is in such chains that the power asymmetry between lead firms and their suppliers is the most acute. While such chains can be beneficial for all parties, the asymmetry may generate negative social, psychological, and environmental consequences for the suppliers, their workers, and the countries in which they operate. These can be addressed through regulatory intervention and/or consumer concern.
- *Hierarchical* governance occurs when the costs of transactions and the amount of knowledge shared are such that a firm decides to develop the products or services in-house. If a firm does not have the capacity to do so, it may lead to vertical integration and the acquisition of a supplier with the necessary know-how (Gereffi et al., 2001: 3–5; Gereffi et al., 2005: 82–90; Gereffi and Fernandez-Stark, 2016: 8–11; Ponte and Sturgeon, 2014: 203–6; Sturgeon and Kawakami, 2010: 10).

Economic upgrading (4) is the ensemble of strategies that firms and countries deploy in order to move into higher-valued tasks in global production networks (Gereffi and Fernandez-Stark, 2016: 12). The GVC literature eventually recognised four economic upgrading strategies: product upgrading, 'namely the shift into the production of a higher value product'; process upgrading, 'improving the efficiency of production systems'; functional upgrading, 'moving into higher value stages in the chain that require additional skills'; and intersectoral upgrading, 'entry into a new value chain by leveraging the knowledge and skills acquired in the current chain' (Fernandez-Stark et al., 2014: 82; see also Lee, 2010: 2995).

As value chains are embedded in various locales, *local institutional context* (5) considers the availability and nature of their inputs into GVCs, such as infrastructure, regulatory and tax regimes, education, workforce, and gender participation. *Stakeholders analysis* (6) examines the participation and involvement in GVCs of actors such as trade associations, trade unions, regulators, governments, and international organisations (Gereffi and Fernandez-Stark, 2016: 14).

Today, GVC analysis is among the best established paradigms in the social sciences and it is a multi-disciplinary endeavour that benefits from the input of a large array of disciplines. GVC discourse is commonly practiced in official bodies: UN agencies such as the World Trade Organization (WTO), the International Labour Organization (ILO), the UN Conference on Trade and Development (UNCTAD), the UN Industrial Development Organization (UNIDO), international organisations such as the World Bank and the Organisation for Economic Co-operation and Development (OECD), and numerous governmental agencies, have all produced or commissioned GVC reports (e.g. Foster-McGregor et al., 2015; ILO, 2016; International Bank for Reconstruction and Development/The World Bank, 2017; UNCTAD, 2013; WTO, 2013, 2016, 2017).

GVCs and Network-Oriented Frameworks

There exist alternatives to the study of international production networks, and some have been applied to research of the media industries. This section compares them to GVC analysis and affirms the suitability of the latter for the research problem on hand and global communication studies in general.

The French *filière* approach encompasses a large body of work often dedicated to the analysis of agricultural value chains in a postcolonial setting, especially in the Sahel and sub-Saharan Africa. However, the approach is more an umbrella than a framework and counts schools of thought that operate with distinctive concepts and methodologies (Raikes et al., 2000: 403).

Another option is Manuel Castells' network theory. Analysing media globalisation, the sociologist observes 'the formation of global networks of interlocked multimedia businesses organized around strategic partnerships' (Castells, 2009: 72). Applying this theoretical framework, Amelia Arsenault notes that media giants collaborate as much as they compete, and they are 'connected to one another . . . through a complex set of partnerships, agreements, cross-investments, interpersonal connections, and much more' (Arsenault, 2012: 119). Network theory's strength is its multi-scalar approach and its recognition of the mutual influence of the local and the global (Castells, 2009: 87–91). It also innovates by highlighting connections among rival firms. The preoccupation of network theory, however, remains close to that of classic political economy, focusing on the reach and power of media giants, and issues such as concentration of ownership and media firm's dependence on advertising and finance. Suppliers – arguably a key part of global networks – remain unaccounted for (Arsenault, 2012; Castells, 2009: 71–99).

Media management scholars offer multiple variants of value chains across the entertainment industries (e.g. Doyle, 2013: 19–21; Hess and Matt, 2013: 38–9; Küng, 2017: 18–23; Picard, 2002: 30–43; Wirtz, 2017: 62–70). Without fail, they use the Michael Porter model, for whom a value chain is a firm's 'collection of activities that are performed to design, produce, market, deliver, and support its product' (Porter, 1985: 36). This approach is reflected in Küng, who writes that 'the value chain disaggregates the activities of *a firm* into sequential stages stretching from the supply side to the demand side' (Küng, 2017: 19, emphasis added), and Picard, for whom 'the concept is useful in considering those activities that are most central to the core activities of *a firm* and those that make the business operational' (Picard, 2002: 33, emphasis added).

The GVC approach is fashioned by multiple influences, but its conceptual roots keep it distinct from Porter's value chain. The latter's framework is *firm-centric*, in the sense that the pivotal point of the analysis is the company's behaviour and activities. Porter's method is intended to be a tool for consultants and managers to execute a firm's strategy, and help it gain a competitive edge by defining its core competencies and extracting the maximum value from its activities. By way of contrast, the GVC framework's point of reference and unit of analysis is the inter-firm *network*. It is more holistic, because it gives an overview of a whole industry and its international structure, focusing on the dynamic between segments and the *relations* among firms.

Global production network (GPN) and GVC analysis are closely related: they share origins in GCC research and an interest in spatially dispersed inter-firm production networks. While both theories are evolving in different directions, they can be used complementarily. The GVC framework is recognised as the most business-centric of the two, and most apt at profiling the DNA of a value chain and unveiling its dynamics. It best suits our purpose, which is to understand the reconfiguration of an industry that is entering the digital age.

GPN research overcomes some of the limits intrinsic to the GVC framework by theorising how production networks connect and intersect with society, geography, and various constituents. It considers a host of extra-firm actors as 'active agents' in production networks (Coe and Yeung, 2019: 782), including the state, labour, trade unions, and intermediaries such as financial firms and standards organisations (Coe and Yeung, 2015: 15, 55–7; Coe and Yeung, 2019: 782–9; Dicken, 2015: 173–225). Reflecting the framework's anchorage in economic geography, GPN scholars conceive 'geography [to] be an active space that shapes the territorial constitution and configuration of these network activities' (Coe and Yeung, 2015: 68). In addition to analysing the spatial configuration of production networks, they examine how networks shape the territories and economies in which they operate (Coe and Yeung, 2015: 67–8; Dicken, 2015: 251–3).

The concept of strategic coupling is used 'to delimit the different way in which regional and national economies intersect with global production networks' (Coe and Young, 2019: 780). GPN research considers production networks as being 'embedded in the broader institutional macro-structures of the global economy' (Dicken, 2015: 52). 'Both history and geography matters', writes Peter Dicken (Dicken, 2015: 52). This involves giving an account of how technological and economic change contribute to reconfigure global production networks, and vice versa. This research applies a GPN perspective to complement GVC analysis in multiple ways, devoting attention to the role of media TNCs (Chapters 3 and 4), technology, standards organisations, and infrastructure (Chapters 5 and 6).

As an academic discipline, international communication worked well when a clear line of demarcation existed between national and foreign media. Adjustments were needed to approach the media industries in an era when lines have blurred and the local and global are entwined. Global communication adopts an epistemological position that is multidisciplinary, holistic, and cosmopolitan. From a theoretical standpoint, it is using the GVC framework to think through – not about – media globalisation. Most examinations of media globalisation are teleological in scope, analysing its impact on culture, markets, firms, and workers. The aim of global communication is to look inside the black box, approach globalisation as a noumenon, and explain it in all its dimensions.

2

The Making of a Digital GVC

The objective of this chapter is to identify the drivers that are reshaping the media industries. At a time when technology and market forces are transforming them apace, understanding firm behaviour and a rapidly changing industry structure is challenging. This chapter singles out three trends: digitisation, consolidation, and vertical disintegration (or de-verticalisation). The first two have long been identified as driving forces in the media industries, while the third has rarely been discussed. De-verticalisation is closely related to the formation of GVCs and will necessitate a longer exposition. I shall explain why GVCs matter for the understanding of global industries and provide an outline of the TV GVC.

At the Origins of Media Globalisation

Is globalisation cause or effect of media industries' transformation? It is an interesting question of an intricate phenomenon that can be compared to an automatic watch movement with a self-winding mechanism. An automatic movement has the capacity to store energy and transfer it to another part of the mechanism. Likewise, globalisation has acquired its own momentum and, once in motion, contributes to changing markets, industry structure, and firm behaviour. For instance, two firms decide to merge in order to enlarge their footprint, which in turn furthers the interdependence of national markets, prompting other companies to internationalise. But what drives globalisation in the first place? What sets the movement into motion and winds the mainspring?

Digitisation

With the advent of streaming, television is turning into a digital GVC. As such, it is part of the digital economy and shares four base technologies that cut across all industries that participate in this growing economy: data collection and network connectivity, cloud computing, big data analytics, and AI/ML (Artificial Intelligence and Machine Learning) (Sturgeon, 2019: 35–41; Chapter 8).

Digitisation plays a key role in the acceleration of the global shift because it alters the internationalisation strategy of media firms. Digital multinational enterprises (MNEs), such as streamers and video platforms, can easily reach online consumers across borders. Internet-based technologies decouple the ratio of foreign sales to foreign assets, meaning that digital MNEs need to make little foreign investment before achieving a high volume of foreign sales (UNCTAD, 2017: 166–73). Tech giants such as Facebook and Netflix have managed to generate significant foreign earnings before making any investment in many of the countries in which they operate. Disney+, for instance, launched in Europe without a team in the region (Chapter 4).

Digitisation makes it easier for MNEs to operate at global scale (UNCTAD, 2017: 179–83). Digital content providers such as A&E Networks, Discovery, Netflix, and ViacomCBS have all shifted their operations to the cloud, facilitating the global distribution of content and coordination of functions such as sales and rights management (Chapter 8). The Internet has simplified the coordination of large supply chains: from electronic mail to online conference platforms and cloud-hosted databases, communication and information flows across borders without hindrance, supporting geographically dispersed networks of production.

Digitisation plays a critical role in the globalisation of television because it facilitates access to the global marketplace, makes it easier to coordinate international activities, and opens the TV industry to digital MNEs that are primarily involved in internet commerce and infrastructure. Another impact of digitisation is convergence, which can be defined as a 'process of technological integration' that involves the destruction and eventual re-organisation of boundaries between industries (Chon et al., 2003: 142). Convergence plays out on several levels. *Device convergence* is the most visible to consumers and occurs when scalable platforms bundle several types of services and content. The leading examples are the smartphone and the game console, which support a wide variety of journalistic and entertainment applications (Han et al., 2009). Digitisation and innovation has also led to *industrial convergence*, opening up the media sector to a variety of industries (Gustafsson and Schwarz, 2013: 11).

Digitisation has opened up television to newcomers, notably telecom operators (telcos) and tech firms. For telcos, the opportunity to get involved arose in the mid-2000s when they realised they could deliver television over the Internet and through their networks (IPTV, see Introduction), using either a live multicast stream for TV channels or unicast protocols for VoD. The first attempts were rarely met with success as telcos were facing stiff competition from cable and satellite operators who had more experience in selling entertainment. The situation evolved to telcos' advantage because of their networks' capacity to deliver high-quality video streams and the rise in mobile connectivity. By 2017, video revenue amounted to US$82.7 billion for the world's fifty largest telcos, a cool 300 million video subscriptions among them. It is a small but growing share of a global telco market that exceeds US$1 trillion (Malim, 2018).

Video represents both an opportunity and a necessity for network providers. Selling fixed and mobile broadband connections is a commodity business. As the only distinctive feature of data pack deals is price, it pushes telcos to a margin-eroding race to the bottom. Bundling video in the offer helps network providers to retain customers and attract new ones by distinguishing their product. It also allows them to sell an 'experience' encompassing entertainment and quality of service rather than just data (Griffiths, 2018). Telcos have two advantages compared to OTT providers: they control quality of service because they operate their own network and have a direct relationship with customers (Griffiths, 2018).

Telcos have several options when entering the video market. They can produce their own content (usually in partnership with a third party), a route taken by operators such as Deutsche Telekom, Orange, or Liberty Global (Maroulis, 2018). Telcos can turn content aggregator and run their own TV service. BT launched BT Sport in 2013; Orange operates OCS in France, an on-demand and linear service with several channels; Deutsche Telekom runs Magenta TV; and Telefónica owns Moviestar+, Spain's largest pay-TV brand. China's three largest telecom providers, China Mobile, China Unicom, and China Telecom all hold IPTV licences. China Telecom is the most advanced triple-play operator (voice, video, and data) with 113 million subscribers to its IPTV service (China Telecom, 2020: 13).

Third, telcos can make deals with content aggregators and carry their service. Most network providers hold carriage agreements with multiple local and international streamers. Conversely, leading streamers hold hundreds of such deals around the globe. These agreements are marriages of convenience. Getting a piggyback from the local dominant telco enables streamers to accelerate international pick up without investing too much in marketing and infrastructure. Telcos can integrate the video services into bundles that make their offer more distinctive and upgrade from commodity to full digital service providers. For both sides, it makes competition less acute and turns potential enemies into frenemies.

In practice, many telcos adopt a hybrid strategy that incorporates all three options. Deutsche Telekom, among others, produces content, runs its own TV service, and carries multiple streaming platforms (Bernfeld, 2018). Finally, telecom providers can acquire media companies, and some telcos have made sizeable acquisitions in the recent past (Table 2.1).

Table 2.1 *Telecom operators' major acquisitions in the media and entertainment sector, 2013–19*

Acquirer	Company acquired	Date	Estimated amount of transaction (US$ bn)
Comcast	NBCUniversal	March 2013	30
Telefónica	Canal+ España	April 2015	0.7
AT&T	Time Warner[1]	June 2018	85
Comcast	Sky	October 2018	39
Telia	Bonnier Broadcasting	December 2019	1

Source: author

Note[1]: AT&T announced in May 2021 plans to spin off its content division and merge it with Discovery. The new entity will remain controlled by AT&T.

5G network deployment, which is necessitating substantial investments, is putting telcos in an even stronger position. With faster download speeds and lower latency, the new standard is sharply increasing mobile video consumption, bolstering network operators' position in the video market at large and facilitating their transition to digital service providers.

The second class of new entrants are tech companies. The first wave included the FAANG (Facebook, Amazon, Apple, Netflix, Google),[1] which are all involved in content production and aggregation (Facebook Watch, Amazon Prime Video, Apple TV and Apple TV+, and YouTube; Chapters 4 & 9). These have been joined by a second wave of platforms including Instagram (2010), Snapchat (2011), and TikTok (2016). Aside from TikTok (Jia and Liang, 2021), most were created in California and brought together the "'NoCal" tech culture' of Silicon Valley and the SoCal culture of Hollywood (Cunningham and Craig, 2019: 47). As a Netflix executive explains:

> We are at a pivotal time in our industry where we stand at the end of the era dominated by the impact, legacy and elegance of that hundred plus year old technology called film and the evolution of what we think of as 'video'. What is really interesting about a company like Netflix is that its culture comes as much from Silicon Valley as from Hollywood. It has deep affinity for creating entertainment and for technology innovation … Its ethos is about the intersection of technology and creativity in order to innovate new forms of storytelling. (Silverman, director, post operations and creative services, Netflix, in Pennington, 2019)

Tech culture comes with distinctive traits and these platforms are 'very comfortable with regularly "rebooting" (starting again), "iterating" (trying again), or "pivoting" (changing direction)' (Cunningham and Craig, 2019: 47). They do all this, but a fourth attribute is their relentless pursuit of scale. According to Eric Schmidt, former long-standing CEO of Google, companies used to grow 'slowly and methodically. Create a product, achieve success locally or regionally, then grow a step at a time by building sales, distribution' (Schmidt and Rosenberg, 2017: 78). This was called 'growth', and it is not something that Google is interested in: 'If you are trying to do something big, it's not enough to just grow, you need *scale* . . . it means to grow something very quickly and globally' (Schmidt and Rosenberg, 2017: 78).

The Netflix founders share the same philosophy. When Randolph was bouncing hundreds of ideas for start-ups to invest in, including customised products, Reed Hastings replied:

> Sure, but you want something that will scale, . . . You want to sell something where the effort it takes to sell a dozen is *identical* to the effort it takes to sell just one. And while you're at it, try and find something that's more than just a onetime sale, so that once you've found a customer, you'll be able to sell to them over and over again. (in Randolph, 2019: 14–15)

The quest for scale is reflected in the technology these firms use, the infrastructure they build (Chapters 3 and 4), and the management practices they adopt. Page and Brin, Google's founders, adopted early on a management technique based on objectives. Called OKRs (Objectives and Key Results), it was developed by Intel and is still commonly used among tech firms. The technique consists of establishing goals that are measurable and realistic, yet set at the edge of attainment and well beyond the business's comfort zone. Its reputed benefits are to align teamwork towards a common objective and set clear priorities for management. The recipe was applied across Google teams (Doerr, 2018: 3–18; Schmidt and Rosenberg, 2017: 177-8; 220–2). Although Google's eventual scale has arguably as much to do with the nature of internet technology and infrastructure as its management culture, the company hit many of its targets. By 2020, it had nine products with at least one billion users: Android, Chrome, Gmail, Google Drive, Google Maps, Google Play, Google Photos, Google Search, and YouTube.

YouTube, in particular, was given its own set of OKRs. In 2012, it was agreed that the platform should reach one billion hours in daily viewing, representing a tenfold increase. Among the measures taken, YouTube's core metric was changed from clicks to watch time, reasoning that the latter was a better reflection of users' enjoyment and engagement with content (Doerr, 2018: 161–3). Youtube's recommendation algorithm was accordingly modified, creating a 'virtuous circle: More satisfied viewership (watch time) begets more advertising, which incentivizes more content creators, which draws more viewership' (Doerr, 2018: 161). The milestone was achieved in 2016 (Kyncl, 2017: 156).

Consolidation

Digitisation and technological convergence have been a major driver of change in the TV industry. It is redefining its perimeter by opening opportunities for businesses that were previously operating outside its realm. It is accelerating media globalisation because tech giants and their video platforms operate across multiple territories. Convergence is leading to the demise of old value–creation models and the rise of new ones, forcing media companies into restructuring activities (Gustafsson and Schwarz, 2013; Hacklin et al., 2013; Wirtz, 2017). Such activities take many forms, from spinning off or selling a portion of the operations to all kinds of strategic alliances (DePamphilis, 2019: 415–40), but often they involve consolidation (or combination), which is when two businesses become one by way of merger or acquisition.

Four types of mergers and acquisitions (M&A) are commonly distinguished: horizontal (combining two firms operating in the same segment of the same value chain, selling a similar type of product), vertical (integrating two companies from the same industry but operating upstream or downstream in the value chain), concentric (bringing together two businesses operating in the same field but which are indirect competitors), and conglomerate (combining companies from different fields of activities) (e.g. Chan-Olmsted, 1998: 36–7). Media economists most commonly refer to the first two types of integration (e.g. Chon et al., 2003: 143–4; Evens and Donders, 2016: 677–8; Sullivan and Jiang, 2010: 28).

A correlation exists between convergence and the successive waves of consolidation that the media industries have experienced in the recent past, particularly in the USA. Before the emergence of the Internet in the 1990s, most M&A transactions occurred within the same business segment and were aimed at scaling up firms engaged in a similar type of activity (Sullivan and Jiang, 2010: 32). By way of contrast, once convergence took hold of the US market, most transactions were aimed at creating synergies across industries (Sullivan and Jiang, 2010: 35). Chon et al. also observed differences in M&A activities before and after the US Telecommunications Act of 1996, whose goal was to break down regulatory barriers between the media and telecommunications industries and facilitate their convergence. The Act changed the structure of the M&A market, increasing the number of transactions between traditional media providers and internet companies (Chon et al., 2003: 149).

Convergence having expanded the perimeter of the media industry to include tech and the telecommunications sector (Oliver and Picard, 2020), many consolidation deals sought to create entities capable of operating in this extended industry. In particular, M&A activities created vertically integrated firms bringing together the networks and customer connections of internet businesses and/or telcos, and the content of media firms. While some of the headline deals between internet and media firms failed in the 2000s (more shortly), the resulting combination of telcos and content owners has created some of the world's largest media companies (Table 2.1).

Horizontal and concentric types of integration remain common. Any large media firm or telco would have gone through decades of primarily horizontal and concentric M&A activities in order to achieve a dominant position in its segment (DePamphilis, 2019: 415–40; Oliver and Picard, 2020). In the telecommunications sector in 2020 alone, T-Mobile and Sprint overcame opposition from several US states to close a merger valued at US$26.5 billion, Vodafone Australia and TPG joined forces in an operation estimated at US$10.1 billion, and Telefónica and Liberty Global formed a joint venture combining their British operations (O2 and Virgin Media respectively) in a US$37.8 billion deal.

Once Comcast had become a fully fledged media firm, it acquired Sky, which presented the advantage of an expanded footprint in Europe. Disney went for scale with the acquisition of 21st Century Fox for US$71.3 billion in 2019. The management reasoned that, in the era of DTC operations, a large library of content is a must, and Fox's programming, such as *The Simpsons* and National Geographic, has duly been integrated into Disney+ (Ball, 2019a). Viacom and CBS joined forces once again in 2019, thirteen years after their split, creating ViacomCBS.

Not all M&A deliver the expected benefits, and Dal Yong Jin contends that as much as 68 per cent of all M&A transactions between 1998 and 2007 failed to achieve their intended outcome (Jin, 2013: 114). Among those, two mega-mergers between AOL and Time Warner, and Vivendi and Universal, went spectacularly wrong (Jin, 2013: 111–26; Peil and Sparviero, 2017). Jin's period covers the end of the dot-com financial bubble, which exposed the shaky ground on which many tech firms' based their business model. However, M&A that seek vertical integration have the highest risk of failure. When John Stankey, AT&T's CEO, decided to spin off WarnerMedia to create a streaming giant with Discovery, he acknowledged that the acquisition was a mistake and the botched integration of Time Warner wiped US$ billions off the company value (FitzGerald et al., 2021; Chapter 4). Management issues and difficulties in execution can also lead to failure, and it is not rare that M&A are driven by financial opportunism or corporate hubris (Junni and Teerikangas, 2019: 5).

While some M&A fail, the ever-growing scale of leading firms in the media and entertainment sector indicates that consolidation and the search for scale are trends that remain significant.

Vertical Disintegration

Digitisation and consolidation attract the attention of scholars and industry observers because they involve public-facing conglomerates, and their business practices have implications for consumers and lawmakers alike (Coates, 2018; Crawford, 2013). While these two trends have been identified, another equally impactful trend is one feeds directly into the globalising process has yet to be analysed: the vertical disintegration of production processes and their segmentation into separate value-adding activities.

Independently from one another, Richard Caves and Allen Scott have already pointed out de-verticalisation in the film industry. The process began with dismantling the Hollywood studio system, resulting in a disintegration of studio film production (Caves, 2000: 87–102; Scott, 2005: 29, 40). The ensuing transition to spot production produced 'several observable changes in the film industry's structure' (Caves, 2000: 96), notably the emergence of specialist suppliers, a more flexible production system, and also a more casual workforce (Caves, 2000: 96–7, Scott, 2005: 120–1). Vertical disintegration has never been analysed in the context of the TV industry and needs a full explanation. The remainder of the chapter contextualises this trend in the context of the global economy, highlights its connection to GVCs, and provides an outlook of the TV GVC.

Vertical Disintegration and the Rise of GVCs

In today's global economy, goods are no longer produced by a single company: production processes are sliced and diced and involve inputs from multiple firms (Foster et al., 2013: 2). This is caused by *organisational fragmentation*, a managerial process whereby multinationals dissect their activities in order to concentrate on core competencies and outsource – often offshore – those service and production tasks that are best done by other companies in decentralised production networks (Contractor et al., 2011a: 6–8).

It is widely acknowledged that outsourcing – defined here as *the externalisation of value-adding activities to contractual partners at home or abroad* – is a dominant business paradigm and commonly practiced by most major firms (e.g. Contractor et al., 2011b; Milberg and Winkler, 2013). Entire industries operate on this model, including fashion and consumer electronics (e.g. Fernandez-Stark et al., 2011; Sturgeon and Kawakami, 2010). Western multinationals know that manufacturing does not offer the same returns as designing and branding. Many companies with substantial market capitalisation – owners of some of the best-known brands – sell products they do not manufacture. Apple, for instance, the world's most valuable company by market capitalisation (which reached US$2.47 trillion at the time of writing), owns no plant and outsources the entirety of its manufacturing operations to Far East subcontractors (Dedrick et al., 2010). As a result, production processes span territories, and sometimes continents, as multinationals allocate tasks according to the local advantages they find in terms of resources, cost, and benefit. Many have become logistics coordinators, expert at managing flows of supplies and information across multiple locations (Curry and Kenney, 2004: 114).

Outsourcing is driven by several factors, including cost reductions in IT and transportation, rapid rates of technological change, skills shortages, and the 'greater codification of corporate knowledge' (Contractor et al., 2011b: 9). A key driver, however, is the process of financialisation that characterises contemporary capitalism. Milberg and Winkler argue that 'the globalization of production and financialization are fundamentally connected' because firms are under tremendous pressure to return dividends to shareholders (Milberg and Winkler, 2013: 27). Facing growing competition in sluggish economies, they opt to focus on core competencies, sell non-core assets, and save operating costs through outsourcing and offshoring (Milberg and Winkler, 2013: 27). In such a context, the ability of outsourcing to deliver cost savings and efficiency gains for businesses overcomes any risk and drawback this strategy may entail.

Furthermore, many products are increasingly sophisticated and complex to manufacture, making it improbable that a single firm has the expertise to cover an entire production process. With the Internet of Things, smart devices from fridges to cars need electronic components to receive, manage, and send data. As a result, automotive and white goods manufacturers, among others, retain the expertise to assemble a variety of components but rely on their supply chain in order to design and produce some of them.

Outsourcing has encouraged the disintegration of production processes, a phenomenon highlighted by economists as the most significant economic and 'organizational development' of recent times (Langlois, 2003: 373). As a result, industries characterised by large vertically integrated corporations have been progressively replaced by GVCs. While Wallerstein underscores the long history of value chains (Chapter 1), they have risen to prominence in the global economy to the point where they constitute a distinctive feature of contemporary capitalism (Feenstra, 1998; Gereffi, 2014, Langlois, 2003; Milberg and Winkler, 2013). Today, they account for a growing share of world trade: 'trade in tasks' (or trade in intermediate goods and services) within value chains is routinely assessed as

Figure 2.1 The making of a global value chain

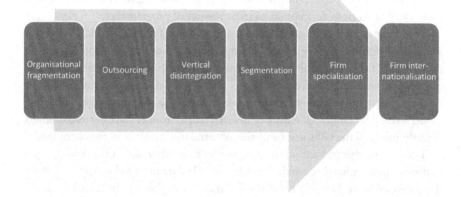

representing more than half the total value of (non-fuel) global exports (Milberg and Winkler, 2013: 37–48; WTO, 2013: 182–3). The 2008/09 financial crisis proved to be a short-lived break in the momentum, and the fragmentation of production has since continued apace to expand in the world economy, representing a significant share of international trade (Timmer et al., 2014). Nor has the COVID-19 pandemic significantly altered the course of GVCs, which have survived other pandemics and multiple conflicts, including two world wars.

As technology and economies evolve, some value chains fade away while new ones emerge. GVC's input-output structure is also subject to change. As vertical disintegration leads to the formation of distinct production stages, some firms seize the opportunity and decide to specialise in an emerging segment. What begins as an embryonic sector can eventually become a fully fledged industry sector in its own right. The process of segmentation has an influence on firm behaviour: once a segment becomes viable, suppliers specialise within it and search for growth internationally (Figure 2.1). In turn, this has an effect on industry structure, and this research argues that the cascading consequences generated by the rise of outsourcing are among the factors that are restructuring the TV industry as a globally integrated system.

The Making of a GVC

Vertical disintegration is a relatively recent phenomenon in the history of television. Until the late 1980s, broadcasters were fully integrated operations. In Europe, they produced what was aired, apart from domestic films and imports from Hollywood, and came fully equipped with studios, generously staffed production departments, and their own philharmonic orchestra. Nor were engineering tasks outsourced: they carried out most of the transmission functions themselves and owned much of the hardware that delivered the signal to the final user. Broadcasters operated on the basis of a vertical-integration model that saw them carry tasks from conception to transmission of programmes.

To a large extent, this model has been dismantled. Whilst broadcasters retain some key functions, they outsource many tasks they once performed. A growing proportion of the programming they air is commissioned, and many transmission and distribution tasks are devolved. Streamers display various levels of integration but carefully choose the tasks they keep in-house and the tasks they outsource. The DTC model is counter-intuitive: it cannot be inferred that a streamer reaching its customers 'directly' fulfils all the tasks and owns the infrastructure involved in the operation.

The pace of change varies from one country to another, and it is acknowledged that more international research is needed. While data need to be expanded there is enough evidence to suggest that the TV industry is globally structured around a GVC (Figure 2.2).

The chain retraces the odyssey a TV programme travels through from inception to reception. It is composed of two connected, but distinct, value chains (content production and media delivery), with aggregators located at the junction between the two. The content production segments correspond to the programme-making phase, which starts with conception and ends when the final production master has been approved. It involves multiple companies located across four key segments (production, facilities, distribution, and aggregation) (Chapter 7). The media delivery supply chain begins when production companies have finished working on the programme and aggregators package it up to reach various audiences. The focus changes from artistic intent to cost management and the search for efficiencies through automation and technology. The key segments are publication, transmission, and reception (Chapter 8).

This model offers a holistic perspective of the TV industry. Unlike media management versions (as discussed previously), it is not biased towards the activities of the lead firm and identifies the segments of the entire input-output structure through which a programme passes from creation to reception. Each segment is a value-adding activity that is a fully fledged sector in its own right.

The TV GVC remains a schematic representation of an industry, which is traversed by several other chains. Reception devices, such as mobile phones and TV sets, are designed and built in separate production networks (Carillo et al., 2015; Lee and Lim, 2018). The transmission segment traverses the wider ecosystem that is the data value chain (Curry, 2016). However, the TV GVC is a model designed to support the analysis of vertical disintegration and further our understanding of its impact on the global restructuring of the TV industry.

Figure 2.2 The television GVC

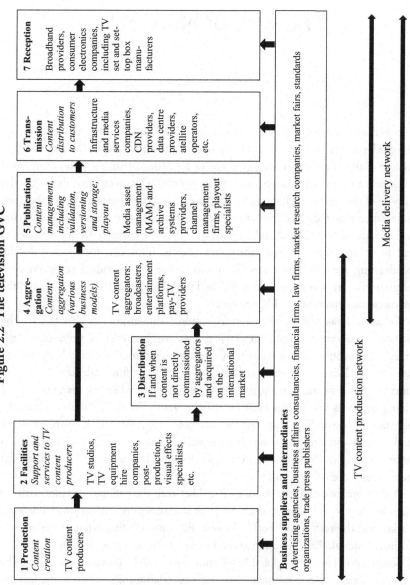

1 Production
Content creation

TV content producers

2 Facilities
Support and services to TV content producers

TV studios, TV equipment hire companies, post-production, visual effects specialists, etc.

3 Distribution
If and when content is not directly commissioned by aggregators and acquired on the international market

4 Aggre-gation
Content aggregation (various business models)

TV content aggregators: broadcasters, entertainment platforms, pay-TV providers

5 Publication
Content management, including validation, versioning and storage; playout

Media asset management (MAM) and archive systems providers, channel management firms, playout specialists

6 Trans-mission
Content distribution to customers

Infrastructure and media services companies, CDN providers, data centre providers, satellite operators, etc.

7 Reception

Broadband providers, consumer electronics companies, including TV set and set-top box manu-facturers

Business suppliers and intermediaries
Advertising agencies, business affairs consultancies, financial firms, law firms, market research companies, market fairs, standards organizations, trade press publishers

TV content production network

Media delivery network

Television GVC

3

The Rise of Networks

The formation of a TV GVC was decades in the making. At the core of the historical process lies the industry's global shift, which began in the last two decades of the twentieth century (the end of the broadcasting age) and accelerated in the new millennium (towards the streaming era). Documenting this shift is the purpose of the next two chapters, which adopt a bird's-eye view to concentrate on those aspects of the shift that are most apparent. Its dynamics and underlying structure are not considered and analysis is restricted to market-facing activities of lead firms and the industry's consumer brands. This chapter focuses on the broadcasting age and broadcasters in the streaming era, providing an overview of the growth in cross-border trade in finished programmes and TV formats, and the international expansion of TV networks.

Television has always had an international dimension, as dictated by the industry's economics. In manufacturing, the marginal cost of production (the added cost involved in the making of one additional unit) remains high as each unit absorbs labour and raw materials. In the TV or film industry, by way of contrast, the cost sunk into the first copy are very high, while the marginal cost of adding copies is low or can even be close to zero (Vogel, 2020: 20). Thus, the incentive of expanding distribution internationally, even if it involves some marketing investment, has always been great, because added international demand makes a strong contribution to profit margins since the marginal cost remains far lower than marginal revenue.

A clear line of demarcation once existed between the national and international when producers and distributors made a clear distinction between their domestic market and the rest of the world. At first, the national dimension prevailed over the international, then the international gained in importance, and finally the line of demarcation blurred as global integration progressed. As communication technologies began to remap media spaces, the relationship between media and territory unravelled. Cross-border trade intensified and firms expanded their reach, progressively reshaping national media systems from within by embedding them in transnational networks of production and consumption. New brands, products, platforms, management practices, and business models emerged, along-side novel consumer choice and cultural experiences.

This research does not assume that the world is flat (Introduction), nor does it presume the end of the local. Due to the rise of social media platforms that encourage participatory culture, local content has never been so abundant. The study postulates that the structuring principles of the TV industry have changed and that the dominant paradigm is global. The local is no longer self-determining but is shaped, to varying degrees, by trans-local forces. Local companies are entangled in international production networks and their trajectory can be affected by the behaviour of multinational firms. It is no longer viable for media companies to remain confined to their domestic market, and their performance depends eventually on their access to the global marketplace. Conversely, multinational firms need access to – and an understanding of – local territories. The formation of a global TV system involves a restructuring of the industry and a power shift from the local to the global, but both are irremediably entangled.

Growth in International Trade: Finished Programming

In terms of sales and acquisition, the TV industry distinguishes finished program-ming and TV formats. Finished programming covers all genres in scripted entertainment, from comedy to drama. While a few TV series are adapted (Chalaby, 2016a), the bulk of the trade consists of tapes (or files) that do not require any adaptation beyond dubbing or subtitling, hence the terminology of 'finished'.

It is an old trade as the incentives for the widest possible distribution of content have always been strong: the incremental costs associated with reaching a larger audience are far lower than the fixed costs involved in developing and producing a new show (Doyle, 2013: 15). The trade went through several growth spurts since its origin. The first wave began in the mid-1950s, the second in the mid-1980s (Havens, 2006: 13–24), and the third in the mid-2000s. During the first phase, television was in its infancy and US exports constituted the essential part of the trade. US distributors' international revenues multiplied nearly tenfold in the course of the period to reach US$100 million in 1970 (Havens, 2006: 18).

During the subsequent spike, the lion's share of the trade remained in American hands, and US producers' revenues increased more than tenfold again, passing 'from $500 million in 1984 to $6.5 billion in 2005' (Havens, 2006: 28). US export landmarks include *Star Trek*, *Dallas*, *Baywatch*, and *Friends*. The boom was spurred on by the liberalisation and concomitant commercialisation of televi-sion in many territories. The most profitable markets for US rights holders were in

Europe, and broadcasters such as Italy's Mediaset, Germany's RTL, and UK's ITV purchased US content in bulk. The period is characterised by the output deals signed with Hollywood studios, which saw them block order large amounts of library material (Torre, 2009). The Kirch group, in Germany, was not afraid of signing huge output arrangements, and its commitments to US studios amounted to US$6 billion by the mid-1990s (Guider and Hils, 1997). The financial burden of these deals contributed to Kirch's eventual bankruptcy. British broadcasters were savvier in their approach but aired their fair share of US fare: the four terrestrial channels (BBC 1, BBC 2, ITV, and Channel 4) scheduled forty-three US series between them in 1997 (Philips, 1997). Pay-TV operators such as Canal Plus and Sky played a dual role in this growth, placing their own orders for their proprietary channels and hosting third party networks that also needed content for their schedules.

Although Hollywood held about 75 per cent of the TV export market in the 1990s (Havens, 2006: 29), regional production centres were emerging. Both Egypt and Japan were exporting drama in their respective regions, while the telenovela trade was dominated by Brazil and Mexico (Havens, 2006: 23, 34). By the end of the decade, Hollywood's market share was in decline as stations started to substitute US imports with locally produced drama (Fry and Hazleton, 1999).

The rise of streaming services has triggered a third boom in scripted entertainment, and the current period is sometimes referred to as a 'golden age' of drama, also known as 'peak TV'. Together with live sports, scripted TV has the unique ability to drive subscriptions, and therefore plays a starring role in the business plans of leading streamers (Chapter 4). The impact of streaming platforms is clear to see, as the number of new scripted series in the English language on US-based online services passed from an annual total of 6 to 160 between 2011 and 2018 (Gallagher, 2018). The annual number of new English-language originals on US television climbed from 266 to 495 during this period, to reach to 559 in 2021 (Schneider, 2022).

Although the USA still dominates the trade in scripted entertainment, other countries export TV series of an international standard and three exporters stand out, all seeing a sharp rise in international sales in the past twenty years. The United Kingdom is a long-standing exporter of TV drama, and historically has benefitted from cultural and linguistic proximity to other English-speaking territories (Weissmann, 2012). However, until the late 1990s, the country's record as a programme exporter was deemed 'lacklustre' and 'a cause for concern' (Roddick, 1998: 20).[1] In 1996, British broadcasters exported £234 million (US$300 million) worth of programming but imported more than twice as much, £516 million (US$660 million) (Roddick, 1998: 20). By 2019, UK exports of finished

Table 3.1 *Korean TV exports, 2016–18 (in US$ millions)*

		2016	2017	2018
Terrestrial broadcasting	Broadcast programme sales	191.4	124.4	131.9
	Format sales	51.2	5.1	3.2
	Other	35.8	44.8	36.1
Programme provider	Broadcast programme sales	63.1	106.2	145.2
	Format sales	3.7	3.7	6.7
	Other	1.9	1.2	3.6
Independent content producer	/	63.9	76.8	151.7
Total		**411.1**	**362.3**	**478.4**

Source: adapted from Ministry of Culture, Sports and Tourism and Kocca, 2020: 27–8.

programmes alone (e.g. *Bodygard*, *McMafia*, *Good Omens*) reached a record high of £957 million (US$1.2 billion)[2] (3Vision, 2019).

Two exporters have emerged beyond the Western world. Turkish drama has become a noted trend, with sales reaching US$350 million in 2018, up from US$10 million ten years earlier (Middleton, 2019d). Sales have spilled outside the natural confines of Turkey's sphere of cultural influence to reach 146 countries across all continents (*Daily Sabah*, 2019). *Hallyu* – the Korean wave – is the term coined in the late 1990s to refer to the worldwide popularity and influence of Korean culture. *Hallyu* covers the full gamut of cultural products, including beauty, cuisine, music, video games, films, TV formats, and TV drama (Kim, 2013a; Park and Lee, 2019). Today, *Hallyu* is a multi-billion dollar export phenomenon that stretches from K-pop artists with billions of views and followers on video platforms to *Parasite*, winner of the Best Picture and three other Oscars at the 92nd Academy Awards in February 2020. K-drama and the Korean television industry lie at the heart of *Hallyu*. Building on hits such as *Winter Sonata* and *Jewel in the Palace* in the early 2000s (Kim, 2013b: 6,7), twenty years later the exports of the Korean TV industry are approaching half-a-billion US$ (Table 3.1).

The trade in finished programmes has undeniably grown in the last two decades. Across the (then) twenty-eight members of the European Union (EU), the origins of fiction on linear television was as follows in 2017: 49.7% of titles originated from the EU, 1.4% from the rest of Europe, 39.0% from the USA, and 9.9% from the rest of the world (EAO, 2018c: 50). Breaking down the EU category, 52% of titles were of national origin, and 48% originated from another EU member state (EAO, 2018c: 51). In summary, 74% of scripted entertainment aired on TV channels across the EU was imported.

Second, the trade began with nearly a sole purveyor and is now *polycentric*. American drama remains world television's stable commodity, but large industrial-scale exporters have emerged. The United Kingdom has made big strides, and it is easily forgotten that it was not always the export powerhouse it is today. In addition to the aforementioned countries, Israel, Spain, and Scandinavia are among the territories with a noted output in scripted entertainment. Nordic Noir has become a distinctive and established genre across multiple markets (Waade et al., 2020). Latin America still exports telenovelas, although they face stiff competition from Turkish soaps, which are available to TV buyers at a similar price point (Hamburger, 2020). Africa's local TV producers are forging partnerships with international companies and their series have begun to travel (*C21 Media*, 2019). *Queen Sono* was Netflix's first African original series and represents a breakthrough for African producers.

While the world has grown accustomed to English-language drama, foreign-language TV series were almost never seen in English-speaking markets. The situation changed in the 2010s when some public service broadcasters, later joined by pay-TV networks and online platforms, began to air original versions of foreign dramas in Western markets. In the United Kingdom, Channel 4 and BBC played a pioneering role. In 2014, Walter Iuzzolino, a former commissioning editor at Channel 4, launched Walter Presents, a streaming service entirely dedicated to foreign-language drama. Today, it operates in all major English-speaking territories, including the United Kingdom, USA, Canada, Australia, and New Zealand (Carugati, 2020). Rakuten's Viki,[3] based in San Mateo, California, holds the streaming rights of shows and movies in more than 200 languages and is known for its selection of Korean drama.

The trade's polycentrism is also reflected in the growth of South-South flows, which expand every time Global South producers sell programming to Asian, Latin American, or African broadcasters and platforms. The nearest indication of this trade's growth is to be found in the statistics of the United Nations Conference on Trade and Development (UNCTAD). Although these data incorporate all creative industries, they reflect the trade's overall growth, and the rise of South-South exchanges. They show a sharp rise in the total value of creative goods exports, passing from US$208.5 billion to US$509.8 billion between 2002 and 2015, an average growth rate of 6.6% per annum. In this period, the annual growth rate of exports in creative goods from developing economies stands at 8.5%, compared to 5.0% for developed markets. As a result, the trade's share of developing countries has risen from 40.5 to 52.0%, while that of developed economies has declined from 58.9 to 47.4% (Table 3.2).

Table 3.2 *Values and shares of creative goods exports, 2002–15 (in US$ millions)*

	2002	2015	Annual growth rate
World	208,493	509,753	6.6%
Developed economies	122,911	241,624	5.0%
Percentage of world exports	58.9.%	47.4%	/
Developing economies	84,365	265,001	8.5%
Percentage of world exports	40.5%	52.0%	/
Transition economies	1,217	3,048	6.8%
Percentage of world exports	0.6%	0.6%	/

Source: adapted from UNCTAD, 2017.

Rights and Financing

In years long gone, TV series were financed and produced domestically without much consideration for international sales. International rights were often referred to as 'foreign', implying a clear distinction between the local and the global and in early TV contracts they could be overlooked altogether. In the United Kingdom, Beryl Vertue, an agent at London Associated Scripts in the 1960s, was able to keep the foreign rights of many sitcoms her company managed on behalf of the rights holders, simply because the BBC was not interested:

> Well because when I was an agent you used to get quite simple short contracts from the BBC, and there was always a clause about, you know, foreign selling the programme abroad sort of thing, and I used to think well they'll never sell that just to cross it out. So the rights never went to the BBC, because I crossed it out, so that's why we had the rights to deal with it. Everyone's much more savvy about it now, they don't give the rights in the first place, you know, because the whole way of doing business here has changed over the years, but in those days it was quite a simple business by comparison. (Vertue, interview 2011)

On this occasion, the rights were attached to *Steptoe and Son* and *Till Death US Do Part*, which were adapted as *Sanford and Son* and *All in the Family* in the USA, the latter achieving cult status (Vertue, interview 2011). This was not an isolated case. The BBC went ahead with *Monty Python* even though, according to John Cleese, 'the entire team was united in the view that their programme would not have appeal whatsoever in the US' (Vickers, 1994: 22). The BBC agreed and ceded all the foreign rights to its creators (Vickers, 1994: 23).

The situation gradually evolved, not least because of Vertue's transatlantic successes, and the licensing of foreign rights began to be integrated into financial plans. In 1981, the BBC signed an output deal with Lionheart Television International, which subsequently handled its US distribution. The company also entered into co-production arrangements with the Corporation, which received £400,000 for the *Edge of Darkness* (Lavender, 1993: 104).

As late as the 1990s, overseas distribution was still 'seen as the cherry on the cake' (Roddick, 1998: 20). Full domestic financing was still an occurrence, but international co-productions were becoming more common. For the first time, country teams discovered other ways to think about and produce drama. Compromises and negotiations impeded creativity, and the finished products were often underwhelming (Considine, 1997; Fry, 1997).

Circumstances have changed once again. Today, drama production is essentially a deficit-funded model, meaning that the sum paid by the primary commissioner is never enough to cover production costs. It is the role of the distributor to plug the gap with co-production deals and/or external financing (in both cases in exchange for a certain amount of international rights), or with international pre-sales. The development of all high-end TV series necessitates complex financial arrangements that involve multiple players, including platforms, broadcasters, distributors, and specialised investment funds. In all cases, high-end drama production cannot be financed without international rights or sales set in advance (Nohr, interview 2020).

A second scenario exists, whereby a global streaming platform meets the full budget requirements, and more. The new model was described by Wayne Garvie, of Sony Pictures Television, in 2015:

> We have recently got the biggest drama commission in British television history which is a show called The Crown. It is going to be a very, very expensive show ... Originally our intention was that we would make it for a British broadcaster and we would look for American co-production money—the traditional model ... [But] then Netflix came in and said we want all rights so we will fund this and we will fund it at a level that is unimaginably high. (Garvie in Doyle, 2016: 636)

In other words, the favourite rights position of streamers is clear: 'when they're commissioning a show they want global rights. That's the way their model works' (Payne, interview 2019). 'We are a worldwide service', Disney+ states, 'we want worldwide rights' (in Crawford, 2021). The presence of SVoD players in the drama market is felt beyond the deals they sign. The increased demand for scripted entertainment has created competition for off- and on-screen talent, raising production costs. While the iconic six-episode *Edge of Darkness* cost the

BBC £2 million in the 1980s (US$3.3 million), the average spend on the 119 TV titles that qualified as high-end in the United Kingdom stood at £9.8 million in 2018, a total investment of £1.17 billion (US$1.55 billion) (Lavender, 1993: 104; Middleton, 2019c). In Europe, the cost of high-end productions steadily climbed to reach up to £3 million (US$3.96 million) per episode. Today, this sum represents an average that is often exceeded (Nohr, interview 2020).

Global platforms can spend much more (Chapter 4). *The Crown* cost Netflix US$10 million per episode (Ryan and Littleton, 2017), but this figure looks modest compared to Apple TV+'s *Masters of the Air* (US$22.5 million per episode, season one, 2021), Amazon Prime Video's *Lord of the Rings* (US$23.3 million per episode, seasons one and two, 2021), Disney+'s *The Mandalorian* (US$16.3 million per episode, season two, 2020), *Wandavision* (US$25 million per episode, season one, 2020), and *The Falcon and the Winter Soldier* (US$25 million per episode, season one, 2020) (Brown, 2021).

The explosion of drama budgets is a sign of international integration: global streamers can sink significant amounts of money in a single production because they can monetise their investment across a large number of territories. The business model of national broadcasters remains different, as Ian Griffiths, an ITV executive, pointed out in 2015:

> The down side of ... SVODs is that it is getting harder for old-fashioned heritage business models like ours, which is based on audience and advertising, to continue to make that same level of investment in that type of content. We can't afford to pay the price that Netflix will pay for content ... Our model is very simple—we get X number of viewers. We know that with around X million viewers, we will sell this much advertising. Therefore we can afford to pay a certain amount of money [for content]. (Griffiths in Doyle, 2016: 638)

In sum, not only global streamers can spend more on drama than national broadcasters, but as they are keeping all the rights, broadcasters are losing access to some of the content they used to rely on for their schedules and on-demand services. They have no option but to find alternatives (Ulin, 2019: 269).

The trade in finished programming mirrors the industry's general evolution towards a global shift. National markets were never autarkic but the major ones were self-sufficient, they are more interdependent today. The trade in finished programming is wider than ever and draws exporters from a larger array of geographies. The way drama is produced has evolved. International sales started as an afterthought and became the cherry on the cake, to eventually be the cake's base layer: TV drama, especially at the high end, must be co-produced or co-financed internationally in order to be greenlit. Global streamers are blurring the distinction between domestic and international rights.

TV Formats

Finished programmes constitute the bulk of cross-border media flows, but a new exchange mechanism has developed: formatting. The timescale of the format trade differs slightly from that of finished programming: it started in the early 1950s, grew in the late 1970s, and exploded in the late 1990s. It does, however, bolster the international TV trade by expanding it into unscripted genres such as game shows, factual entertainment, reality TV, and talent competitions. A TV format can be defined as the *structure* of a show that can generate a distinctive narrative and is licensed outside its country of origin in order to be adapted to local audiences (Chalaby, 2016: 13). From humble origins, the trade has become a multi-billion-dollar business that is essential to the industry. As a result, and unbeknown to audiences, the origin of many of their favourite TV shows lies abroad.

The TV format trade was initiated by a contract signed by the US rights holders of CBS's *What's My Line*, a comedy panel show, and the BBC on 29 June 1951. For the first time, and after years of haggling, a broadcaster agreed to pay for the idea and package of a show – its format – as opposed to something tangible such as a tape or script. The contract pins down the notion of the format as the right to remake a programme for a given territory that exists alongside other rights attached to the programme. This led to the formation of a new class of rights, on the back of which the international TV format trade grew.

Thereafter, the TV format trade developed, albeit at slow pace. Well into the 1980s, US producers were the trade's main purvey, which remained confined to game shows. ARD (Germany), RTF (France), RAI (Italy), TVE (Spain), Radio Luxembourg, Sveriges Radio (Sweden), the BBC, and ITV (UK), all adapted American game shows, plus some from fellow European broadcasters. Few among them shared the BBC's belief that they should pay for the packaging of a programme, and most of their adaptations were unlicenced. Broadcasters in Latin America and Australia operated under similar assumptions. Public policies were another restraint on the format market because they envisioned television as a national medium: broadcasters, particularly the public service ones, were given the mission to promote national culture and strengthen national identity. This role did not square with entertaining the masses with *Double or Nothing*, *Tic Tac Dough*, or *Queen for a Day* (Chalaby, 2016b: 19–28).

The format trade perked up with, on the demand side, the dismantling of public monopolies and development of commercial television and, on the supply side, two distribution agreements that internationalised the Goodson-Todman catalogue, the world's largest library of game shows (*The Price is Right*, *Password*, *Family Feud*, *Card Sharks*, *Blockbusters*, etc.). In the first sign that Marc Goodson was paying any interest to overseas markets, he divided the worldwide format rights of his library into two chunks, giving Europe and the Middle East to Fremantle, a US-based distributor, and the rest of the world to Reg Grundy, an Australian producer. These agreements ensured a much wider distribution of the Goodson shows, and helped transform the format trade into a lawful business (Moran, 1998, 2013).

The trade was further developed by contributions from other TV producers, such as Chuck Barris (*The Dating Game, The Newlywed Game*), Merv Griffin (*Jeopardy!, The Wheel of Fortune*) and, in Europe, Action Time (UK), Joop van den Ende's JE Entertainment and John de Mol Productions (The Netherlands). The format trade professionalised during this period. The United States sent 'flying producers' whose job was to help local teams set up their game shows. Marc Goodson, among others, was insistent that broadcasters stick to his guidelines and his producers travelled the world armed with sample scripts, set plans, and sample questions (Chalaby, 2016b: 28–32).

Although the format trade had progressed by leaps and bounds, it remained a little-known mechanism of TV distribution. Game shows – never a prestigious genre – formed the backbone of the trade, and at least three quarters were of US origin. Format producers and distributors operated at the fringes of the industry, knocking on doors with bags of tapes selling them as one would sell brushes.

The format revolution that heralded the global shift occurred at the turn of the millennium. It was brought on by a combination of factors. Commercial broadcasting developed in Central and Eastern Europe, the Middle East, and across Asia and Latin America. Fledgling broadcasters noticed that their audiences preferred local shows to imported ones, but local programming required knowhow and resources, both in short supply at the time. They realised that the best solution would be to rely on concepts that came with a pre-established method of production and guidelines.

In mature markets, television was becoming more competitive and broadcasters welcomed the opportunity to acquire formulas that had been tested in other territories and that enabled them to de-risk their schedules. TV producers internationalised and progressively realised that TV formats could help them achieve scale (Chapter 7).

The invention of a new genre, reality TV, and its associated sub-genres, factual entertainment and talent competitions, propelled the format trade to new heights. A reality TV programme has no formal script and consists of a succession of set situations and turning points that weave drama by interlacing narrative strands. It is, essentially, a structure that contains a series of narrative elements, techniques, and characters that, together, form a distinct show. These elements are discrete, and thus reproducible and formattable. Indeed, the history of reality TV and TV formats is closely entwined (Chalaby, 2016b).

Table 3.3 *World's top 20 travelling TV formats, 2020*

Programme title	Year of origin	Country of origin	Distribution company	Total number of adaptations
Who Wants to Be a Millionaire?	1998	UK	Sony Pictures Television	102
Deal or No Deal	2000	The Netherlands	Banijay Rights	85
Got Talent	2006	UK	Fremantle	78
The Voice	2011	The Netherlands	ITV Studios	70
Family Feud	1976	USA	Fremantle	68
MasterChef	2005	UK	Banijay Rights	65
Dancing with the Stars	2004	UK	BBC Studios	63
Minute to Win It	2010	USA	Banijay Rights	62
Survivor	1997	UK	Banijay Rights	58
Are You Smarter Than?	2007	USA	MGM	57
The X Factor	2004	UK	Fremantle	56
Idols	2001	UK	Fremantle	56
Money Drop	2010	UK	Banijay Rights	55
Cash Cab	2005	USA	All3Media	52
Wheel of Fortune	1975	USA	CBS	49
Weakest Link	2000	UK	BBC Studios	49
Next Top Model	2003	USA	CBS	48
Big Brother	1999	The Netherlands	Banijay Rights	48
You Can't Ask That	2016	Australia	ABC Commercial	47
Come Dine with Me	2005	UK	ITV Studios	46

Source: K7 Media, 2021: 21.

Although formats were crossing borders in growing numbers by the late 1990s, many TV executives had yet to take notice. The role of heralding TV formats to the world fell to four shows: *Who Wants to Be a Millionaire?*, *Survivor*, *Big Brother*, and *Idols* (Bazalgette, 2005; Chalaby, 2016b: 50-61). *Millionaire* broke all kinds of records: it is the fastest-selling format ever (it sold to ninety territories less than two years after its launch in September 1998), and currently has the highest number of adaptations (Table 3.3). It also established the basic principles of the global TV franchise: consistent branding, territory-by-territory licensing, and extensive ancillary rights.

Survivor is the original adventure reality game show. It has been produced in more than forty countries and has gone through thirty-eight seasons in the USA alone up to 2019 (company source). *Survivor*'s historic contribution is the weekly elimination process, an unparalleled mechanism of drama construction for unscripted entertainment. *Big Brother*, which was among the first reality shows to incorporate such a process, innovated in multimedia storytelling and the use of several platforms to generate revenue. It was influential and inspired a long line of formats that use a similar premise, up to and including ITV's *Love Island*. On its twentieth anniversary in September 2019, *Big Brother* was still in production in eighteen markets (Brzoznowski, 2019).

Popstars may have been the first reality version of the amateur show, a tradition that started with sound broadcasting in the 1930s, but the planetary success of *Idols* stole its limelight. By the end of the 2000s, the format had gone to 156 series in 43 markets, breaking audience records in many territories. *Idols* was also the first iteration of a long line of reality-skewed singing competitions that stretches from *The X Factor* and *The Voice* to *The King of Mask Singer*. Many of its format points, such as the skills-based performance, the panel of judges, the public vote and the elimination process were extended to other talent competitions, such as *Dancing with the Stars* and *Got Talent*.

Together, these four shows marked the history of the medium by demonstrating the potential of the format as a distribution mechanism and opening up international trade to unscripted shows. Reality formats – and talent competitions in particular – became a global entertainment phenomenon. Many of these competitions have seen at least fifty local adaptations and most territories have aired one or several versions of these formats (Table 3.3).

Today, hundreds of shows are adapted at any one time, reaching a cumulative value (in terms of distribution and production fees) of several billion dollars per year (FRAPA, 2009). The leading formats can see up to 100 adaptations (Table 3.3). From a handful of companies in the 1990s, hundreds create, produce, or distribute TV formats today. The leading global TV studios sell thousands of hours worth of format every year, and Banijay alone has thousands of registered formats in its catalogue. Format producers have their own awards, events, and conferences.

Formats have become an integral part of broadcasting schedules. In Europe, eighty-four channels aired 28,386 hours of formats (the equivalent of 338 hours per channel) by 2013 (*TBI Formats*, 2014: 23). Most top-rated unscripted programmes worldwide are formatted, such as these ubiquitous talent competitions. The trade is no longer limited to game shows and reality TV, as scripted entertainment from telenovelas to British comedies and Israeli series have joined the format revolution and are remade locally (Chalaby, 2016a; Verevis and Perkins, 2015).

TV Formats and the Global Shift

The TV format business is deepening media globalisation on several counts. For viewers, TV formats are as any other local shows, but they follow transnational patterns of production. A programme can only become a format once adapted outside its country of origin. As Michel Rodrigue, one of the industry's founding fathers, explains:

> A format is not a product, it is a vehicle, and thus the only *raison d'être* of formats is the international market ... The format is a vehicle which enables an idea to cross boundaries, cultures, and so on, and to be localised in every place it stops. (Rodrigue, interview 2008)

However, formats do not merely fly across borders: they change as they do so and always involve an interplay between the local and the global. They are a kernel of rules that are immutably blended with elements that adapt in travel. In addition, the knowledge that underpins them is also transnational in scope. Production bibles lay out format rules and consultant producers explain or, if necessary, enforce them. Bibles also contain a certain amount of local knowledge, as they can be updated with information accumulated in the territories where the show is produced. If an idea that is tried in one market works, it is passed on, and if it fails, licensees are warned against it. Leading brands such as *The Bachelor* or *Dancing with the Stars* organise international conferences for licensees, and share knowledge on intranet websites.[4]

The format trade has increased the volume of cross-border TV flows. As seen, broadcasters have long imported Hollywood films and TV series, but once made light entertainment by themselves. Today, broadcasters seek answers to their scheduling issues abroad and the flagship shows they air at prime time are often the local adaptations of global brands. They are transnationally more interdependent because they rely more on international TV studios, and they make programming decisions based on the ratings performances of shows in other territories.

The evolution of the TV format business echoes that of finished programmes in its polycentrism. During the game show era (pre-1990), US producers dominated the market with 62% of international format sales. The focal point of format origination shifted to Europe with the rise of unscripted genres such as factual entertainment and reality TV. In the 2000s, the United Kingdom dominated the market with 43% of sales, followed by the USA (20%) and the Netherlands (12%). The following decade saw the United Kingdom retain its dominant position with 30% of the market, but in second position came Israel (16%), followed by the Netherlands (15%) and the USA (13%) (K7 Media, 2019: 15). 2020 data put the

UK's market share at 42.1%, followed by the Netherlands, 10.3%, and USA and South Korea, 10.1% each (K7 Media, 2021: 7).

Further data underline the trade's growing scope. Exports from outside these four countries account for 27.5% market (K7 Media, 2021: 7). Format originators can be found in every world region (Khalil, 2017; Ndlela, 2017; Uribe-Jongbloed and Pis Diez, 2017), and Asian producers are performing particularly well. Among them, Japanese and South Korean firms have the expertise and connections to remain among the top producers. Two of the best-selling formats of recent years come from South Korea (*The King of Masked Singer* with forty-two adaptations since 2015 and *I Can See Your Voice* with seventeen sales so far). Japan has a longer tradition of format exports, and best sellers include *Hole in the Wall* and *Dragon's Den* (forty-five and forty-three international sales since the 2000s) (K7 Media, 2021: 21, 27). In contrast to recent past, Asian formats are finding their way into Western markets: 31 of the 41 Asian formats sold in 2020 were bought outside the region, and the USA alone has acquired 11 (K7 Media, 2021: 30).

Transnational TV Networks

Television was invented as a national medium (or even local in the USA). Cable and satellite distribution gave broadcasters the first opportunity to reach a larger audience. This section offers an overview of the development of international TV channels, starting with Europe, before considering other world regions.

The first European communications satellites launched in the 1980s, prompting a small number of pioneers to reach for a pan-European audience. These included public service broadcasters such as the francophone TV5 and European Broadcasting Union's (EBU) Eurosport, American broadcasters (CNN, Discovery, and MTV), and Murdoch's Sky Channel. Many ventures have long disappeared (e.g. Europa, ITV's Super Channel, Music Box, Screensport, among others) as the going was tough for channels that went against the national grain (Tydeman and Kelm, 1986: 179–209). The challenges were such that industry analysts thought that international TV networks had little prospect on the continent (e.g. Alonzi, 1998; Barker, 1993).

At the root of the problem was the very small size of the reception universe, the potential audience. Direct-to-home satellite technology was in its infancy and no more than 25 million European homes were connected to cable in 1991, a fraction of the 132 million TV households in Western Europe (Woodman, 1999). Furthermore, in the absence of an international regulatory framework, cross-border stations were entirely dependent on national legislation, which was rooted on protectionist policies and contained many entrenched monopolies. Managing international TV rights was also challenging, and acquiring them was often impossible in the first place. Most rights owners viewed transnational TV networks with suspicion. Among them, Hollywood studios held 'the policy of not selling to TV channels which deliberately cross frontiers' (Cox, 1985). The pan-European advertising market was weak, and even multinationals showed little interest. Brand names changed across the continent, as did packaging and product cycle. Most multinationals like Nestlé or Unilever devolved marketing to their local subsidiaries, which passed on the advertising budget to a local agency (Chalaby, 2009: 7–53).

The planets finally aligned for pan-European TV channels in the 1990s, when the barriers and obstacles receded as new technologies broke through: digitisation facilitated the formation of large-capacity international communications networks, a viable international copyright regime was created (not least through the 'SatCab' EU Directive adopted in 2003), regulation evolved (e.g. the Television without Frontiers EU Directive voted in Paris in 1989), the number of cross-border subscribers expanded, and advertisers began paying attention. This led to rapid growth of transnational TV channels across a wide variety of genres, including news and business news (Bloomberg, CNBC, CNN, Euronews, etc.), factual entertainment (e.g. the Discovery and National Geographic suite of channels), entertainment (AXN, HBO, and Fox-branded channels), children's television (such as Cartoon Network, the Disney brands, and Nickelodeon), sports (Eurosport, ESPN), music television (MTV, Viva, etc.), and films (e.g. Studio Universal, Turner Classic Movies) (Chalaby, 2009; Collins, 1992; Esser, 2002; Negrine, 1988).

Many pan-European TV channels have progressively evolved into networks of localised channels, enabling them to blend the local with the global. Local channels can adapt to a specific cultural and linguistic environment, develop their own schedules and positioning, and add a bit of their programming. At the same time, they benefit from the network's strengths, sharing with other stations a brand, a 'look and feel', most of the programming, and all the resources and infrastructure (Chapter 10).

These networks never surpassed terrestrial TV channels in ratings but by the early 2010s they had carved a position on every pay-TV platform in Europe. In 2013, 98 international brands delivered across 1,010 local channels, bringing a total income (advertising and carriage fee) of US$4.3 billion for their owners (Chalaby, 2016c). Pan-European TV networks did particularly well in certain genres, notably factual entertainment (e.g. Discovery, National Geographic), music television (MTV), and children's television (e.g. Cartoon Network, Disney, Nickelodeon).

There was a total of 1,074 localised TV channels across the EU in 2017 (Tables 3.4 and 3.5). US conglomerates ran an average of 81 channels in the EU, but taking into account the subsequent acquisitions of 21st Century Fox by Disney and Sky by Comcast, the average is slightly higher today (provided the number of channels has stayed the same). The same study calculated that localised TV channels represented 32 per cent of all TV channels available in the EU in 2017 (EAO, 2018a: 19–20).

The development of pan-regional TV networks is particularly advanced in Europe. European markets are attractive, and the continent is characterised by strong transnational governance. The EU's forward-looking Television without Frontiers Directive offered the world's first regulatory framework for international TV channels. Revised numerous times since 1989, it is today known as the Audiovisual Media Services Directive. The Directive ensured EU-wide reception of TV services, thereby enacting the single market for audiovisual services (Collins, 1998).

Pan-regional TV channels are a worldwide phenomenon. Africa's regional networks emerged in the 1990s, following the contours of the three main linguistic zones. TV5 Afrique and Canal Horizons served the region's francophone populations, South African Broadcasting Corporation's SABC Africa covered the English-speaking countries, while RTP Africa was available across the lusophone nations (Mytton, Teer-Tomaselli and Tudesq, 2005). Today, Africa's connectivity may not meet the standards of the most advanced markets, but the continent's satellite TV industry is thriving and includes a mix of Western and home-grown brands. The area's largest regional pay-TV provider is MultiChoice, a South African company that operates a major satellite TV service and multiple TV channels across sub-Saharan Africa.

Transnational television had the most impact, culturally and politically, in the Middle East. With the emergence of regional communications satellites, the international airwaves became a battlefield for competing news agendas. For audiences, pan-Arab news stations were the opportunity to hear a different voice and bypass their regime's stronghold on national media and journalism. None of these voices has been more impactful – and more documented – than Al Jazeera (El-Nawawy and Iskander, 2002; Sakr, 2005; Seib, 2012; Zayani, 2005). The Qatari station launched in 1996, followed by the English version ten years later. The 1990s also saw the rise of direct-broadcast satellite providers with a region-wide reach, such as Arab Radio and Television (ART), Showtime Arabia, and Orbit. Today's leading regional providers are Dubai–based Orbit Showtime Network (OSN) and Qatar–based beIN Media group. Both platforms mix proprietary channels and third party global TV brands.

Satellite technology profoundly changed television in South Asia. Three satellite platforms emerged in India in the 1990s: Sony, Star TV, and Zee TV. Until

Table 3.4 *US TV network brands established in the EU, ranked by number of localised services, 2017*

US parent company	TV network brands	Localised versions
Discovery	Animal Planet, Discovery Channel, Discovery History, Discovery Science, Discovery Turbo, Discovery World, DMAX, Eurosport 1, Eurosport 2, Eurosportnews, ID – Investigation Discovery, TLC	161
21st Century Fox	24 Kitchen, Baby TV, Fox, Fox Comedy, Fox Crime, Fox Life, Fox Movies, Fox Sports, Nat Geo People, NGC – National Geographic Channel, Wild – Nat Geo Wild, Sky 1, Sky 3D, Sky Atlantic, Sky Cinema, Sky Cinema Comedy, Sky Cinema Family, Sky Cinema Hits, Sky Sport 1, Sky Sport 2	136
AMC Networks	A&E, AMC TV, Canal Hollywood, Canal Panda, CBS Reality, Extreme Sports Channel, Film Café, FLN – Fine Living Network, Food Network, Horror Channel, JimJam, Megamax, MGM, Minimax, Odisea, Spektrum TV, Sport 1, Sundance Channel, The Outdoor Channel, Travel Channel, TV Paprika	109
Viacom	Comedy Central, Comedy Central Extra, Comedy Central Family, MTV, Nick Junior, Nick Toons, Nickelodeon, Paramount Channel, VH1, VIVA	101
Warner Media	Adult Swim, Boing, Boomerang, Cartoon Network, Cartoonito, Cinemax, Cinemax 2, HBO, HBO 2, HBO 3, Nova TV, Ring TV, TCM – Turner Classic Movies, TNT – Turner Network Television	97
Sony Corporation	AXN Black, AXN Channel, AXN Spin, AXN White, Fightbox, Filmbox, Filmbox Extra, Filmbox Family, Filmbox Plus, Filmbox Premium, Pop!, Sony Entertainment Television, Sony Sci-Fi, Sony Turbo	75
Walt Disney	Disney Channel, Disney Cinemagic, Disney Junior, Disney XD	50
Comcast Corporation	13th Street, Diva, E! Entertainment, Movies 24, SyFy, Universal Channel	44
A&E Networks	A&E, Blaze, CI – Crime and Investigation, H2 – History Channel 2, History Channel, Lifetime	27
Liberty Global	QVC, UPC	8

Source: European Audiovisual Observatory (EAO), 2018a: 38.

Table 3.5 *European TV network brands established in the EU, ranked by number of localised services, 2017*

EU parent company	TV network brands	Localised versions
Kinnevik	3+, CTC, Nova TV, Trace Sport Stars, Trace Urban, TV1000 Balkan, TV1000 East, TV1000 Premium, Viasat Explore, Viasat Film Action, Viasat Film Comedy, Viasat Film Family, Viasat Film Hits, Viasat Film Premiere, Viasat Fotboll, Viasat Golf, Viasat History, Viasat Hockey, Viasat Motor, Viasat Natue, Viasat Series, Viasat Sport	122
Albert Bonnier	C MORE First, C MORE Fotboll, C MORE Golf, C MORE Hits, C MORE Hockey, C MORE Live, C MORE Series, C MORE SF, C MORE Sport, C MORE Stars	36
United Media	N1 TV, SK Golf, SK Sport Klub	27
Bertelsmann	Auto Motor Sport TV, Film+, Film+2, RTL 2, RTL Crime, RTL Living, RTL Passion, RTL+	22
RCS Management	Digi Animal World, Digi Film, Digi Sport, Digi World	13
Da Vinci Media	Da Vinci Learning	11
Duplicato Media	Cinestar Action and Thriller, Cinestar Premiere, Cinestar TV	10
Vivendi	Canal+, Canal+ Family, Canal+ Series, Canal+ Sport, TeleToon+	10
Mega Max Media	Kidzone, Kidzone+	8
Telecom Srbija	Arena Sport	7

Source: EAO, 2018a: 39.

the mid-1990s, they had a greater impact domestically than regionally as, outside India, only the Philippines and Thailand had significant numbers of households equipped to receive transnational television via satellite (400,000 and 393,000 respectively). In Indonesia, Malaysia, Brunei, Myanmar, and Vietnam, these numbers were negligible (Thomas, 1998: 228). In the next decade, the number of homes with cable or satellite reception reached millions, and these three Indian providers, together with Hindi entertainment, began to dominate the region (Page and Crawley, 2005: 138–41, Thussu, 2005: 161). In parallel, pay-TV platforms emerged in the smaller markets, bringing to the region international channels such as the BBC, Cartoon Network, ESPN, HBO, Discovery, HBO, and MTV (Thomas, 1998).

Today, Sony Pictures Networks India, Star (a Walt Disney subsidiary), and Zee Entertainment are bona fide global broadcasters able to reach subscribers in any part of the world. Sony and Zee are available in 167 and 173 countries, respectively (company sources).

Global TV Brands

TV channels have different reasons and strategies for crossing borders, and the extent of their reach differs widely (Chalaby, 2005a). International networks come in all shapes and sizes: some are in a handful of countries, some are pan-regional, others have achieved a global presence. The first channel to achieve global distribution was CNN in 1989, when the news network was given access to a Soviet satellite (Chalaby, 2005b: 27–8, 173–5; Flourney and Stewart, 1997). Thirty years later, CNN International reaches 388 million households, and the localised channels are available to more than two billion people across 200 territories (company source). Al Jazeera English, BBC World News, China's CGTN – China Global Television Network, France 24, and Japan's NHK World, count among the other news channels with global reach (Gilboa, 2005; Paterson and Sreberny, 2004).

Rights and monetisation issues make the distribution of entertainment channels more complicated, but some brands have achieved a wide presence. In factual entertainment, these are the Discovery, National Geographic, and BBC branded networks. Discovery Networks International operates over 60 brands, localised in over 400 distribution feeds in 50 languages across 220 territories, distributing up to 14 channels in any particular market (Discovery, 2019: 14). In Europe alone, 372 million people watched the Tokyo Olympic Games across its TV and digital services, including Eurosport (O'Halloran, 2021). In children's television, Cartoon Network, Nickelodeon, and the Disney branded channels have also achieved near-worldwide distribution.

Conclusion

This chapter focused on the origins and the broadcasting side of television's global shift. Trade in content has grown manifold in volume and diversity since the 1950s. Commerce in finished programming has developed in successive waves, while the business in TV formats exploded in the late 1990s, increasing the transnational interdependence of both broadcasters and producers. Both trades have progressively become more polycentric, with participation widening to a growing number of exporting nations. TV channels began to internationalise in the 1980s, and after a difficult start achieved a large distribution. Transnational TV networks eventually became common on pay-TV platforms across the world, and some broadcasting brands became global. The TV industry began its global shift before the Internet made its mark; Chapter 4 will examine the impact of the new distribution technology.

4

The Rise of Platforms

Streamers accelerated the shift initiated by broadcasters. Global integration is not merely a matter of size and reach of lead firms but a question of technology and infrastructure that are deployed, scope of supply chain, nature of suppliers, and the connections among all these geographically dispersed components. This chapter, however, focuses on the streamers themselves and the brands that consumers interact with.

This chapter will offer an overview of the streaming landscape and focus on the distinctive feature of the TV industry in the digital era: the rise of platforms. First, it will contextualise the advent of streaming by raising the following question: is it an evolution or revolution in the history of screen entertainment? I will argue that, on one hand, streaming is built on the industry fundamentals of non-rival consumption, introduced by cinema, and convenience, heralded by broadcasting. On the other hand, platforms extend these qualities to such an extent that they have changed the way the TV industry operates. Platforms can only operate at scale, and this new governing principle has been a driving factor in the acceleration of television's global shift.

This chapter will then examine the importance of scale, before introducing the concept of the platform to explain how it is achieved. It will distinguish three types of streaming platforms (internal, multi-sided, and transaction), which it will connect to three business models (SVoD, AVoD, and video sharing).

Streamers and Broadcasters in the New TV Industry

Online platforms have stolen the limelight from pay-TV providers, but the latter continue to play a key role in the TV ecosystem. In 2019, the pay-TV market was valued at US$393 billion worldwide, while global streaming was worth US$42.6 billion, about 11 per cent (Grand View Research, 2020; MarketWatch, 2019). Both markets are set on different trajectories. While double-digit growth is expected for streaming for the foreseeable future, pay-TV services are set for a decline in developed economies and modest growth elsewhere. In the USA and Europe, pay-TV peaked in the late 2010s and subscriptions have begun to fall. In the USA, the leading pay-TV providers lost 1.7 per cent of their subscribers in 2018 and 5.4 per cent the following year, shedding a total of 6.5 million customers in two years (O'Halloran, 2020b). In most emerging economies, pay-TV is still growing, albeit at a slower pace than in the past (O'Halloran, 2019). However, SVoD subscriptions being cheaper than pay-TV services, the size of the market fails to do justice to the growing popularity of online platforms. Globally, there are more than 700 million SVoD subscriptions, and they are set to overtake pay-TV in more than thirty countries (Holleran, 2020). Thus, even though the gap is closing, pay-TV still weighs more economically than online entertainment services.

Streaming is a disruptive technology in the sense that consumers use these services, to a variable extent, as substitutes for others. This behaviour manifests itself with cord-cutters, those consumers who cancel their multichannel subscription, precipitating the decline of pay-TV services in certain markets. Changes in consumer behaviour triggered by the availability of streaming has inevitably lead to revenue falls for certain media firms and, in certain cases, their collapse (Chapter 9). However, there is a certain complementarity between pay-TV and streaming services, especially when the latter need the former to access viewers. SVoD services such as Disney+ and Netflix have signed hundreds of agreements with partners among pay-TV operators, gaming consoles, mobile phone manufacturers, and wireless carriers in order to accelerate their penetration rate. Netflix has international partnerships in place with pay-TV operators such as Sky and Liberty Global, giving the streamer direct access to consumers in those European territories that these carriers operate. In sum, it is likely that streamers and pay-TV providers will co-exist for the foreseeable future.

Streaming: Evolution or Revolution?

The word 'streaming' is often associated with 'revolution'. But is such a claim justified? Historically, entertainment has gone through two revolutions. In the nineteenth century the entertainment sector was thriving: theatres and music halls were erected in great numbers and sophisticated touring circuits were operating in France, the United Kingdom, and the USA (Bakker, 2008: 40). But performances were live, a constraint for artists and audiences alike, and an obstacle to the sector's industrialisation. In London's West End, in-demand stars made scheduled appearances in different theatres on the same night, forcing them to travel as fast as they possibly could from one venue to the other. The advent of motion pictures changed everything:

When Charlie Chaplin was eight, he performed in three large music halls an evening. Ten years later, in 1915, each night he could be seen in thousands of halls across the world. The remarkable transformation of spectacting into a non-rival setting where Chaplin could be watched in many places simultaneously was made possible by motion pictures. They industrialized entertainment by automating it, standardizing it, and making it tradable. (Bakker, 2012: 1036)

Motion pictures turned entertainment into a non-rival good whose consumption by one person does not prevent simultaneous enjoyment by others, thus considerably lowering the marginal cost of providing the same entertainment to additional viewers (Vogel, 2020: 20). In addition, cinema was the first technology to internationalise entertainment. The reproducibility of the film reel made entertainment tradable, soon creating an international market for films (Bakker, 2008: 164).

Broadcast television built on this principle of non-rival consumption: the reception of a TV signal by a household does not prevent others from tuning in, and the cost of additional reception from the same transmitter for the broadcaster is zero. Television, though, added one key component: *convenience*. Television is among the commercial and industrial success stories of the twentieth century because it brought entertainment into the living rooms of millions. When the BBC resumed post-war operations, the opening programme introduced television as follows:

To those of you who are seeing television for the first time, and who therefore are the people for whom this film is primarily intended, we'd like to sound a note of caution. Television is essentially the entertainment of the home viewer, and it is the family group that our producers and artists normally consider to be their audience. And so, if your first introduction to television is not by your own fireside, do believe me when I say that you will enjoy it so much more when you meet us once again in the intimacy of your home, when you are sitting relaxed in your own armchair. (BBC, 1946)

Television shifted the consumption of entertainment from public to private. At a flick of a dial, news bulletins, entertainment programmes, films, and some dazzling variety shows became available in viewers' homes. The convenience of the medium progressively improved. Videocassette recorders, which became widely adopted in the 1980s, were the first time-shifting technology. Next came cable TV, which first delivered near VoD by providing content carousels where films started every fifteen minutes or so. As cable got faster, providers offered true VoD, well ahead of the Internet (Ingold, 2020).

On one hand, streaming is built on non-rival consumption and convenience and does not change these fundamentals. On the other hand, it extends these principles and scales them up to such an extent that it is changing the way the industry operates. Broadcasting enabled non-rival consumption *in a family setting* where all members of a household share a TV set. Someone in the household would make a choice and the others would have to abide by it. Albeit that TV sets have multiplied in family homes, streaming is available on all types of connected devices, making content easily accessible for every household member. Streaming extends non-rival consumption from the family to the individual: broadcasting made entertainment private, and streaming makes it *personal.*

Streaming is successful because it is extraordinarily convenient. As streamers have their entire catalogue online, viewers can choose what they want, when they want, and as often as they like. They can watch it anywhere inside or outside their home and while commuting and traveling. Being both convenient and personal, streaming has become the popular mode of delivery, and a variety of business models is based on the concept, forcing entertainment conglomerates and broadcasters to pivot towards DTC services. Streaming, however, is also a massive overhaul. In the digital era, television has adopted a new way of distributing content: platforms. Through them, content providers can achieve unprecedented scale, propelling the global age of television.

Streaming: Television at Scale

Some of the earliest streaming services were established by broadcasters, whose platforms fall under the BVoD label (Introduction). Channel 4's 4oD and BBC iPlayer, both in the United Kingdom, launched in 2006 and 2007, respectively. Since then, in Europe as elsewhere, all TV networks stream and broadcast. Originally conceived as catch-up services, many of these platforms feature original content aimed at young viewers today.

Broadcasters' platforms fulfil an important role and have no vocation to cross borders, but streaming works best at scale. Scale is among the reasons streaming is contributing to the industry's fast global integration. Broadcast television was a national medium that progressively internationalised, streaming is a global industry that is progressively localising.

On paper, streamers are a plethora. Considering SVoD alone, 197 services are accounted for in Europe (EAO, 2017: 19), mostly the online services of local broadcasters. In terms of market share, the SVoD space is heavily concentrated, and five providers were collecting 89 per cent of streaming revenues in Europe in

2018: Netflix, 52 per cent; Amazon Prime Video, 21 per cent; Sky, 4 per cent; HBO, 3 per cent; and Viaplay, 3 per cent (Briel, 2019). In India, home to multiple online services, two platforms, Disney+ Hotstar and Netflix, collected 78 per cent of the SVoD market revenues in 2020 (*Rapidtvnews*, 2021).

Television internationalised well before streaming because of the economics of the medium. The sunk costs of producing a TV series or film being high, rights owners have strong incentives to distribute their content as widely as possible (Chapter 3). But scale was difficult to achieve. In the initial stages of the global shift, TV channels struggled with the practicalities of establishing international distribution. A cable TV executive recalled the difficulties in expanding European distribution of a music channel:

> There was no infrastructure in each of the markets for soliciting the cable operators. Barclay and I would traipse around the medium-sized towns of Belgium, Holland and Switzerland in a rented car. In some cases we would have a phone number of the local electricity company (in many cases the same as the cable operator) but sometimes we had nothing. On arriving at such a town we would follow the pylons to the main switching site or look for the gas tanks of the local utility combine. Sure enough, in a portakabin in the gas works we would find some charming local employee who was Mr Cable Operator. Our war-cry was 'give us a channel'; more often than not, he did so. (Richard Wolfe in *Cable & Satellite Europe*, 1994: 44)

Communications satellites facilitated international distribution, but it remained complex and expensive compared to the Internet. By way of contrast, streaming works best at scale because the technology it uses has exceptionally low marginal distribution costs. The Internet makes it cheap and easy to globalise entertainment services not merely because of the way the network has been designed but the way these services deploy it. Streaming companies, while they typically have a good understanding of technology, very rarely own the Internet infrastructure they use: they outsource distribution to cloud suppliers, who in turn monetise their infrastructure across multiple industries and thousands of users, making it possible for streamers to add countries or entire world regions to their distribution rosters simply by clicking an 'enable' button (Chapters 5, 6, and 8).

Netflix provides a case in point. For twelve years, the entertainment service did not step out of its domestic market. Management followed the 'Canada principle', which stipulated that 'if [they] took the amount of effort . . . Canadian expansion would require and applied it to other aspects of the business, [they]'d eventually get a far greater return than 10 percent' (Randolph, 2019: 208). But in 2010, three years after pivoting to streaming, the company initiated its international roll-out, starting with, precisely, Canada, followed by a selection of European and Latin American countries. The company added a few more territories until Reed Hastings, the chief executive officer, announced the following at the Las Vegas Consumer Electronic Show in 2016:

> Today ... I am delighted to announce that while we have been here on stage at CES we switched Netflix on in Azerbaijan, in Vietnam, in India, in Nigeria, in Poland, in Russia, in Saudi Arabia, in Singapore, in South Korea, in Turkey, in Indonesia, and in 130 countries ... Today, right now, you are witnessing the birth of a global TV network. (in Lobato, 2019: 1–2)

Several years of preparation preceded the flick of the switch, but an expansion of this scale and speed would have been impossible a decade earlier. A year following the announcement, the service's number of international subscribers (57.8 million) was already higher than the domestic figure (52.8 million), and its revenues from international streaming were fast approaching US revenues (US$5.1 billion against US$6.1 billion as of 31 December 2017; Netflix, 2018).

The scale and international coverage of leading streamers is without precedent in the history of TV aggregation. Previously, the world's largest pay-TV operators, DirectTV in the USA and Sky in Europe, hovered around the 20 million–subscriber mark. In the SVoD market, by way of contrast, Disney+ hit 100 million subscribers just over a year after its launch in November 2019. Buoyed by the COVID-19 pandemic, Netflix surpassed 200 million subscribers at the end of 2020 and Amazon Prime Video soon thereafter. Apple TV+ launched in November 2019 and was immediately available in excess of 100 territories (Table 4.2).

Entertaining a global audience is an expensive business and the content investment of platform owners has reached new heights (see also Chapter 3). In 2020, the world's largest content investor was Walt Disney with a US$28.3 billion outlay. The combined 2020 spend of Warner Media and Discovery (which jointly operate Warner Bros. Discovery) stood at US$20.8 billion. Netflix came third with a US$ 15.1 billion content bill for the same year (Brown, 2021). Amazon's acquisition of MGM Studios for US$8.45 billion means that 4,000 films (including the James Bond franchise) and 17,000 hours of TV programming have changed hands (Porter, 2021). It also creates an entity with a content budget of US$11.8 billion (Brown, 2021). The content investment of other platform owners in 2020 remains consequential: US$7.5 billion for ViacomCBS, US$6.0 billion for Apple, and US$1.4 billion for Facebook (Brown, 2021).

In the video-sharing space, YouTube also operates at global scale. Founded in 2005 in San Mateo, California, the platform was acquired for US$1.65 billion in stock by Google in October 2006 (Burgess and Green, 2018). Today, over two billion logged-in users visit YouTube each month; they watch more than one billion hours of video every day, 250 million hours of which are viewed on TV screens. More than 500 hours of video are uploaded every minute (the equivalent of 82 years of content every day), and the library has an estimated 10 billion videos. With local versions in over 100 territories and navigation available in 80 languages, users upload and watch videos virtually everywhere. The platform has millions of creators to whom it makes payments in over 90 countries. The number of channels with more than one million subscribers is growing by 65 per cent year on year, and the number of channels with a six-figure income is growing by 40 per cent year-on-year. Over half a million channels live-streamed for the first time in 2020, accounting for over 10 million new streams on the platform. YouTube's advertising revenue is commensurate with the attention it commands, growing from US$15.1 billion in 2019 to US$19.8 billion in 2020, and, at time of writing, is projected to reach circa US$28 billion in 2021 (company source; Alphabet, 2021: 27; Hale, 2019; Kyncl, 2017: 71).

Two factors can delay the internationalisation of an online entertainment service. First, streamers need to hold content rights in the relevant territories. When commissioning new programmes, leading platforms seek to acquire the global rights, at least for the duration of the first licence period, usually three years (Middleton, 2021; Payne, interview, 2019). But for entertainment conglomerates and broadcasters that sell international rights to third parties, launching a DTC service overseas has implications for their business model and balance sheet.

Disney+ provides a case in point. Walt Disney launched its DTC service in five territories (USA, Canada, the Netherlands, Australia, and New Zealand) in November 2019, making available most titles from a variety of libraries, including Disney films and animation, Disney Channel originals, Pixar, Marvel, the whole *Star Wars* franchise, and National Geographic. In all, the platform offered 500 films, 7,500 hours of TV content, plus a few new releases. This comes at a cost as Disney has had to retain (or regain) the streaming rights of titles it could have (or indeed had) sold to third parties. The 'intra-segment licensing transactions' that cover the theoretical cost of keeping these rights in-house amounts to US$1.5 billion in 2020 and are projected to rise up to US$2 billion per year until 2024 (Walt Disney, 2019b: 61). Walt Disney made the necessary investment because, as a senior executive stated, Disney+ was conceived as 'a global product with universal appeal – one that we will launch in just about every major market over time' (Walt Disney, 2019b: 8).

The cost implications of retaining or acquiring rights, however, is among the reasons that can delay or even prevent international expansion. Because HBO content is profitably licenced to streamers and broadcasters around the world,

HBO Max started its international roll out in 2021, well behind the competition, and will not launch as a stand-alone entity before 2025 in the European territories where its parent company, WarnerMedia, has signed an output deal with Sky. For management, it is a matter of regret that HBO Max is not available in 190 countries and they have promised 'to make sure we set a record for how fast we go global' (Middleton and Easton, 2021).

Disney-owned Hulu – launched in the US market in 2007 – offers a variety of bundles to 39 million domestic subscribers. Disney executives were hesitant about its international development and wanted to ensure 'that [their] losses are manageable' before making a final decision (Walt Disney, 2019b: 63). Ultimately, they decided to keep Hulu as a domestic service and roll out Star, an adult-oriented streaming service without third-party content originating from India.

NBCUniversal's Peacock launched as an AVoD platform in July 2020 in the US market and has garnered 20 million domestic users in one year. So far, international distribution is limited to Sky's European customers. NBCUniversal's brands such as *Law and Order* and *Chicago* are popular with broadcasters worldwide and provide a significant sales income. Should the company use these shows to support Peacock's international expansion, broadcasters' interest would wane and their sales value would decline (Comcast, 2020).

The international development of DTC services is further complicated when US-based media conglomerates are operated by telcos, as is the case with NBCUniversal (Comcast) and, until recently, WarnerMedia (AT&T). Both companies bundle their online platform with pay-TV, wireless and broadband products, and both have a fair amount of leverage with US customers in the states and cities in which they enjoy a dominant position (Crawford, 2013). Such is not the case in other markets, which can only slow down or impede the foreign penetration of their DTC services.

Losing ground to market leaders is among the reasons that pushed AT&T to spin off WarnerMedia, its content division, to create a US\$ 150 billion streaming giant with Discovery. Warner Bros. Discovery is unfettered by legacy assets and has the required size to compete internationally with leading on-demand entertainment services (Fontanella-Khan and Nicolaou, 2021). Comcast has opted for a similar strategy and has joined forces with ViacomCBS to launch SkyShowtime, an SVoD service that is aimed at the European countries where neither group has a strong presence. Comcast acknowledges that in the current circumstances the joint venture is the best solution to 'quickly scale internationally and monetize content across Europe' (Sky Group, 2021).

Not all streaming services have a vocation to become international, but those that do achieve unparalleled scale at remarkable speed. There is one common explanation for this evolution: the rise of platforms as a content distribution mechanism.

The Rise of Platforms

What is a platform, and how many varieties exist in the TV industry? The first fundamental distinction is between streaming platforms and virtual Multichannel Video Programming Distributors (vMVPDs). The former are aggregators of content (by way of acquisition and commissioning), the second are 'aggregators of aggregators' that use the Internet to reach viewers and bring together third–party branded streaming services with live and on-demand TV channels. Amazon Fire TV, Hulu Live, YouTube TV, fuboTV, and Roku count among the market leaders. While most of these vMVPDs operate in multiple markets, the rights situation they face is more complex than for content aggregators and thus they operate on a territory-by-territory basis. Other providers include mobile apps, such as the Apple TV app (not to be confused with Apple TV+, the brand's own platform). The streaming-only subscription options of pay-TV providers, such as DirecTV Now (USA) and Sky Go (Europe), can also be considered as vMVPDs.

Then there are platforms. From Airbnb to eBay and Amazon to Uber, they have become pervasive in the digital economy (Kenney et al., 2021; Kenney and Zysman, 2016; Srnicek, 2017). They have also become a distinctive trait of television's streaming era.

The discourse on platforms is far from unified and encompasses a variety of disciplines, including industrial design, management studies, and economics, which offer competing perspectives. The typology adopted here bridges those different approaches and will enable us to give the best account of the variety of streaming platforms. Based on Annabelle Gawer's typology, five types of plat-forms can be distinguished (Gawer, 2009). An *internal platform* is developed within the context of one firm; it is a technological architecture that combines core elements deployed across a stream of products and variable elements that are used at the periphery of the system. These platforms share two features. The first is modularity, as system components are designed to combine with others and slot in a multitude of product variants (Baldwin and Woodard, 2009: 25). The second is the economies of scope they generate both in production and innovation, since a product issued from an existing platform is cheaper to develop and produce than an entirely new one (Gawer, 2014: 1242). *Supply chain platforms* bear similarities but are developed as a joint effort by several firms, which then use the components in their own product ranges.

An illustration is provided by the automotive industry, where the norm is to design platforms whose core components can be deployed across a wide range of models or brands. The platform is internal when its components are shared among brands within the group (e.g. Volkswagen's Audi, SEAT, Škoda, and VW), and becomes part of a supply chain when developed in common with another group (e.g. Porsche's Cayenne and Volkswagen's Touareg) (Gawer, 2009: 52–4; Steinberg, 2019: 83–6).

Industry platforms' are products, services, or technologies that are developed by one or several firms, and that serve as foundations upon which other firms can build complementary products, services, or technologies' (Gawer, 2009: 54). These platforms usually form *ecosystems* such as those created by Apple, Google, and Microsoft, which involve multiple participants (Gawer, 2009: 54). Ecosystems share features with modular chains (Chapter 1): their governance is not devoid of hierarchy and power asymmetries, and their architecture is characterised by a high level of codification, standardisation, and interoperability (Jacobides et al., 2018). However, they differ in key aspects: in ecosystems, firms have direct access to the consumer market and can develop their own complementary brands and products. They are *participants* or *complementors* in a market rather than *suppliers* in a chain. They have more autonomy and visibility than suppliers, even though their participation is subject to rules and parameters set by the platform *architect*.

The fourth type is *multi-sided platforms*. Economists have observed that some markets involve two (or more) sets of agents. These markets, Rochet and Tirole write, 'are characterized by the presence of two distinct sides whose ultimate benefit stems from interacting through a common platform' (Rochet and Tirole, 2003: 990). The canonical examples are video game consoles and debit cards. Video game publishers are attracted by a large market of gamers who own a particular console, and gamers are drawn by a wide-ranging choice of games. The same goes for a debit card, whose success depends on 'both consumer usage and merchant acceptance' (Rysman, 2009: 125).

Not all multisided platforms involve external providers and consumers who engage in transactions among one another. Newspapers and commercial broadcasters who bring together audiences and advertisers provide such an instance (Rochet and Tirole, 2003: 992). By way of contrast, *transaction platforms* coordinate interactions among consumers and a set of external producers. All the properties listed on Airbnb, and all the products sold on eBay, are owned by external providers who interact directly with consumers. Like industry platforms, transaction ones create ecosystems of vendors and participants, but their role 'is purely to facilitate transactions between different sides of the markets without the possibility for other players to innovate on complementary markets' (Gawer, 2009: 57–8). Transaction platforms are distinctive because they are 'pure exchange or trading platforms' that operate digitally (Gawer, 2009: 57), and can be conceived as *interactive ecosystems that coordinate transactions among two or more groups of agents* (Parker et al., 2016: 1–15; Steinberg, 2019: 95–125).

Multisided and transaction platforms are characterised by network effects across the platform's markets that imply that, in principle, its value to participants increases as their numbers grow: YouTubers attract viewers, viewers attract YouTubers and advertisers, all side growing mutually. Network effects generate 'economies of scale for the platform and economies of scope for the various groups that transact with each other' (Baldwin and Woodard, 2009: 26), and trigger 'a self-reinforcing feedback loop that magnifies incumbents' early advantages (Gawer, 2014: 1241). These advantages combine for the market leader, making it virtually impossible for competitors to challenge their dominant position. Thus, competition between platforms often results in winner-take-all situations and oligopolistic market outcomes (Sturgeon, 2019: 44).

Based on this typology, three varieties of platform can be distinguished in the TV industry. The digital equivalent of internal platforms prevails in the SVoD market (Table 4.1). Netflix, for instance, is engineered as a platform, using proprietary digital technology and cloud infrastructure to capture data and mass customise its catalogue (Chapters 5 and 8). Users do not interact with any external provider and may not even be aware of Netflix's supply chain (Chapter 7).

Internal platforms can be joint ventures. Faced with increasing competition from global streamers, broadcasters are developing common platforms: BritBox was set up by the BBC and ITV in 2017, and Salto, which is only available in France, was launched by three local broadcasters (France Televisions, M6, and TF1) in 2020.

AVoD platforms are two-sided as their business model is predicated on bringing together viewers and advertisers (Table 4.1). These are nothing new and were preceded by the seventeenth-century newspaper and the twentieth-century broadcasting station. All evolve around the same premise: the acquisition of content in order to aggregate an audience, which is then sold to advertisers. For instance, when NBCUniversal streams the Tokyo 2020 Olympics on Peacock, the

Table 4.1 *Type of platform by streaming business model*

Type of platform	Internal platforms	Multi-sided platforms	Transaction platforms
Business model	SVoD	AVoD	Video sharing
Leading	Disney+	Hulu	TikTok
incumbents	HBO Max	Peacock	Twitch
	Netflix		YouTube
Participants	/	Advertisers, viewers	Advertisers, content providers, viewers

Source: author

broadcaster buys the rights from the International Olympic Committee (IOC) and then sells the games as inventory to advertisers. NBCUniversal is the sole mediator between advertisers, viewers, and the IOC.

Video-sharing online services are transaction platforms because they involve multiple transactions among three sets of participants: advertisers, external content providers, and viewers (Table 4.1). Advertisers run targeted campaigns and pay the platform owner to do so. However, the platform keeps a percentage of the advertising income (around 45 per cent in the case of YouTube) and returns the rest to external content providers. The amount of money they receive is calculated according to monetisation formulae specific to each platform. YouTube, for instance, takes into account metrics such as the number of times a video is watched and the number of times that ads are viewed on the video. The country in which these views occur has a strong influence on advertising income, as YouTube cost per 1,000 impressions ('cost per mille' – CPM) varies strongly from one territory to another.[1] Streamers also take a cut from subscription income (e.g. YouTube Premium) and channel memberships. In addition, advertisers can enter into various partnership agreements with content providers pertaining to sponsorship and merchandising. Overall, the platform has paid more than US$30 billion to creators, artists, and media companies in the last few years (company source). Viewers, on their side, can rate, share, subscribe, or sponsor, the streamers they have most affinities with.

Platform Business Models

Streaming platforms tend to avoid direct competition by aiming to serve unmet needs and underserved markets, a strategy called white space mapping. In terms of business model, the broad choice is between SVoD, AVoD, and video sharing, and the variations that exist within each. In addition, platforms pursue distinct content strategies.

SVoD

Subscription Video on Demand has become one of the main ways of monetising video in the digital age. The SVoD platforms that have opted for international expansion are achieving scale and global reach at pace (Table 4.2).

The SVoD principle remains the same for customers, who gain access to a whole catalogue for a set fee. Media owners, however, have multiple reasons to enter this space, and three approaches to SVoD can be distinguished in terms of

Table 4.2 *Leading international SVoD platforms, by number of subscribers, November 2021*

	Netflix	Amazon Prime Video	Disney +	Apple TV+	HBO Max	Paramount+
Launch date	April 1998	September 2006	November 2019	November 2019	May 2020	March 2021
Total subscribers	213 million	204 million	118 million	40 million[1]	70 million	48 million[2]
Footprint	worldwide	Worldwide	The Americas, Northern and Western Europe, selected countries in Asia-Pacific	worldwide	39 territories across the Americas and the Caribbean – 61 territories by end of year	The Americas, Nordic territories, Australia

Source: author

Note[1]: This is an industry estimate as Apple has not released its number of video subscribers. The company posted 660 million subscribers across all its services as of June 2021 (Brown, 2021).

Note[2]: combined with Showtime

business strategy (Ball, 2019b: 3).[2] The first is unique to Netflix in the sense that the firm is entirely dedicated to SVoD and has no other sources of income.

The second group of aggregators are *macro-bundlers*, which not only bring several video services under one roof, but for whom SVoD is 'a large-scale platform upon which other services and products can be sold' (Ball, 2019b: 6). This is the case of both Hulu and HBO Max in the US market. While Hulu's SVoD service is attractively priced at US$5.99 per month, the price climbs to US$54.99/month when sixty-five live and on-demand channels are added. Hulu also serves as a gateway for multiple add-ons such as third-party subscription services. HBO Max is similarly bundled to higher-tiered plans, and the parent company's wireless offerings.

Finally, there are three *super-aggregators*: Amazon, Apple, and Disney. The importance of video varies among them, but their SVoD operation is invariably part of a larger ecosystem. Amazon Prime Video offers its own content to subscribers, and the platform also sells TV channels for an added fee and movies on a transactional basis. In addition, the platform is connected to its parent company's e-commerce business. An anecdote reported to me by a senior TV executive drives the point home; Amazon Prime Video's director of content was asked if he knew how many people were watching *The Grand Tour*, considering the amount of money the show had cost him. He claimed not to care, as the main purpose of the service was to drive retail sales. Amazon found out that customers on Amazon Prime spent on average 50 per cent more than others and wanted to retain them. The answer was Amazon Prime Video. The specific purpose of *The Grand Tour* was to attract men in their thirties and above with a fair amount of disposable income. This story may be apocryphal, but this particular programme is among many that squarely aim at this particular demographic.[3] Amazon Prime Video plays a role in a larger organisation and does not need to be viable.

Apple TV+ serves a similar purpose in another ecosystem. First, Apple's subscription service is part of a bundle of video services offered by Apple via its Apple TV app that includes TV channels and streaming services, and a selection of movies accessible on a transactional basis. Apple's hope is to become a super-bundler and replicate the dominant position of iTunes, whose market share has been in sharp decline since the advent of streaming services (Ball, 2019b: 7). Second, while Apple TV+ is available on a variety of manufacturers' devices, a one-year subscription is free with the purchase of any Apple device, thus support-ing hardware sales by adding a distinctive feature to the brand (Dams, 2019a).

Video monetisation is at the heart of Disney's business model but, through franchises, the company has always been apt at bundling multiple products. Theme parks, resorts, cruise ships, experiences (e.g. National Geographic exped-itions), and merchandising was the company's highest reporting segment before the COVID-19 pandemic, representing 37.7 per cent of its total revenue (US$26.2 billion for a total of US$69.6 billion; Walt Disney, 2019a: 93). It is in this context that Disney+ must be understood: as a hub to the company's digital content and video services (possibly ESPN and Hulu), and as a portal to the company's vast portfolio of products and experiences. As Ball writes: 'Generating $70 or $100 a year from Disney+ is irrelevant when you can use the service to drive a $5,000 Disney cruise vacation' (Ball, 2019b: 9).

AVoD

Cross-border AVoD platforms have yet to acquire the prominence of their SVoD counterparts. AVoD includes BVoD, which are streaming services that tend to operate nationally, as illustrated by Hulu. In addition, the vast majority of AVoD platforms have adopted a hybrid monetisation model, offering ad-free premium versions. However, the market is gaining momentum as advertisers are shifting their budgets online: globally, AVoD platforms generated US$5 billion from advertising in 2010, US$6 billion in 2015, and US$26 billion in 2020 (Aguete, 2021).

The sector's *international* leaders are Rakuten's Viki, ViacomCBS' Pluto TV, and Fox's Tubi (Table 4.3). The last two were relatively slow to expand beyond the confines of the US market, and began to reach overseas territories in 2021.

Table 4.3 *Leading international AVoD platforms, by advertising revenue, 2021*

	Viki	Pluto TV	Tubi	Facebook Watch
Launch date	December 2010	August 2013	April 2014	August 2017
Parent company	Rakuten	ViacomCBS	Fox	Meta (Facebook)
2020 Advertising revenue (US$ million)	55	49.5	33	/[1]
Footprint	Worldwide	The Americas, Europe	Australia, Canada, Mexico, USA	Worldwide

Sources: author; Brown, 2021 (advertising revenue).
Note[1]: Facebook does not disaggregate its advertising revenue, which stood at US$84.2 billion in 2020 (table 9.3).

Table 4.4 *Leading international video-sharing platforms, by number of monthly users, November 2021*

	YouTube	TikTok	Dailymotion	Twitch
Launch date	February 2005	June 2017	March 2005	June 2011
Parent company	Alphabet	ByteDance	Vivendi	Amazon
Number of monthly users	Over 2 billion	Over 1 billion	Over 300 million	140 million
Footprint	Worldwide	Worldwide (banned in India and Pakistan)	Worldwide	Worldwide

Source: author

Similarly, Amazon's IMDb TV, which launched in the USA in January 2019, became available to UK customers less than three years later. Amazon operates another ad-based streaming service, MiniTV, in India. AVoD is also the model chosen by social media networks, such as Facebook (and, therefore, its own streaming platform, Facebook Watch), Instagram, and Snapchat.

Video Sharing

While video-sharing platforms rely on advertising as a source of revenue, they form a distinctive space in the ecosystem. In this sector, platform leaders benefit from particularly strong network effects, which generate economies of scale on the platform side and economies of scope for participants. As these platforms are digital, these effects are exacerbated by their scalability: the ability to expand rapidly and adapt capacity in order to support increased usage.

The sector is therefore characterised by the presence of a powerful incumbent (YouTube), and challengers need to find new functionalities to thrive (Table 4.4). Twitch has achieved this by occupying the live streaming space and becoming popular with gamers; ByteDance's TikTok lowered the participation threshold by focusing on short videos.

Platform Content Strategies

Platforms use distinct content strategies. The distinction between premium and non-premium content is problematic as the exact line of demarcation is impossible to establish. There is, however, a difference between videos generated by users that platforms get for free, and high-end TV series and major sports events whose rights are licenced for millions or even billions of dollars (e.g. EAO, 2018b). As a general rule, non-premium content is monetised through AVoD and premium programming through SVoD. Peacock is among the exceptions, as the NBCUniversal entity primarily generates revenue through advertising.

Another content difference exists among platforms that pursue a generalist approach versus a niche strategy. Amazon Prime Video and Peacock cover everything from live sports to drama. With Peacock, NBCUniversal's intent is to create the equivalent of a broadcast TV network delivered on the Internet (Steve Burke, chairman of NBCUniversal, in Comcast, 2020).

At the other end of the spectrum lie platforms that have opted for a niche strategy. Some services focus on a genre, such as ESPN+ (sports) or Twitch (gaming), whilst others deliver content of specific origin (e.g. BritBox or Mitele Plus Internacional) (Table 4.5). Some niche platforms thrive, others struggle. There is a limit to the number of platforms consumers will subscribe to (a phenomenon known as subscription fatigue), and specialists compete against platforms with deep pockets that can easily encroach into their space if and when they detect sufficient interest from viewers (Bylykbashi, 2019). Thus, some niche services have a short shelf life; Afrostream, DramaFever, Filmstruck, and Shomi count among those that have ceased operations (Bylykbashi, 2019; Ofcom, 2019: 68).

The Global Shift: From Networks to Platforms

Chapters 3 and 4 have focused on the TV GVC's lead firms and examined television's global shift from a market perspective. National media systems have progressively integrated with one another and embedded in transnational networks of consumption, distribution, and production. Cross-border media flows have intensified and become more complex. Finished programmes travel in greater numbers and TV formats became common in the late 1990s. More territories are involved in the production and export of TV series and formats. While drama was predominantly produced for domestic audiences, their distribution has progressively internationalised. Today, global streamers are blurring the dichotomy between local and international by acquiring worldwide rights when commissioning content. Trade has grown in importance and connects markets.

TV channels began crossing borders in the 1980s, the most persistent mutating into transnational TV networks, combining global capability and local adaptability. These networks, while present on most pay-TV platforms, never surpassed the ratings of national broadcasters. The shift from broadcasting to streaming, and

Table 4.5 *Leading international niche streaming platforms, 2021*

Platform	Genre	Ownership (country)
Acorn TV	British-style content	AMC Networks (USA)
Blomberg TV+	Business news	Bloomberg L.P. (USA)
BritBox	British TV shows	BBC & ITV (UK)
Crunchyroll	Anime and manga	Sony (Japan)
DAZN	Sports	Access Industries (USA)
Discovery+	Real-life entertainment	Discovery (USA)
ESPN+	Sports	Disney (USA)
Hayu	Reality TV	NBCUniversal (USA)
Irokotv	Nollywood and African content	Iroko Partners (UK)
Mitele Plus Internacional	Spanish content	Mediaset (Spain)
MTV Play	Music and reality TV	ViacomCBS (USA)
NextUp	Comedy	NextUp Ltd (UK)
Shahid	Arabic content	MBC (Dubai)
Shudder	Horror, thriller & suspense	AMC Networks (USA)
Starz Play	TV series and movies	Lionsgate (USA)
Sundance Now	Indie shows and films	AMC Networks (USA)
Twitch	Gaming	Amazon (USA)
Viki	Asian TV shows	Rakuten (Japan)
Walter Presents	Non-English drama	Channel 4 & Global Series Network (UK)
Wavve	Korean drama	SK Telecom, KBS, MBC, SBS (Korea)

Source: author

from TV networks to platforms, has moved the centre of gravity from the national to the global. Streaming technology and platform economics dictate that online entertainment services work best at scale. All the leaders in the AVoD, SVOD, and video-sharing spaces have an international footprint and are setting new benchmarks in terms of investment and revenue. On platforms, content travels seamlessly without even appearing in trade statistics. YouTube's most popular videos are viewed billions of times, and Netflix's series are equally popular in a wide variety of territories (Parrot Analytics, 2019). Beyond lead firms lies a complex technological and industrial system (Chapters 5 and 6), and a web of global production networks that connect them to suppliers across borders (Chapters 7 and 8).

5

Technology Designed for Scale

The relationship between media and technology is symbiotic. As Daniel Defoe remarked: 'The preaching of sermons is speaking to a few of mankind, printing books is talking to the whole world' (in Eisenstein, 1980: 316). It is technology that separates media from interpersonal communication and which differentiates it from one century to another: the invention of the rotary press brought newspapers to the millions, the transmission of sound and image by electromagnetic waves signalled the advent of broadcasting, communications satellites expanded the reach of TV networks, and cloud computing is powering the transition from broadcast networks to streaming platforms.

Television was born a national medium. Broadcasters exchanged programmes and set up international associations but operated within national boundaries. Their signal covered the length and breadth of the country, from capitals to the remotest parts of the countryside. Foreign broadcasters were not allowed to transmit on national territory and attempts to do so were seen as breaches of sovereignty. Television was tied up with the national project and no other cultural institution was more central to the intent of engineering national identity (Scannell, 1990). In Europe, state monopolies were in place to ensure that nobody interfered with this design.

'Technological change', writes Peter Dicken, 'is unquestionably one of the most important processes underlying the globalization of economic activity' (Dicken, 2015: 75). In the unravelling of the relationship between nation and television, three technologies have played a crucial role: communications satellites, the Internet, and cloud computing. Taken as a whole, digital technologies represent a new 'techno-economic paradigm' as they 'have such pervasive effects on the economy as a whole that they change the "style" of production and management throughout the system' (Freeman, 1987: 130). The first purpose of this chapter is to offer an overview of each technology and examine key components and features of the twenty-first-century *global communications network*. Its second objective is to highlight the role of standards in contemporary technological systems. These systems require the collaboration of multiple firms, and international communication would not exist without the agreements that enable various pieces of software and hardware to interface with one another.

Communications Satellites

With the Cold War, both the Soviet Union and the USA faced a growing need for cross-border communications and military capabilities. It prompted them to look to new technologies, leading in turn to the space race. An opening salvo was fired by the Russians with the launch of Sputnik in October 1957. The US government responded by creating two agencies soon thereafter, which would play a hugely important role in the development of globalising technologies: the Advanced Research Projects Agency (ARPA) and the National Aeronautics and Space Administration (NASA) (Galloway, 1972: 9–16).

Technology breakthroughs followed rapidly. The first (sound) communications satellite, an ARPA project called SCORE (Signal Communication by Orbiting Relay Equipment), was launched in December 1958. This was followed by Echo 1, the first passive communications satellite, sent into space by NASA in August 1960. In July 1962, Telstar 1 and six purpose-built ground stations in the USA, Canada, the United Kingdom, France, Germany, and Italy, provided the first transatlantic television pictures. Telstar 1 had space for one television channel and, being in a non-geosynchronous orbit, could only relay images for about twenty minutes a day. Tracking and receiving the signal was a technological win made possible by state-of-the-art computing and sizeable ground antennas. The British earth station is still located in Goonhilly (Cornwall), and its antenna – known as 'Arthur' – is 25.9 meters in diameter and weighs 1,100 tonnes (Labrador and Galace, 2005: 33–47).

Television transmission requires satellites that revolve in the same direction as the earth's rotation, remaining in one orbital position 36,000 kilometres above the planet's equator, and able to communicate continuously with ground stations. The first geostationary satellite was Syncom 2; it launched in July 1963 and was used to relay pictures from the 1964 Tokyo Olympics. The world's first commercial satellite, Intelsat 1 (also named Early Bird 1), was placed into geostationary orbit in April 1965, and led to the birth of the communications satellite industry. It was managed by Intelsat, an international consortium based in Washington, DC, established by eleven signatories (telecom organisations designated by their governments) in 1964. Although the US government held the majority of voting shares, the consortium expanded to 76 members in 1971 and 114 in 1997. Intelsat had public service obligations and enacted Resolution 1721 (XVI) of the United Nations (December 1961), which states that 'communication by means of satellites should be available to the nations of the world as soon as practicable on a global and non-discriminatory basis' (Galloway, 1972: 147–64; Labrador and Galace, 2005: 49–58).

Intelsat developed its fleet of spacecraft and achieved coverage across the three major oceans with its third satellite in July 1969. Although the first global satellite system was primarily built and used for voice telephony, the Intelsat spacecraft was able to establish TV links. These are the satellites that covered the first global media event, delivering images to a worldwide audience of the moon landing on 20 July 1969 (Galloway, 1972: 148; Labrador and Galace, 2005: 58).

Following in the footsteps of the Soviet Union and the USA, Europe began building its own communications satellite system in the 1970s. Europe's first satellites were developed by the European Space Agency. It instigated the European Communications Satellite programme (ECS), which would eventually be managed by Eutelsat, Europe's international satellite organisation. The first ECS satellite launched in June 1983 and became operational in mid-February 1984. ECS 1 opened an era of cross-border television in Europe as its ten transponders were immediately filled with TV services such as francophone TV5 and 3Sat, the German-language equivalent. When the capacity on ECS 1 was three times oversubscribed it became clear that video applications would constitute a large slice of the communications satellite market. However, none of the satellites of the ECS family (four spacecraft were eventually successfully launched) had been designed for video distribution. Like all communications satellites, ECS spacecraft were intended for the relay of telecommunications signals, that is, point-to-point applications such as public telephony and data transmission (Chalaby, 2009: 14–25).

So far, satellite signals were relayed to either broadcasters or local cable operators. Viewers the world over would watch global news and sports events on their public and terrestrial TV stations. The next big step arrived when communications satellites became involved in point-to-multipoint communication and distributed channels directly to consumers. It became a possibility with the advent of powerful satellites that could send a stronger signal to earth, and the improved performance of satellite dishes' receiving device (known as the low noise block downconverter – LNB). These dishes had to become small enough (roughly 60 cm in diameter) to be sold on the consumer electronics market.

Two new classes of communications satellites emerged: direct to home (DTH) and direct broadcast satellites (DBS). The latter were developed by a host of European nations, such as France's TDF, Germany's TV Sat, Nordic's Tele-X, and the Italo-British Olympus. DBS were high-power spacecraft that were complex and expensive to build and run (Tydeman and Kelm, 1986: 86–130; Williamson, 1988). Some of these craft were eventually launched but proved to be expensive, over-engineered white elephants that failed to attract interest from media owners and viewers alike. DTH craft were medium-power satellites, cheaper to procure and operate than the DBS version (Tydeman and Kelm, 1986: 86–130). Allocating less bandwidth per transponder, DTH satellites slightly compromised on quality but were able to carry more channels. Ultimately, they proved to be the only viable option for satellite broadcasting. While European nations passed the bill for their failed projects to the taxpayer, alone in Europe one small Luxembourg-based start-up took the right stance. Its story is significant on two counts: it eventually became the world's largest satellite operator, and it provides an illustration of the connection between innovation and entrepreneurship (see also Chapter 9).

Société Européenne des Satellites: Pioneering the DTH Industry in Europe

Between 1959 and 1979, the ITU (International Telecommunication Union) organised a series of conferences that allocated radio frequencies worldwide (Williamson, 1988). The 1977 World Administrative Radio Conference (WARC), which was attended by 111 delegations at the ITU headquarters in Geneva, apportioned the frequency bands assigned to satellite broadcasting (11.7–12.2 GHz for Europe, the Middle East and Africa). Following an approach agreed at previous gatherings, the 1977 WARC allocated frequencies according to an 'a-priori plan' that aimed to give all ITU members 'equitable access' to radio frequencies and geostationary orbital slots (Codding, 1990: 100–4). Based on this principle, the WARC 77 agreement apportioned each nation with a piece of the geostationary orbit and associated frequencies. European countries received enough capacity for five satellite TV channels each on average.

The government of Luxembourg was looking at alternative sources of revenue and employment for its declining steel industry when it decided to seize the opportunity offered by the WARC 77 allocations. Luxembourg was home to Europe's sole international broadcaster of the pre-satellite era, CLT, which had the expertise to support such a project. Overcoming sustained opposition from France, Germany, Eutelsat, and even the EU, Luxembourg's satellite venture was incorporated in March 1985 as the Société Européenne des Satellites (SES). What happened next not only ensured the company's bright future, it changed the direction of the communications satellite industry.

British Telecom (BT) was a signatory of Eutelsat and Intelsat, but unlike its European counterparts was partly privatised in 1984. The telco was aware that several US cable networks were looking for European distribution and had made its own investment in cable channels. It first approached Eutelsat with the proposal of procuring a craft purpose-built for television distribution. When rebuffed, BT approached SES and the two companies came to an agreement: the latter would procure and operate the satellite, and the former would build ground facilities and sell capacity on the transponders. SES's first satellite, Astra 1A, was operational by February 1989, and BT leased all its transponders. SES's first – and most demanding – customers were two of Europe's most powerful media magnates, Leo Kirch and Rupert Murdoch.

Astra 1A amounted to a paradigm shift on several counts. First, SES demonstrated the viability of the DTH market, and other satellite and pay-TV operators would follow suit. Second, SES began a fruitful and ongoing collaboration with Sky, Europe's leading pay-TV platform. Prefiguring the current DTC strategies of most media firms, Murdoch embraced DTH because he grasped that the technology offered him an opportunity to reach customers directly and bypass cable operators, which he often branded 'middle men' (in Chalaby, 2009: 71). Third, the rise of SES rolled back governments' involvement in the communications satellite business, and forced Eutelsat and cable operators to be more responsive to market forces.

SES' main competitor, Eutelsat, eventually entered the DTH market and both operators went on to develop Europe's most popular video neighbourhoods (Table 5.1). These are built by co-locating satellites in the same orbital position, thereby increasing their capacity and the choice of channels for viewers. Capacity was further increased by the number of transponders growing from around ten in

Table 5.1 *Leading European video neighbourhoods, 2021*

Satellite operator	Eutelsat	Eutelsat	SES	SES
Orbital position	13° East	28° East	19.2° East	28.2°/28.5° East
Number of satellites	Hotbird 13B, Hotbird 13C, Hotbrid 13E	Eutelsat 28E, Eutelsat 28F, Eutelsat 28G	Astra 1KR, Astra 1L, Astra 1M, Astra 1N	Astra 2E, Astra 2F, Astra 2G
Number of TV channels transmitted	1000	850	1040	462
Audience/reach (households)	135 million	17.9 million	118.4 million	45.7 million

Source: author, based on industry data

the 1980s to sixty-four today. It received another boost with digitisation. Since spacecraft do not distinguish between analogue and digital signals, entire satellite fleets were converted to the new type of transmission in the 1990s. This enabled broadcasters to package around ten digital channels per transponder where one analogue network had fit previously. This is how hundreds of TV channels came to be broadcast from a single orbital position, a feature that is essential to the pay-TV market. Most viewers watch a handful of channels, but pay-TV platforms grew by offering attractive content and a wide choice that covered a variety of taste in culture, sports, and entertainment.

Henceforth, the DTH market developed strongly in Europe, with operators establishing a foothold in many territories. The market went through several false starts in the USA, before DirecTV and Echostar began operations in the mid-1990s (Labrador and Galace, 2005: 135–9). Elsewhere, pay-television and the DTH industry are still growing, and multiple video neighbourhoods serve various DTH communities around the world, such as Intelsat's 68.5° East (553 channels, Africa), 166° East (199 channels, Pacific Rim & South Pacific), or 302° East (365 channels, Mexico).

Communications Satellites in the Digital Age

While internet-driven connectivity and undersea fibre networks carry the bulk of international video traffic (Chapter 6), communications satellites remain at the heart of the video chain, providing solutions for both 24/7 and live transmission. Altogether, Eutelsat broadcasts 6,788 TV channels and reaches 274 million homes, while SES transmits over 8,365 channels to 361 million households. Live broadcast and streaming are growth areas, and SES delivers more than 8,400 hours of online video streaming each year (Eutelsat, 2020: 12; SES, 2021: 17). Some transnational TV networks rely on hybrid distribution solutions that mix undersea cables with video neighbourhoods to reach territories in multiple continents.

The largest televised events are beamed live to audiences worldwide via satel-lite. It began with the first landing on the moon in July 1969. Today, some sports events such as the Olympic Games, FIFA World Cup, and the ICC Cricket World Cup attract billions of viewers. Since the first Gulf War in 1990/91, news organisations rely on satellites to gather news and deliver it. War and foreign correspondents book 'occasional' satellite capacity in order to deliver live image and commentaries from conflict zones or any remote location. While, in the past, a small crew and a satellite newsgathering van were required to uplink to a satellite, today field reporters do it with equipment that fits in their backpack. Some music festivals and ceremonies, such as the Academy Awards ceremony (the Oscars), also use satellite feeds to reach a live international audience.

Beyond television, communications satellites play a role in internet connectivity. They are used to deliver broadband to remote areas and are increasingly integrated into mainstream data flows. A major cloud provider, Amazon Web Services (AWS), has connected six earth stations directly to satellites, both simplifying and accelerating the data transmission path (Mohney, 2020).

Internet Distribution

Media delivery was changing before the Internet became a vehicle for video distribution. Cable and communications satellites increased the number of transmission paths, and the first time-shifting technologies, such as VoD, existed before streaming (Chapter 5). IP transport remains a game changer: it comprehensively transformed media delivery, helped bring about a video ecosystem that far exceeds, both in terms of volume and complexity, the broadcasting ecology of the recent past, and opened up the era of streaming media. In turn, streaming altered consumer behaviour and business models alike, together with the contours of an entire industry.

Streaming: Origins

Streaming is the delivery over the Internet of audio or video files from origin server to connected end users who can access the content in a constant fashion while it is delivered. It is commonly distinguished from downloading, where content must be saved by the end user before being accessible. Under equal conditions, streaming is quicker and more convenient than downloading, since the latter requires a certain amount of storage space that not all users have access to at any point in time.

In terms of data transmission, streaming consists of the digitisation of an analogue TV signal. The process involves sampling of the signal at regular intervals and the quantisation of each sample, which itself consists of constraining each sample from a continuous (and large) to a discrete (and specific) set of values. The outcome is a high-rate and continuous data stream, whose fulfilment has two requirements. First, the bandwidth has to be available continuously and be 'at least equal to the signal's data rate' and, second, 'the file and storage system must be of the streaming type and must have a capacity sufficient to handle all video streams' (Tobagi et al., 1996: 87).

Streaming on a massive scale became a possibility only with advances in compression. The Moving Pictures Experts Group (MPEG) published its first standard in 1992, which would be used in DVDs and MP3s. The codecs within MPEG-1 eliminated redundant information, such as the same blue sky across multiple samples, thereby considerably reducing the stream's rate (Tobagi et al., 1996: 86–7).

Several US-based companies (notably Microsoft) and start-ups were working on streaming technology in the early 1990s. Among them, Starlight Networks (Mountain View, California) developed the first proprietary video transport protocol, and one of the first network–based video applications. The most advanced version of StarWorks, as Starlight's software was called, was commercialised in 1993. It included components for both the server and client desktops, cost US$18,495, and allowed for connection of up to twenty-eight users over a local area network (LAN) (Smalley, 1993: 42).

At this point, streaming as an entertainment application was not envisaged. Starlight itself saw the primary markets in the corporate world and education: 'This [streaming] capability will be used by corporate environments to broadcast the address by the company president . . . Other uses will include distance learning applications where remote classrooms can view the lecture being presented in another place' (Tobagi et al., 1996: 99).

The next step was to create a similar application over the World Wide Web. In the early to mid-1990s, the Web was primarily a research network that had yet to be commercialised. Rob Glaser, an executive who had stepped down from Microsoft, stumbled onto Mosaic, a browser whose first version was released in 1993. Convinced he had seen 'the future', he wondered if he could create for audio and video what Mosaic did for text (Glaser, 2015). He set up Progressive Networks (later RealNetworks), which released RealAudio in April 1995. It was an audio streaming application that could be plugged in to Netscape, the browser that followed Mosaic. Five months later, the company set up the world's first live streaming event: the radio broadcast of a baseball game between the Seattle Mariners and the New York Yankees for ESPN SportZone subscribers.

The video compression format, RealVideo, followed suit in 1997, and RealNetworks commissioned a short tap-dancing film from Spike Lee to use as a demo (Glaser, 2015). The same year, RealNetworks launched its own content delivery network (CDN, see more shortly). This could 'support up to 50,000 simultaneous streams . . . and was the first major effort to try and bring video to the masses via a dedicated content delivery network' (Rayburn, 2016).

RealNetworks dominated streaming in the second half of the decade, capturing up to 85 per cent of the market (in terms of streaming content) and – estimates vary – between 50 and 75 million of registered users worldwide (Forbes, 1999;

Glaser, 2015; Rayburn 2016). The industry, however, was beginning to change as streaming was attracting the interest of large companies. Microsoft, which had been working on video technology since 1993, launched its own player, NetShow, in 1996. The following year, it licenced some of RealNetworks' technology, which it promptly dropped after acquiring another streaming start-up, VXtreme. In 1999, a newer version of NetShow became part of Windows Media, and was bundled to the company's operating system (Rayburn, 2016).[1]

Meanwhile, a series of events demonstrated and spurred the popularity of streaming: the death of Diana, Princess of Wales, in August 1997, led to a sharp rise of video requests on BBC Online (which used RealNetwork's servers and had a capacity for 20,000 concurrent video streams), President Clinton's four-hour testimony before a grand jury in August 1998, and NetAid in October 1999. The purpose of NetAid was to harness the power of the Internet in order to alleviate poverty, and the first event was three simultaneous concerts taking place at Wembley Stadium (London), Giants Stadium (New York), and the United Nations' Palais des Nations in Geneva (Gittlen, 1998; Rayburn, 2016).

By the turn of the millennium, RealNetworks remained a dominant force, but its prominence was waning. Microsoft was gaining market share, as did new entrants such as Apple, which added a streaming media format to its QuickTime 4 application in 1999. The most widely distributed streaming application became Macromedia's Flash Player. It was a free browser plugin whose popularity grew fast as it 'seamlessly marr[ied] interactivity, Web 2.0 and streaming media for the first time' (Zambelli, 2013).

The burst of the internet bubble caused the streaming market to crash. Start-ups that had borrowed large amounts of money found out they did not have a viable business model and, unable to raise new funds, were filing for bankruptcy. Most streaming vendors disappeared, as Rayburn recalls: 'To put it in perspective, at the 2000 Streaming Media West trade show, there were over 700 exhibitors on the show floor. When the show was started back up again in 2004, there was a total of 24 exhibitors' (Rayburn, 2016).

Streaming Technologies: Rise of a New Dawn

When the industry reopened for business, streaming was broken. Without the prospect of earning revenue online, media owners were withholding content from the Web. Downloading seemed the way forward and Apple was affirming its presence in media distribution. iTunes, the firm's downloading application, which had launched in 2001, was supporting video four years later. By 2007, the Cupertino-based firm announced that iTunes 'has sold over 2.5 billion songs,

Table 5.2 *Streaming services launched in the mid-2000s, by launch date*

Platform name	Launch date	Launch country
Vimeo	November 2004	USA
Google Video[1]	January 2005	USA
Dailymotion	March 2005	France
YouTube[2]	April 2005	USA
Todou[3]	April 2005	China
Crunchyroll	May 2006	USA
Amazon Video	September 2006	USA
Youku[4]	December 2006	China
Netflix	February 2007[5]	USA
Hulu	March 2008	USA

Source: author
Note[1]: shut down in August 2012; *Note*[2]: acquired by Google in November 2006; *Note*[3]: merged with Youku in March 2012; *Note*[4]: merged entity Youko Todou acquired by Alibaba in November 2015; *Note*[5]: streaming launch.

50 million TV shows and over two million movies, making it the world's most popular online music, TV and movie store' (Apple, 2007). Downloading was made further popular by the peer-to-peer file-sharing applications (often using the BitTorrent protocol) that users turned to in order to illegally obtain copies of copyrighted material. Kazaa was among the most visited file-sharing networks with an estimated 60 million users in 2003 (Woody, 2003).

Yet, barely a few years after the bubble burst, ten streaming platforms launched within a short timeframe (Table 5.2). While a few have not survived, many are still thriving. In order to reach their current size, these platforms had to scale up, and they grew alongside internet infrastructure and video technology. Four techno-logical evolutions are especially relevant.

HTTP Adaptive Streaming

In the mid-2000s, Drew Major's Move Networks came up with a 'new video delivery paradigm', now known as HTTP (Hypertext Transfer Protocol) Adaptive Streaming (HAS), which would enable streaming to scale up to new heights (Bentaleb et al., 2019: 562). Traditional streaming methods used protocols such as Real-time Transport Protocol (RTP/UDP) which pushes content to client servers, or end users. With HAS, it is the client who requests the content over HTTP and pulls it from a server. The server partitions the file into separate segments (known as 'chunks' that are typically between 2 and 10 seconds) and encodes each segment at multiple bit rates. When starting the session, the client downloads a manifest that details each segment and their different versions, and then 'repeatedly fetches the most appropriate segment among the available representations from the server' (Bentaleb et al., 2019: 563). This method enables the stream to adapt to the client's key parameters such as processing power and available bandwidth (Bentaleb et al., 2019: 563; Seufert et al., 2015).

Adaptive bit rate can accommodate any device, from a smartphone to a 64-inch 4K (Ultra High Definition) TV, selecting the version most suited to its processing power and memory capacity. HAS is a dynamic process that can also adapt to transmission environment variables. At first, the device may not know how much bandwidth is available and will select a low bit rate. But as the device is pulling packets, it is measuring them, and will choose a higher bit rate if conditions allow. Conversely, if a viewer is in a household where someone else is starting to download a game, her device will adjust the bit rate to the available bandwidth (Bentaleb et al., 2019: 563).

The benefits of adaptive streaming are multiple. First, it uses resources efficiently and optimises the stream's quality level, thereby improving viewers' quality of experience (Jarnikov and Özçelebi, 2011; Seufert et al., 2015). Second, the economic case is compelling. As HAS uses 'conventional Web servers or caches available within the networks of Internet Service Providers (ISPs) and Content Distribution Networks (CDNs)' (Bentaleb et al., 2019: 563), it can leverage existing HTTP delivery infrastructure and does not necessitate the deployment of specialised servers. Access to CDNs, in particular, greatly facilitates the scaling up of streaming platforms and their international distribution (next section).

Video-Coding Formats

The transmission of digital video would be impossible without compression due to the large amount of data the process demands. For example, the storage of the raw data of one hour of 4K video would take up to 150 discs, while the same compressed data only requires one disc (McCann, 2020). The only place where files are uncompressed is inside a broadcast facility where there is plenty of bandwidth available. As content leaves the studio, it goes through a series of compression and decompression phases until it reaches the end user.

The specifications of coding formats are implemented in codecs (an acronym for coder/decoder), which are the software or hardware technologies used to make the transmission of digital video feasible by compressing down the audio and video to a pre-agreed level to suit available bandwidth in the transmission medium

(Chapter 8). The compression efficiency has doubled every decade since the 1990s. The first widely adopted format was MPEG-2, which was standardised in 1995. It was mostly used for DVDs and supported the transition from analogue to digital television (McCann, 2020). The next generation of coding formats is known as Advanced Video Coding (AVC), and the family's two key standards are H.264 and MPEG-4 Part 10, which were co-published in 2003. H.264 was widely implemented as it offers much improved compression performance, squeezing the same video in terms of image quality into a far lower bit rate than its predecessors (Richardson, 2010: 83). H.264 has since been revised many times. Despite the emergence of new generations of compression standards, it remains widely in use due to licencing issues with some of the most advanced codecs (McCann, 2020).

Content Delivery Networks

A CDN is a network of servers whose role is to improve the speed and reliability of content delivery by storing content as close as possible to end users. When a user's device sends a request for content, it is directed to the CDN's nearest front-end (or edge) server. The CDN will recover the first request for a particular piece of content from the originator (origin or source server), and will then cache or replicate a copy at a particular edge location. Subsequent requests from this location (or any nearby location that will result in the lowest latency for a user) will no longer travel to origin but will be dealt with by the CDN's front-end server. For instance, the second (and subsequent) request(s) for *Chilling Adventures of Sabrina* from a London-based Netflix customer will no longer travel to California but will be routed to a data centre in London (Telehouse North in Docklands, in this instance). The CDN will replicate the operation as many times and in as many locations as necessary, storing content on its network of edge servers, as close as possible to where end users live.

CDNs represent 'a seismic shift in how the Internet is interconnected' and their rapid deployment is down to the multiple benefits they offer (Stocker et al., 2017: 4). CDNs are designed to answer the scale implications that unicast creates: by routing much of the traffic to the nearest Point of Presence (PoP), a CDN offloads an enormous amount of data onto local networks and enables the scaling of IP content distribution. By reducing travel between source and destination, CDNs help trim latency (delay) and improve the viewing experience that is essential in the competitive world of VoD consumption. In sum, streaming platforms would be unable to distribute content at scale and internationally without CDNs, which form an integral part of the media delivery value chain (Chapter 8).

Proto-CDNs were proxy servers that acted as intermediaries between origin server and users by caching content nearer the latter. The first CDNs appeared in the late 1990s and delivered online documents (Pathan et al., 2008: 10). The second generation of CDNs emerged in the following decade, when their focus and key application became video delivery (Pathan et al., 2008: 10). By 2005, the CDN industry was well established and the market value of video delivery (stream and download) 'was estimated at between US$385 million to US$452 million' in the media and entertainment sector alone (Čandrlić, 2012).

The CDNs that emerged in the 2000s were developed either by tech firms offering a bundle of web and cloud-oriented services or specialist suppliers that focused on content delivery to the edge of the network, where end users are. AWS' CDN, Amazon CloudFront, is among 169 cloud products provided by the firm, while Google's Cloud CDN sits alongside 89 other services offered under the Google Cloud brand. Other providers are smaller companies with a narrower focus on content delivery and edge computing, such as Akamai Technologies (Table 5.3). While the latter is often acknowledged as the industry's pioneer and leader, its market dominance is increasingly challenged by larger providers. Microsoft is the latest tech giant to add a CDN option to its cloud-based products, launching its network in 2018 (Chapter 8).

The Cloud

The cloud is a global network of remote servers that can be used for a variety of computing needs. While the cloud is not an entity it does operate as a 'single ecosystem' of interconnected servers (Microsoft, 2020). The cloud is called 'private' when the servers, possibly run on-premises, are accessed by a sole user, 'public' when servers are shared and accessed through the Internet by a variety of users, and 'hybrid' when both cloud types are combined. The bulk of the cloud is public, though, and by common understanding the term refers to computing services offered by third-party providers to users who pay as they go (Chapter 8).

Cloud computing plays an increasingly central role in the media industries. Internet-based applications encode, store, transfer, encrypt, and distribute files, support asset management operations, and facilitate collaboration and editing through file sharing. The adoption of the technology is growing exponentially among a wide array of media firms along the entire value chain, from content creation to media management and video delivery. For instance, rendering, an image synthesis process widely used in animation, necessitates a huge amount of computing power that can only be done on the cloud; archives, which can take up a lot of storage, are increasingly migrated to the cloud; video delivery in the OTT

Table 5.3 *Key CDN providers, by launch date*

Launch date	CDN provider (firm or division)	CDN/edge Focus	Headquarters
1998	Level 3 Communications[1]	/	Broomfield, Colorado, USA
1998	Rackspace	No	San Antonio, Texas, USA
1998	Akamai Technologies	Yes	Cambridge, Massachusetts, USA
1998	ChinaCache	Yes	Beijing, China
1999	Speedera Networks[2]	/	Santa Clara, California, USA
2000	CDNetworks	Yes	Singapore
2000	Wangsu	No	Shangai, China
2001	Limelight Networks	Yes	Scottsdate, Arizona, USA
2002	CacheFly	Yes	Chicago, Illinois, USA
2002	Imperva	Yes	Redwood Shores, California, USA
2005	Medianova	Yes	Prague, Czech Republic
2006	EdgeCast Networks[3]	/	Santa Monica, California, USA
2008	Amazon CloudFront	No	Seattle, Washington, USA
2008	Google Cloud	No	Mountain View, California, USA
2009	Cloudflare	No	San Francisco, California, USA
2009	MaxCDN[4]	Yes	Los Angeles, California, USA
2010	Microsoft Azure (CDN: 2018)	No	Redmond, Washington, USA

Note[1]: acquired by CenturyLink in 2017; *Note*[2]: acquired by Akamai in 2005; *Note*[3]: acquired by Verizon in 2013 and now known as Verizon Media Platform; *Note*[4]: now StackPath.
Source: author

space is done through CDNs, another cloud application. Cloud computing is particularly useful for processing and analysing the large bodies of data that streaming platforms collect continuously.

In all segments of the value chain, the cloud facilitates remote collaboration and workflows by removing location-specific dependencies and making processes accessible from multiple locations (Atkinson, 2017; Kilpatrick, interview 2019). The cloud facilitates the transnationalisation and deterritorialisation of production processes, which is a great benefit for media companies operating from multiple locations and across markets. During the COVID-19 pandemic, the cloud enabled workers to remain productive at home and has become an essential tool in business continuity.

As with other digital technologies (HAS, compression algorithms, and CDNs), media companies began using the cloud in the 2000s (Kilpatrick, interview 2019; Plunkett, interviews 2017). Today, the industry's leading survey

(100,000 + responses worldwide) shows that a majority of media firms prefer to externalise computing services (Devoncroft, 2018). While pure OTT players have long completed their cloud migration, most American and European broadcasters are in the process of migrating workflows to the cloud too. In the United Kingdom, those broadcasters that have streaming platforms operating from the cloud include the BBC (iPlayer), Channel 4 (All 4), and UKTV (UKTV Play), as do Turner, Fox, and Comcast in the USA. Some broadcasters have gone further and moved their *entire* playout and delivery operations to the cloud. Discovery Networks has closed its own VoD operations and moved 300 TV channels onto cloud, streaming them globally from Northern Virginia. A&E Networks' approach was more regional, first moving its North American channels, then its European ones, to the cloud (O'Halloran, 2020a; Chapter 8). Likewise, ViacomCBS is migrating its entire broadcast operations, 425 linear TV channels and 40 media centres in total, to the cloud.

The flexibility and capacity of cloud computing allow media companies to complete a variety of tasks *at scale*. In the case of Discovery and A&E, cloud distribution enables them to reach hundreds of millions of viewers and subscribers across the world more efficiently. Netflix provides another case in point. Before migrating to the cloud, Netflix was developing – as was common at the time – its own monolithic ecosystem, a large application that contained the entirety of its functions needed to run the service. All the components were interconnected and shared the same codebase and database. It was expensive to run, cumbersome to develop (one small change had repercussions across the entire application), difficult to fix (faults took a long time to be diagnosed and repaired), unreliable (when one component failed, the entire application crashed), and virtually unscalable (because of memory requirements) (Evans, 2016).

When moving to the cloud in 2008 (Chapter 8), Netflix opted for an architectural style known as microservice, which is defined as follows: 'The microservice architectural style is an approach to developing a single application as a suite of small services, each running in its own process and communicating with lightweight mechanisms' (in Evans, 2016). Everything Netflix does, recollecting what viewers watch, predicting what they will watch next, building film rows that match their preferences, finding the right video file to play, identifying subscribers, charging them, etc., is a microservice. Netflix is made up of about 700 such microservices that are autonomous and loosely coupled (Hahn, 2015). This architecture is more resilient as faults can be isolated and it is easier to manage and upgrade as self-contained services can be coded, tested, deployed, and supported independently by dedicated teams (Hahn, 2015). These advantages, combined with those of cloud infrastructure, make this ecosystem imminently more scalable than a monolithic application.

Without the cloud, Netflix and other global streamers could not serve tens of millions of subscribers, stream billions of hours of content every month, and collect data about every single human–computer interaction, all on a world scale. Because of its globalising capabilities, cloud computing is as significant in the history of international communication as the telegraph and communications satellites.

Technology, however, only can be widely deployed in communications networks when it is commonly available and understood, and when the terms and conditions of its use have been agreed upon by all participants in the value chain. This role is played by standards, the object of the following section.

Standards

GVC and GPN scholars have underlined the growing importance of standards in value chains. The former mention them in the context of chain governance, the latter count standards organisations among the intermediaries that support international production networks (Chapter 1; e.g. Coe and Yeung, 2015; Ponte and Sturgeon, 2014). All agree that without standards most industries could not be as globalised as they are (Coe and Yeung, 2015: 56).

Standards have always featured in the screen industries but have become essential to operations. No organisation has full oversight over the streaming delivery chain (Chapter 8), and thus participants rely entirely on common interfaces and technical standards in order to cooperate in the delivery of files and signal from source to end user. This section unveils the key standards that support the TV GV and shows how standards organisations themselves have progressively internationalised.

Standards are born of virtue and necessity. Throughout the twentieth century, the men and women who formed the standardisation movement held the firm belief that open standards were fundamental to social progress. These standards accelerated the pace of innovation, facilitated collaboration among firms and colleagues, kept societies open, and international trade flowing. The most prominent figures in the movement were evangelical about their work (Russel, 2014: 6–21). Olle Sturen, the long-standing Secretary-General of the International Organization for Standardization (known as ISO, a pseudo-acronym), embodied this philosophy. He stated his agenda in his first speech to ISO Council in 1969: 'Political nationalism will most probably prevail as long as we live. Economic nationalism is about to disappear. And technical nationalism has disappeared!' (Sturen, 1997: 67). Sturen, an avowed internationalist, thought that '[s]tandards free mankind; they don't chain us ... the alternative to world standards is world chaos – and chaos is what the 1700 ISO committees around the world are working diligently, unsung and almost unnoticed, to avoid' (in Yates and Murphy, 2019: 198).

Standards are also a necessity, and the world economy needs tens of thousands of them to function properly. Most products and processes are standardised, from an A4 sheet of paper to 5G, the latest generation of wireless technology. Without standardised components, sound and picture would not cross borders. The exhibition of a motion picture, a YouTube video, the live streaming of a sporting event, an international news feed, all necessitate hundreds of standards to occur.

While standards have contributed to shape economic globalisation, globalisation has changed their nature. National standardising organisations were set up in the industrial nations during the first half of the twentieth century. International bodies, such as the ITU, were already active, but most standards were national in scope and relatively few exchanges took place at the international level (Yates and Murphy, 2019: 52–125).

The standardisation movement began to internationalise in the 1960s. Developing nations set their own standardising bodies and were in search of a framework in which to embed their rules. The growth of international trade also spurred the need for common standards, as firms needed sets of norms to exchange goods and collaborate on production processes. Multinationals found out that inconsistent, and at times incompatible, local standards slowed down their cross-border activities (Sturen, 1972: 236).

It is around this time that ISO embarked on a vast expansion, multiplying the number of members and committees. By 1997, fifty years into existence, the ISO had published more than 10,000 standards, which were increasingly global in scope in their application. The way the ISO set standards also marked a departure from national practices. Witness the famous standard for freight containers, which in due course would contribute to transform the world economy by dramatically reducing long-haul shipping costs (Levinson, 2006):

> When we began this TC 104 project [the ISO committee on containers], one of the first problems we ran into was various countries trying to have the international standard reflect their own national practices. We really didn't want to do that. We weren't just looking to affirm what existed, we were creating something new. (Grey, 1997: 42)

The standards movement entered its third phase in the 1990s out of the necessity of finding common rules in the internet era. Standards are no longer solely generated by intergovernmental agencies such as the ITU or quasi-governmental international organisations set up by national standardising bodies, but by 'standardization consortia [that] are typically formed by large global companies', whose membership rules are based on relevance and interest rather than nationality (Yates and Murphy, 2019: 266). According to Jean-Christophe Graz, the new breed of standards set by these bodies are instances of 'transnational hybrid authority' that are 'based on the ambiguous juxtaposition of instances of power transforming the relation between transnational capitalism and territorial sovereignty' (Graz, 2019: 25). The World Wide Web Consortium (W3C), founded by Tim Berners-Lee, is a typical example of such a consortium. Existing international organisations, such as the ITU, or the Internet Engineering Task Force (IETF), have also progressively changed their membership rules and procedures (Yates and Murphy, 2019: 260–6).

Today, standard-setting bodies include global consortia, as well as governmental and intergovernmental organisations. The scope of their work varies in terms of clout and purpose. They can issue engineering guidelines, technical specifications, recommended practices, and up to fully fledged standards that outline the agreed ways of making a product, managing a process, or delivering a service. Many standards are voluntary and agreed upon by actors in industry, but some have regulatory implications. In the field of information and communication technologies (ICT), compatibility standards are those that matter most (Krechmer, 2014). These standards aim to ensure the interoperability of all software and hardware that need to talk to one another for communication to occur.

According to the ITU, there are 'over 300 bodies working in some capacity on ICT standards' (ITU, 2019a). The ITU itself has more than 4,000 recommendations in force, which become mandatory if and once adopted by national governments (ITU, 2019b). In particular, the ITU plays a crucial role in the allocation of radio frequencies. As seen, the 1977 WARC contributed to shape the global communications system, but seventy-five other radio conferences, covering everything from wireless radio to Wi-Fi networks, have taken place since 1903.

Several organisations are setting standards for broadcasters. The New York-based Society of Motion Picture and Television Engineers (SMPTE) issues internationally agreed and recognised standards related to moving-imagery engineering, that covers everything from films to IP-based workflows. The SMPTE has set 800 standards and generates 50 new standards annually (SMPTE, 2019). Broadcasters' associations are also involved. Regional organisations such as the ABU (Asia-Pacific Broadcasting Union) or the EBU (European Broadcasting Union) have technical programmes that set standards for their members in coordination with other international standards setting bodies.

Streaming is highly dependent on standards because IP-driven file delivery involves a multiplicity of operators, and none has overall responsibility over the video chain (Chapter 8). At its most basic level, streaming relies on general internet protocols that have been agreed on internationally, such as HTML (Hypertext Markup Language) and its recent iteration HTML5, and HTTP, enabling audio and video to be streamed over conventional web servers. W3C and the IETF are among the standard-setting bodies for the Internet.

Streaming also necessitates industry-specific rules, and the common benefit of reaching consensus through standards is acutely illustrated with codecs. At first, multiple proprietary formats were developed by firms such as Adobe, Apple, Google, Microsoft, as well as the camera vendors (Sony and Panasonic). These companies went for a land grab by claiming ownership over the technologies they developed, but it became apparent that multiple proprietary formats hampered scale and market development. This was followed by a concerted industry effort to reduce the number of formats, standardise them, and then implement standards-based file delivery. It fell to the Moving Picture Experts Group (MPEG), whose role is to set standards for audio and video compression and transmission, to work out a compromise. As of October 2020, 132 meetings have taken place, each bringing together more than 400 participants representing more than 200 companies (MPEG, 2020). Within participating firms, it is the role of chief technology officer (CTO) to drive standardisation by coordinating with other organisations in order to agree on common approaches. Over the years, the group has delivered a widely used family of standards, notably MPEG-2, MPEG-4 and MPEG-DASH (Dynamic Adaptive Streaming over HTTP), which standardised the codecs used for adaptive streaming (Plunkett, interviews, 2017).

Technology and standards combine to deliver content within and beyond frontiers. But all of this would remain theoretical without the bricks, mortars, and cables that make innovations and technical know-how a reality. Generally unbeknown to audiences, the global TV industry, and the modern video ecosystem at large, depends on a vast infrastructure, which is examined in Chapter 6.

Infrastructure Built at Scale

Technology is the application of science and knowledge to accomplish a task inside a domain. The purpose of a codec, for instance, is to compress video in the context of IP-driven video distribution. Infrastructure consists of the *material elements* that actualise technology: it is the buildings, cables, servers, switches, and routers needed to transport data packets from point A to point B; it is the firms, machinery, engineers, and technicians who design, build, update, and repair these material components. This chapter examines the cloud infrastructure that sustains streaming, focusing on two key components: undersea cable networks and data centres. The final section describes the video ecosystem that technology, standards, and infrastructure have brought into existence.

The Cloud Infrastructure

The cloud (so called because engineers used to draw a cloud to designate the Internet in their sketches of telecommunications networks) is both a set of technologies and an infrastructure. It is the combination of hardware and software technologies designed to handle and process data on a large scale. Cloud infrastructure consists of two main components: undersea cable networks and data centres.

Sky Above, Sand Below, Terabytes Within

Vint Cerf, one of the Internet's founders, and Google's chief internet evangelist, once expressed his surprise at the amount of undersea cable the Internet necessitates (Cerf, 2019). It is certainly ironic that the underpinning of the 'cloud' – and the digital world at large – lies 20,000 leagues under the sea. These submarine cables carry 99 per cent of the voice and data traffic worldwide (Chesnoy, 2016: 4).

The current fibre optic networks connecting continents are the latest incarnation of a long evolution. The first submarine cables were laid to connect the national telegraphic systems that developed in Europe and North America from the mid-nineteenth century onwards. The first international connection was established between London and Paris in December 1851, with a Dover to Calais cable running under the Channel (Fouchard, 2016: 24). Another engineering feat was accomplished when the first trans-oceanic cable was successfully laid between Ireland and Canada, connecting London and New York. The original cable laid in 1858 worked only briefly, and the connection was permanently established via two cables (one new, one retrieved) eight years later (Fouchard, 2016: 24–7; Winseck and Pike, 2007: 19–25).

At first, the weakness of the electric current and frailty of the line cast doubts on the cable's commercial viability. Transmission was incredibly slow and messages had to be sent several times over. Queen Victoria's courtesy message to President Buchanan on 16 August 1858 prompted seven clarification requests from the receiving operator ('Repeat from beginning of message to "desires"', etc.) (Fouchard, 2016: 25; HMSO, 1861: 232). Due to improvements, cable systems expanded across all world regions. In the 1870s, commercial services connected Europe, Asia, and Australia (Ash, 2014). By the turn of the century, hundreds of thousands of nautical miles of cables had been laid. Together, they formed a fledgling global communications network, albeit imperfect from a technological viewpoint and unbalanced from a political one (Ash, 2014; Fouchard, 2016; Hills, 2002; Standage, 1998; Winseck and Pike, 2007).

Coaxial cables, the second generation of submarine cables, began to be laid in the 1950s, before being progressively replaced by fibre optic cables in the 1980s (Fouchard, 2016: 35–50; Starosielski, 2015: 38–54). These cables have been continuously upgraded and their capacity has since increased 'by a factor of 20,000' (Chesnoy, 2016: 14). Recent cable systems can transmit well over 100 terabytes (one million bytes) per second (Tibts/s) over long distances. For instance, Google's transatlantic cable between the USA and France, launched in 2020, has a capacity of 250 Tibts/s (Hecht, 2018; Jowitt, 2019). There are more than 400 subsea fibre optic cables in service around the world, travelling more than one million kilometres (km), and the industry's annual revenue is estimated at US$13 billion in 2020 (Chesnoy, 2016: 4; MarketsandMarkets, 2020). The year set a new record in subsea investments, with 35 new cables totalling more than 100,000 km having been added to existing routes (Stronge, 2020).

Inevitably, considering their insatiable appetite for bandwidth, tech giants have become involved in the industry. First they leased capacity, then they invested in subsea projects, and now they are commissioning their own private cables. The third option gives them full control over their cables and exclusive use, if needed, of the available bandwidth (Hecht, 2018; Jowitt, 2019; Kava, 2020). By 2018, four tech giants owned collectively, solely, or in consortium, some 143,772 miles (231,384 kilometers) of cables: Google, 63,605 miles; Facebook (now Meta), 57,079 miles; Amazon, 18,987 miles; and Microsoft, 4,104 miles (Cooper, 2018). Since then, Google has completed two substantial subsea projects, adding 16,833 km of private cable to its portfolio. The first cable connects Virginia Beach (USA) to Saint-Hilaire-de-Riez (France), and the second, Los Angeles to Valparaiso, Chile (Jowitt, 2019).

Facebook and Google take part in the Open Cables Working Group (OCWG), which seeks to maximise cable capacity and promote open industry standards (OCWG, 2019b). The aim of the two tech giants is to achieve scale and ensure scalability (to scale up capacity when needed). Facebook's specific objective is to design and build 'a scalable, high capacity, cost-effective subsea network to meet [the company's] growing bandwidth demand' (OCWG, 2019a), while Google's technical lead of subsea fibre optic systems is 'focused on ensuring a cost-effective, highly scalable network that is easy to grow and operate' (OCWG, 2019a).

The outcome is a network of unprecedented scale in terms of geographical reach, speed, and capacity.[1] News of the death of William III, King of Great Britain, at Kensington Palace (London) in March 1702, allegedly took forty-eight days to reach Massachusetts in the thirteen colonies (Rantanen, 2009: 48). Steamers reduced the journey to ten days in the nineteenth century, before the electric telegraph produced another breakthrough. At a pace of one word a minute, it took several hours to transmit Queen Victoria's message to President Buchanan in 1858. The pace improved to ten words per minute in 1867, to reach fifty words per minute in 1880 (Fouchard, 2016: 33). In the 1920s, growing competition from wireless encouraged cable companies to upgrade their equipment, and a new transatlantic cable achieved 1,500 words per minute (Fouchard, 2016: 30).

By the turn of the millenium, the accepted latency in satellite transmissions between two locations across hemispheres (e.g. Australia to the United Kingdom) was three seconds, past which an investigation was run (Moir, interview 2005). Today, the transmission time between the USA and Europe via subsea fibre optic cable is 20 milliseconds (0.02 second); add 10 milliseconds for Asia (Chesnoy, 2016: 6).

Communicating across continents is incredibly faster, and cheaper. The telegraphic rate between Britain and North America was fixed at US$10 per word in the 1860s (Winseck and Pike, 2007: 25). Rates declined thereafter (Table 6.1), and bulk purchase would bring prices further down. But the telegraph was too costly for common folk and remained the preserve of news organisations, governments, and large businesses.

Table 6.1 *Cable rates from Britain to selected countries (per word), 1890 vs 1902*

Country	1890 (US$)	1902 (US$)
USA	0.25	0.25
Australia	2.37	0.75
Japan	2.00	1.94
Brazil	1.50	0.75
China	1.77	1.87
India	1.00	1.00
Nigeria	2.41	1.70
East Africa	1.93	0.75
Jamaica	1.45	0.75

Source: adapted from Winseck and Pike, 2007: 147.

Table 6.2 *Median prices per month at 10 Gbit/s, selected subsea cable routes, 2015 vs 2019*

Route	2015 prices (US$)	2019 prices (US$)
London–New York	4,500	2,800
London–Johannesburg	60,000	16,000
London–Singapore	20,000	8,000
Singapore–Mumbai	50,000	20,000
Miami–São Paulo	28,000	7,000
Los Angeles–Tokyo	11,000	5,000
Los Angeles–Sidney	40,000	18,000

Source: Boudreau, 2016; 2020.

Today, unit cost is calculated differently: it is the transfer rate of 10 gigabytes per second (Gbit/s) of data per month, moving to 100 Gbit/s on key routes. Capacity increases and compression progress have made unit prices steadily erode over the decades, and while prices vary by geography, they are converging as they decline (Table 6.2). To these costs, the expense of port and terrestrial transit through cable landing stations and terrestrial fibre optic networks must be added. Five billion words can be stored on 10 Gbit, or the equivalent of 10 hours of video streaming in normal conditions.

The current capacity is without common measure with that of telegraphic cables, a fact that has not escaped the industry's actors. When Google announced its new transatlantic cable, the firm declared that the transmission speed of the cable meant that, in little more than a century and a half, cable systems have evolved from a pace of one word a minute to being able to 'transmit the entire digitised Library of Congress three times every second' (Jowitt, 2019).

Data Centres

Data centres are at the heart of global computing infrastructure and play a crucial role in communications networks. It is where data is collected, stored, protected, managed, processed, accessed, and distributed. Data centres vary in terms of occupancy, role, and size.

In terms of occupancy, a broad distinction exists between enterprise and colocation data centres. The former are operated by a sole owner who runs them for their own purpose, while the latter are occupied by various end users who lease a certain amount of capacity and processing power.

Another difference exists between data centres that are part of the Internet's backbone and those that sit at the edge of the network. Those placed at the core of the network are primarily designed to handle vast amounts of data, while those at the edge are smaller facilities that are installed as close as possible to end users (usually in urban centres). Their mission is to improve connectivity and reduce latency. Edge facilities are used and/or built by internet service providers, social media networks, and global entertainment services. Once integrated into CDNs, they play an important role in streaming provisions and are critical in improving users' quality of experience.

For the data centres that belong to the core of the network, the key parameter is efficiency of workload processing. The trend is leaning towards 'hyperscalers', infrastructures of massive scale. A total of 625 hyperscale facilities were in operation by 2021, and the number is growing apace (DCD Magazine, 2021). Hyperscalers accommodate tens of thousands of racks and hundreds of thousands of servers, which are hosted in data halls that can exceed 100,000 square feet, spread over facilities of several million square feet, and built on campuses occupying hundreds of acres. For instance, a Google data centre in Iowa is built on more than 300 acres of developed land, the equivalent of 235 American football fields (Kava, 2020). Hyperscalers are also unique in their architecture and management, and the way they approach the challenges that come with workloads of such scale in terms of power sourcing, energy conservation, cooling methodology, resilience, scalability, and standardisation (Carlini, 2020: Miller, 2019).[2]

Regarding hyperscalers, 38 per cent are located in the USA; 10 per cent in China; 6 per cent in Japan; 5 per cent in the United Kingdom; and 5 per cent in Germany, with Australia, Canada, Singapore, India, Hong Kong, Brazil, and

France completing the list of popular locations (Synergy, 2020: 1). No more than two dozen operators run hyperscale data centres. In the twelve months leading up to March 2021, they invested US$149 billion on infrastructure and their revenues exceeded US$1,700 billion (DCD Magazine, 2021). They include cloud service providers (Amazon, Microsoft, Google, and IBM), and other tech firms such as Alibaba, Apple, Baidu, Facebook, and Tencent. Only the leading cloud providers, however, have achieved global coverage with a presence in all regions (Synergy, 2020: 1; Chapters 8 and 9).

Sustainability and the Global Communications Network

Submarine cables and data centres are the linchpin of the global communications network. However, data also travels across long-haul terrestrial fibre optic cables and some routes include communications satellites. At the end of their transnational odyssey and as they approach end users, data packets transit through edge locations and local area networks (LANs) (which may or may not be wireless).

By all accounts, the growth of the data infrastructure industry has been staggering, and forecasts point to compound annual growth rates in double digits in all market segments (fibre optic cables, hyperscale data centres, colocation, edge connectivity, etc.) for the foreseeable future (e.g. Technavio, 2020). Current expansion is being driven by the adoption of smart technologies that involve devices (cars, home appliances, wearables, etc.) connected 24/7 to the Internet. Artificial intelligence, augmented reality, and virtual reality all consume vast amounts of data. 5G, the fifth generation of the mobile connectivity standard, is also increasing the pace and quantity of data consumption. Data centre and cloud service providers support a fast-expanding Internet: global internet bandwidth usage was 100 gigabytes *per day* in 1992, 100 gigabytes *per hour* in 1997, and 100 gigabytes *per second* in 2002 (Cisco, 2018: 5). Twenty years later, global bandwidth usage stands at 786,000 gigabytes (786 terabytes) per second (Sandvine, 2022: 11)

The impact on the environment of all this data consumption has raised question marks about its sustainability. Estimates vary widely according to the multiple ways of measuring the energy consumption of the Internet (Morley et al., 2018). Looking at conservative numbers, data centres would consume 5 per cent of global electricity, with streaming alone amounting to 3 per cent of global electricity usage (DCD London, 2019). In mitigation, the IT infrastructure is increasingly efficient. Google, for instance, managed to achieve 550 per cent more computing in its data centres with only 6 per cent of additional energy between

2010 and 2018 (Kava, 2020). Smart technologies, by making homes, cities, and transport systems more efficient, can save up '10 times the carbon emissions they generate' (Morley et al., 2018: 128). Tech giants in the public eye, such as Alphabet, Facebook (now Meta), and Microsoft, are among the world's largest investors and purchasers of renewable energy and have markedly lowered their carbon footprint (Kava, 2020).

Conclusion: A New Video Ecosystem

Infrastructure, technology, and standards combine to form a global communications network of unprecedented reach and scale. The consequences are far-reaching as the ability to move large amounts of data to and from almost any location on the planet at lightning speed strikes at the heart of multiple economic, political, and cultural processes.[3]

A key feat of the global communications infrastructure is to support a globalised video ecosystem, which includes an expanded television industry. Television has two delivery modes (broadcasting and streaming), and while broadcasters use both modes, the industry now comprises pure OTT players (Introduction; Chapters 2 and 8). However, the new video ecosystem expands well beyond the TV industry per se: video originators have multiplied and include firms and organisations whose business model is not solely based on video monetisation: social media networks, news agencies, online newspapers, educational institutions, brands (e.g. Red Bull), sports leagues (e.g. NBA, NFL), and sports federations (e.g. UEFA), count among the new video sources.

While the number of video originators expands, so does video consumption, driven by the affordability and convenience of streaming and VoD. VoD is a 24/7 universe where users expect to stream or download programming anytime and anywhere, regardless of where they are. At home, handheld smart devices are leading to multi-screening (the same person multitasking on multiple screens) and multi-watching (different members of the household watching their own screen). The spread of video-sharing platforms and streaming services has led to new forms of video consumption, such as binge watching (consuming several episodes of a TV show at once), casual watching (fleetingly watching mundane content on video-sharing apps), and background streaming (listening to music while conducting another activity). Connected handheld devices are expanding the frequency of viewing: in households, streaming occurs in short but frequent sessions throughout the day and up to (an extended) bedtime (Widdicks et al., 2019).

Table 6.3 *Global application traffic share, 2021*

Application	Traffic share (of total internet traffic)
YouTube	14.61%
Netflix	9.39%
Facebook	7.39%
Facebook Video	4.20%
TikTok	4.00%
QUIC	3.98%
HTTP	3.58%
HTTP Media Stream[1]	3.57%
BitTorrent[2]	2.91%
Google	2.79%
Total	56.42%

Source: Sandvine, 2022: 13

Note[1]: long tail of content aggregators, includes broadcasters' streaming services; *Note*[2]: file sharing, which can be used to illegally accessed copyrighted content.

Table 6.4 *Global mobile application traffic share, 2021*

Application	Traffic share (of total mobile internet traffic)
YouTube	8.67%
Generic QUIC	7.88%
App Store	7.03%
TikTok	6.44%
BitTorrent	5.64%
Facebook	4.81%
iCloud	4.00%
Apple Software Update	3.94%
Facebook Video	3.71%
Discord Voice	3.69%
Total	55.8%

Source: Sandvine, 2022: 16

Streaming video represented 53.4 per cent of overall internet traffic in 2021, ahead of all other categories such as social (12.69 per cent), web (9.86 per cent), or gaming (5.67 per cent) (Sandvine, 2022: 12). The global share of the leading video applications is substantial (Table 6.3). Worldwide, users watch one billion hours of YouTube videos and 165 million hours of Netflix shows each day. Combined, these two services take up almost a quarter of internet capacity. There are regional variations: in Asia-Pacific, Facebook and Facebook Video are in first and second position and together represent 36.17 per cent of internet traffic; in the Americas and Europe, Netflix comes on top with 19.85 per cent and 16.1 per cent of bandwidth usage, respectively (Sandvine, 2022: 19–21). In both regions, Amazon Prime and Disney+ make their appearance in the top ten (Sandvine, 2022: 19–20).

Video streaming also dominates mobile networks, with YouTube, TikTok, BitTorrent, and Facebook Video all among the top ten applications in terms of traffic, but Netflix drops out of the list (Table 6.4).

This amount of video traffic and consumption would not be possible without the technology and infrastructure that the IT industry has put in place. The global communications network is built for scale and speed, two attributes that are contributing to redefine the TV industry and underpin its globalisation. The challenge now is to explain how this globalised media system works.

7

Content Production

This chapter addresses the segments that constitute the programme-making phase of the TV GVC, that is, facilities, production, and distribution. These segments cover the route a programme follows from creation to final production master. Production companies are located at the core of this network, and they have their own suppliers in the facilities segment. The distribution segment consists of businesses or divisions that specialise in finding the best possible home, at the best possible rate, for producers' content.

This chapter provides an in-depth analysis of each segment of the programme-making phase and includes aggregation. It examines firm behaviour and explains why the search for scale plays such a determining role in the strategies of firms. It highlights three key trends that characterise the chain's programme-making production network: internationalisation, consolidation, and vertical integration, emphasising that they occur in the wider context of industry segmentation. The chapter looks back at the formation of ten global TV studios (or TV production majors), taking Banijay as a case study. Finally, it defines the role and nature of content aggregation in the TV GVC.

The Facilities Segment

This segment consists of companies that supply services to TV producers, such as providing studio space, film crews and gear, props, and costumes, in addition to finding locations, flying drones, and fulfilling post-production tasks. This segment has one particularity: firms congregate in clusters. When working on a shoot or providing services in a studio, suppliers collaborate on a daily basis for weeks or months on end. Clusters arise because of producers' need for multiple specialist firms to participate in large projects. Among suppliers, clusters facilitate interaction as they share knowledge about gear, staff, and forthcoming projects among a population of predominantly small firms. In a sector characterised by casual patterns of employment, the presence of multiple businesses and facilities within a locale makes it easier for below-the-line crews to move from one project to another. Conversely, companies have access to a large pool of skilled and nomadic workers such as camera operators, grips, prop masters, set decorators, lighting technicians, location managers, or makeup artists. Clusters are complex ecosystems that grow organically and are difficult to recreate *ex nihilo*. The largest film and TV production hubs are located in Mumbai, India and Los Angeles, USA. Smaller international production hubs include Miami-Dade County, USA and London, United Kingdom (Caldwell, 2008; Scott, 2005).

Taking the United Kindom as a case study, the facilities segment consisted of 1,300 businesses employing in excess of 50,000 people for a combined turnover of £2.2 billion in the 2010s (Pennington, 2011: 14). TV studios are among the services the sector caters for. These are the factory floors of the TV industry that come with a wide range of facilities (stages, production suites, workshops, dressing rooms, etc.) (Kempton, 2020). A complex such as Elstree Studios hosts specialist suppliers that offer additional services integral to a shoot, such as prop-hire and kit-hire businesses (which also supply the crew that operate the rental equipment), special effects and prosthetics experts, and action vehicle suppliers.

While British broadcasters retain some studios for daytime programmes and open-ended serial dramas such as soap operas, they have sold most of their larger facilities, which they deemed non-core to the business. The Greater London area comprises a wide range of film and TV studios of all sizes (Kempton, 2020). The largest complex is Pinewood Studios, which boasts 24 stages that extends to 59,000 square feet for the 007 Stage. The studio's operator, Pinewood Group, is a consolidator and owns several facilities: in addition to Pinewood and Shepperton Studios, both in the Greater London area, it operates studio complexes in Atlanta, Toronto, and the Dominican Republic, offering in all over one million square feet across 74 stages (company source).

The drama boom driven by the streamers is causing British studio space to be in high demand and is turning the country into a global production hub. Netflix has signed a long-term deal for space at Shepperton, and Comcast (via its British subsidiary Sky) is building a 32-acre facility near Elstree.

Post-production covers, notably, video and audio editing (cutting and assembling raw footage), colour grading, special visual and sound effects, and the preparation of the completed work in the required formats by the producer's clients. While the editing process predominantly takes place once shooting has completed for scripted programming, it is increasingly integrated into production workflows across the reality TV genres. The latter shows have a very high shooting ratio (they shoot many more hours than they need for the final version) and storylines are shaped during post-production on the firms' powerful non-linear editing systems. Fixed-rig productions using remote control cameras to unobtrusively film in sensitive areas such as secondary schools, maternity wards, or A&E units also generate a vast quantity of material in need of editing (Sargent, interview 2010). The growing integration of post-production tasks to workflow has upgraded the status of post houses in the supply chain, and they see themselves more as partners than mere suppliers to their clients (Bickerton, 2019b).

London's post-production houses have historically clustered around Soho and have recently spilled over to Shoreditch, in the East End (Pratt and Gornostaeva, 2009); staffing varies from fewer than ten to a few hundred. In theory, anyone with a Mac can carry out post-production tasks, which tempts some of the sector's clients to take the work in-house. Reality, however, is more complex. Post-production remains an outsourced activity because it requires creative and technical skills, and continuous investment in technology. Rapid technological evolution means that software and hardware quickly become obsolete, and workflows and skill sets need constant updating. Leading outfits such as The Farm, Envy, or Molinare are thriving because they have state-of-the-art facilities and large teams of creative staff. Nonetheless, technological advances ensure that barriers to entry to the industry remain low, and post-production houses are under constant pressure to do more for less (Sargent, interview 2010). Post-production is an activity requiring frequent interactions with clients and is carried out locally. Deluxe, which was present in thirty-eight territories, was an exception. But it went through a major restructuring plan and sharply reduced its footprint after filing for bankruptcy in 2019 (Bickerton, 2019a).

The facilities segment comprises other specialisms. The archive sector provides footage of historic events, wildlife, sports, news, and current affairs to both producers and broadcasters. These companies exploit large libraries of content that have been digitised and are available online. There are also research companies that dispense market intelligence and ratings analytics. The leader remains Nielsen, funded in 1923 and listed on the New York Stock Exchange. It provides the national measurement service in the USA and Canada and analyses viewing habits across 100 territories. Some younger companies specialise in mining data sets generated by social media networks to gather insights into consumer demand and streaming consumption. There are also trade press publishers, trade fair organisers (e.g. Reed Midem, which owns the MipCom and MipTV annual events in Cannes), and business affairs and commercial consultancies that help media firms sell or buy assets, or raise finances.

The TV GVC is connected to other value chains and the facilities segment is one of the contact points where it meets the pro-electronics GVC, that is, the equipment manufacturers. Camera systems, monitors, projectors, and other accessories are made by global firms such as Canon, Panasonic, or Sony. The largest manufacturer of professional motion picture equipment is Arri, founded in

1917 in Munich. Sennheiser, also from Germany, makes audio equipment such as microphones and headsets. Post-production houses rely on audio and video editing suites, and the leaders in editing and engineering technology are US-based Avid and Blackmagic Design, from Australia.

TV Content Production: Internationalisation and Consolidation

The TV content production segment is the core of the programme-making phase. TV production requires skills in project management and finance, as well as creativity. In most countries, the segment is populated by two types of producers: those that are independent, and those owned or controlled by vertically integrated groups. Historically, the first TV production sectors developed in Australia, Western Europe, and the USA. As the sector depends upon a few buyers, its health and shape rest, to a large extent, in the hands of regulators. In the USA, it flourished when the Financial Interest and Syndication Rules prevailed, which had been introduced by the Federal Communications Commission two decades earlier in order to prevent US networks from owning the programmes they aired in prime time. Their repeal in the 1990s weakened the rights position of producers vis-à-vis broadcasters and media conglomerates (Kunz, 2007: 77–8; Lotz, 2007: 82–97).

In the United Kingdom, the sector began to develop in 1982 when the government decided to set up Channel 4 as a 'publisher-broadcaster' that was required to commission its programming from independent producers (Darlow, 2004; Potter, 2008). Following further regulatory support, the sector grew and was supplying 10,000 hours of programmes to the United Kingdom's terrestrial channels by the mid-1990s (Jones, 1995a). It had an annual turnover of £722 million and employed 12,000 staff, but was predominantly made of small businesses: out of 800 producers, only 100 had a turnover that exceeded £2 million (Jones, 1995b: 9).

It was during this decade that the TV production companies operating in the most advanced markets began to consolidate and internationalise. TV formats played a key role in the expansion of their footprint. Leveraging the Goodson-Todman catalogue (Chapter 3), Grundy was operating in seventeen territories by the mid-1990s. In the Netherlands, Joop van den Ende and John de Mol joined forces and created Endemol, which rapidly built an international TV production network. Pearson came next, a London-based media company, which bought Grundy in 1995 and All American Communications two years later, acquiring a large catalogue of game shows at a stroke.

The 'super-indies' followed. They were small-scale consolidators – despite the label – that brought several production companies under one roof and combined them with a distribution arm. Firms like RDF Media (founded 1993), Shed Productions (1998), Shine (founded by Elizabeth Murdoch in 2001), and All3Media (2003), were all UK-based consolidators that made several domestic and international acquisitions (Chalaby, 2010).

Elsewhere in Europe, TV producers were on a similar trajectory. Propelled by *Big Brother*, Endemol was pursuing its international expansion by way of organic growth and acquisitions. Attracted by the UK rights position, the group developed a strong presence in the country. Stockholm–based Zodiak Media Group, Paris-based Banijay Entertainment, and Amsterdam-based Eyeworks joined the ranks of international consolidators.

Broadcasters began to invest in content production in the 2000s with two objectives in mind: to secure their content supply chain, and to diversify and internationalise their revenues. The second aim became a key driver only once they sensed that digital media were a potential threat to their business model. RTL Group bought the TV production assets of Pearson and renamed it FremantleMedia. The producer grew internationally on the back of unscripted shows, which broke audience records wherever they travelled: *Idols*, *The X Factor*, and *Got Talent*. BBC Worldwide, the corporation's commercial arm, used *Dancing with the Stars* and shows such as *The Weakest Link* and *Top Gear* to establish a network of production bases in key markets. ITV built on the international legacy of former ITV regional franchise holders Carlton Communications and Granada and expanded its own international network of production companies. ProSiebenSat.1 created Red Arrow Entertainment and embarked on a similar path.

Sony Pictures Entertainment was the first Hollywood studio to commit to multi-territory film and TV production. Its TV division, Columbia TriStar International Television, was producing local content across Asia, and in Brazil, Germany, and the United Kingdom by the mid-1990s. Sony Pictures Television (the division's new name), subsequently added seventeen production companies to its roster, including *Who Wants to Be a Millionaire?*'s 2waytraffic. The other studios joined the fray later. They were used to selling franchises with universal appeal and perceived local production and adaptations as a threat to their lucrative finished programming business. The reality wave, and the ratings of some unscripted shows such as *Survivor* or *American Idol*, convinced them otherwise. NBCUniversal and Warner Bros. set up international television production arms and made a few acquisitions in the second half of the 2000s. The biggest investment came from 21st Century Fox, which acquired Shine for an estimated £415 million in 2011.

By the end of the 2000s, fourteen *global TV studios* (or TV production majors) were in operation (Chalaby, 2016: 114). There are deemed 'global' because of their scale, the integrated nature of their international operations, and the role they play in the production and distribution segments of the TV system. They had local production facilities in eleven territories and controlled more than twenty labels on average, enabling each of them to exchange information, share ideas, run production hubs, produce their own formats, and sell finished programmes worldwide. Collectively, they owned most of the best-known TV brands.

In the last decade, consolidation has continued unabated, the most acquisitive companies being Banijay, ITV Studios, Modern Times Group, Red Arrow Entertainment, and Warner Bros. The latter acquired Eyeworks, a production major that was present in seventeen territories when acquired for US$270 million in 2014. ITV Studios built a vast network of production companies, bringing sixty labels under one roof across twelve territories. Its main acquisition was Talpa, the Dutch company founded by John de Mol and maker of *The Voice*. The British broadcaster commands significant capacity in the USA, where it is the leading producer of unscripted programming. Stockholm–based Modern Times Group bought Strix, a large Nordic producer comprised of multiple businesses, to form the Nice Entertainment Group. Red Arrow Studios brought together sixteen companies across seven countries, building a strong presence in the USA, the United Kindom, and Germany.

The most active group has been Banijay: following successive waves of acquisitions that have brought together six consolidators, it has become the world's largest independent TV production major. Its formation sheds light on the entanglement of multiple geographies in successive rounds of consolidation:

1. Zodiak Television began life with the fusion of two Swedish TV production groups, Jarowskij Enterprises AB and MTV Mastiff Produktion AB in 2004. Zodiak Television AB joined thereafter and gave its name to the eponymous group. Three years later, the Stockholm-based group held majority holdings in eighteen businesses. Its footprint was concentrated in Scandinavia but the company was making inroads in other markets.

2. De Agostini, originally a publishing firm, acquired Italy's largest independent TV producer, Magnolia, followed by France's Marathon, before turning its attention to Zodiak in 2008 (and adopting the latter's name). At this juncture, Zodiak spanned thirty companies and was present across the Nordic region, continental Europe (Belgium, France, Italy, the Netherlands, Spain), the United Kingdom (four companies), Eastern Europe (Poland and Russia), and India.

3. In 2010, Zodiak scooped RDF Media Group, one of the British super-indies, which consisted of forty-five operating units spread across seventeen territories.

4. Paris-based Banijay, founded in 2008, had an acquisitive mindset from the start and owned fourteen production companies across ten markets (including Germany, Nordic territories, Spain, Australia, and USA) within two years. The 2016 merger of Banijay and Zodiak created the world's largest independent content creation group (operating under the Banijay banner) with a revenue of around 1US$ billion.

5. UK-based Shine began its international expansion in 2007 with Reveille, an American distribution company noted for adapting *Ugly Betty* and *The Office* for US audiences. Two years later it had start-ups in Germany, France, and Australia before getting hold of Metronome Film and Television, the largest production group of the Nordic region with fifteen companies across northern Europe. In 2011, Shine established itself in Spain, bringing the group to twenty-six operating labels across ten markets.

6. Endemol pioneered the international production model and was already in ten countries by the end of the 1990s. Using a multitude of formats to grow internationally, it was operating eighty labels across thirty territories by the 2010s.

7. 2014 saw the merger between Shine, Endemol, and Core Media, a US-based content company that had bought several producers, notably 19 Entertainment (*American Idol*). This merger created a global power-house of 120 production labels, 68,000 hours of finished programming, and 4,300 formats in its catalogue.

8. In 2019, Banijay agreed to buy the Endemol Shine Group in a transaction estimated at US$2.2 billion. Just before the operation, Banijay owned sixty-one production labels across sixteen countries. The combined group brings together 180 companies across 23 territories, 90,000 hours of finished tape, and thousands of formats under one roof. The main shareholders are Vivendi, which holds 32.9 per cent of the stock; LDH, a holding company controlled by Stéphane Courbit (52 per cent); and Italian group De Agostini (company sources; Mahon, interview 2014; Porte, interview 2009; Roth, interview 2008; Wood, 2010; Zodiak Television, 2008).

M&A activities have brought down the number of global TV studios from fourteen to ten in the last decade (Table 7.1). Large conglomerates do not disaggregate their revenue down to TV production and programme sales, but at least four majors exceed US$1 billion in income. In sum, the segment has seen both horizontal and vertical integration: producers aggregate among themselves to reach a bigger scale, and all majors bar one are integrated to a broadcaster or media conglomerate.

Table 7.1 *Top ten global TV studios, by estimated size and revenue, 2020*

Company	Type of company/ ownership	HQ (intl. TV production division)	2019 Revenue (production and global sales)	Number of production labels	Production footprint	Metric highlights
Banijay (including Endemol)	Independent	Paris	US$2.9 billion (est.)[1,2]	180	23	90,000 hours of programming, at least 4,300 registered formats
ITV Studios	Integrated/ITV	London	US$2.4 billion	60	12	46,000 hours of programming, 4,616 programmes available, including several unscripted global TV brands
Fremantle	Integrated/RTL	London	US$2.0 billion	33	30	12,000 hours or programming, 100 billion views on YouTube
BBC Studios	Integrated/BBC	London	US$1.4 billion	2	7	Among the largest catalogue, 2,000 hours produced annually, owns many global brands
Red Arrow Entertainment	Integrated/ ProSiebenSat.1	Munich	US$731 million	16	8	4,400 titles in catalogue sold in 200+ territories
All3Media	Integrated/ Discovery– Liberty Global	London	US$641 million	28	6	6,500 hours of programming
Sony Pictures Television International Production	Integrated/Sony Pictures Television	London	/	24	12	Global brands include *The Crown* and *Who Wants to Be a Millionaire?*

Table 7.1 (*cont.*)

Company	Type of company/ ownership	HQ (intl. TV production division)	2019 Revenue (production and global sales)	Number of production labels	Production footprint	Metric highlights
Warner Bros. International Television Production	Integrated/ AT&T Warner Media	London	/	3	14	Owns leading brands, including *The Bachelor* and *Cold Case*
NBCUniversal International Studios	Integrated/ Comcast NBCUniversal	London	/	5	3	Global brands include *Downton Abbey* and *The Real Housewives of...*
NENT Studios[3]	Integrated/ Nordic Entertainment Group	Stockholm	US$244 million	32	17	Licences sold in 240 territories

Source: author; *Note[1]:* estimated figure combines Banijay's and Endemol's 2018 revenues; *Note[2]:* exchange rates for companies not reporting in US$ as of 31 December 2019; *Note[3]:* NENT Studios is part of the Nordic Entertainment Group, the streaming and broadcasting company formed after Modern Times Group (MTG) split into two entities. Nordic Entertainment kept the television activities and MTG turn itself into an e-sports company.

Benefits of Scale

The advantages brought by scale are not clear-cut in the TV production segment. The barriers to entry remain relatively low and hundreds of small TV producers operate in the sector. It is not infrequent for TV executives to leave large majors and start their own company. Size does not prevent producers from working with global streamers, albeit a presence on the US West Coast helps, as most of their senior commissioners remain located there. Scale is not without challenges either. Large firms have a legacy infrastructure and, in the case of Banijay, a very large debt, which needs servicing. Running operations become complicated and the outer parts of empire often have issues that need to be fixed. As David Flynn, Youngest Media's co-founder, notes, 'endless consolidation is just a corporate complexity that takes you away from the core mission of us all, which is creativity and ideas' (Flynn, interview 2019). He adds that many bright new ideas have not come from majors but from a new breed of companies that have the time to focus on creativity and innovation, rather than on challenges that come with scale and consolidation (Flynn, interview 2019).

Nonetheless, consolidation is happening, and not merely for the wrong reasons. First, by common accord in the industry, distribution is 'inherently and inescapably a scale business' (Graham, interview 2010).[1] Buyers are more likely to find what they need in a large and diversified catalogue complemented with third party properties. Scale is also a way of diversifying a production company by engaging in multiple genres. Television is a cyclical business and genres fade away before returning – in a slightly different format – years later. For instance, the reality TV wave has come and gone, but unscripted shows will return in greater numbers once streamers work out what works for them. In their early consolidation stages, production groups purposely acquire companies that specialise in genres that lie outside their core output in order to de-risk the business and reduce its exposure to fads and cycles.

Large TV studios generate cash flow from their stock of formats and tapes, and reinvest some of it to generate new content assets. They have central development funds, which they spend on developing projects. They can spend more money than smaller independents on presenting their ideas to streamers, who tend to expect more development up front. Lucas Green, Banijay's head of content, explains that the producer does not hesitate 'to invest money in pilots and development in order to bring shows to life' (Green, interview 2019). They also have the resources to deficit-finance expensive drama with potential for global distribution (Payne, interview 2019; Chapter 3). While, in theory, global TV studios can take more risks, this comes with a word of caution from Cathy Payne, the chief executive of Banijay Rights:

If you've got scale you can take more risk. Though the biggest trap to any integrated production and distribution business [is investing] in shows that wouldn't get made otherwise. So sometimes they say oh, we should do it for the group ... I'm going, well, go to the market, will anyone else give you the money? ... You can get carried away in your own world and say I should back every one of my shows. You have to only back the shows that you think can make the money back. (Payne, interview 2019)

A key benefit of scale is that it gives producers the opportunity to stay longer in the content value chain. They can distribute their own content through integrated distribution arms, saving themselves the fees. In addition, they put to good use their network of local production offices (Table 7.1). With regard to formats, single-country producers operate under the rules of the licensing model: when foreign producers or aggregators express an interest in adapting one of their shows, they have no other option but to sell the adaptation rights. The licence fee falls between 7 and 8 per cent of production costs, which can be a modest sum when shows are cheap to produce. Thus, this model depends on a steady pipeline of formats and is not viable in the long run. Independent companies that pioneered format distribution, such as Distraction Formats (Montréal) or Target Entertainment (London), closed their doors a long time ago.

Instead, majors can keep the intellectual property in-house by producing the format in as many territories as possible. In certain countries, production fees can be as high as 40 per cent of the show's total budget (Carter, interview 2008). The upside gets even better when a ratings bonus and a (variable) share of ancillary revenues (e.g. licencing and merchandising) are negotiated into the contract. While this model also requires a steady stream of formats, the value capture alone justifies the risk and costs involved in the running of an international production network.

Major TV studios also leverage their transnational network to enhance creative processes. Local teams exchange ideas and collaborate on projects, and have access to resources should they need support to finalise a concept or programme (Chapter 10). Scale has an influence on the issue of power between producers and aggregators (Chapter 9). Although it does not change the fundamentals of the relationship between the former and the latter, it goes some way in helping producers address the power asymmetry between the two parties. The preferred rights position of streamers is known: they seek global rights for the duration of the licensing period (Chapter 3). However, flexibility is often possible and a large producer is more likely to have the wherewithal to soften this position and emerge from negotiations with a more attractive proposal, such as the reversion of some rights (e.g. AVoD, linear) after a holdback period (Payne, interview 2019).[2] In addition, should the streamer be keen to keep the rights, a large TV studio can ensure that it remains a partner throughout its production footprint (Green, interview 2019; Payne, interview 2019). Should a global streamer order a format from Banijay, the producer would insist on producing any local version commissioned (Green, interview 2019).

Another solution consists of setting up a central hub to host the production of multiple local versions. It does not require a network of local production offices, but it is predominantly practiced by major studios. The concept was invented by Adventure Line Production (ALP), a French company long integrated into the Banijay Group. ALP used a Napoleonic fort built on a bay off La Rochelle (France) to shoot an adventure game show called *Fort Boyard*. When the format sold abroad, ALP naturally used the same location to host teams from across Europe, shooting up to four episodes in one day (Porte, interview 2009). The benefit of this practice is to create economies of scale that considerably lower production costs.

Today, many TV majors practice the central hub idea by setting up operations in low-cost countries. The time zone is an additional factor in choice of location if the show has a live element. ITV Studios has built hubs for *The Chambers*, *Love Island*, and *I'm a Celebrity ... Get Me Out of Here!* Endemol Shine (now with Banijay) has used hubs for *Wipeout*, *The Fear Factor*, and *All Together Now*. Some formats (e.g. *Survivor*) have several hubs and clients may choose the one that fits their budget and time zone. Central hubs suit streamers, who get localised versions at a lower cost. Netflix has two shows based on central hubs: *Ultimate Beastmaster* (Santa Clarita, CA) and Studio Lambert's *The Circle* (Manchester, UK) (Fry, 2019).

Distribution

The role of distribution is to coordinate content production and content aggregation. A distributor's core remit is to wring every last drop from the intellectual property they represent, whether it belongs to their parent company or a third party. In the latter case, they need to access the distribution rights, which often necessitates the development of a long-term relationship between the two parties. With the multiplication of genres, rights, windows, and platforms, distribution is an increasingly complex activity requiring expertise in finance, marketing, and commercial law.

The rights attached to a TV show are extensive. On the broadcast side, they include interactive, adaptation (formats), linear or non-linear. Non-linear come in multiple variants: premier day (first 24 hours), reverse EPG (viewers hitting playback, valid for one week), and catch-up. Catch-up are available in different options: rolling five (thirty days catch up), in-season stacking (all episodes made available until end of season), and box set (full franchise, e.g. season one to nine). Rights extend to all types of digital platforms (e.g. streaming) and methods of delivery that do not yet exist. Ancillary rights cover, among other things, the licensing and merchandising deals. The sale of these rights needs to be coordinated among different buyers and territories. If a TV series has been sold as a ready-made tape and then adapted in certain territories, the distributor must be mindful of where each version will be seen and needs to put in place a carefully choreographed sequence of holdbacks and releases (Jackson, interview 2012; Nohr, interview 2020).

Regarding financing, the production costs of top-end dramas are rarely fully covered by broadcasters' budgets, and distributors need to find a way to bridge the gap. This practice, known as deficit funding, requires a distributor to find multiple financing sources, and it can decide to advance some of the funds itself (Chapter 3). Whoever participates in the financing owns some of the intellectual property but shares the commercial risk.

Several forces at play are complicating the task of distributors. First, consolidation (e.g. Disney and Fox) is taking 'content and content providers out of the open market' (Payne in Fry, 2020: 14). The integration of many distributors into large TV studios and media conglomerates is siloing content supply chains and, similarly, is putting some content out of reach of independent distributors (Middleton, 2019a). While independent distributors are still thriving,[3] the segment is dominated by integrated consolidators today; all the TV studios listed in Table 7.1 have global distribution divisions.

Second, while the digital market has increased the number of rights and the number of clients for producers (as well as the overall amount of money flowing into content production), some trends in this market are creating issues. Global entertainment platforms and their inclination to hoover up rights has reduced the number of windows (the 'release sequence' of content across a number of platforms and territories) in which these rights can be monetised (Doyle, 2016: 629).

This has a series of implications for distributors as the existing rights ecology is being dismantled and the 'traditional aftermarkets' of TV programmes are receding (Ulin, 2019: 269). As explained by Andy Zein, head of formats at Warner Bros:

> In the past distribution and rights businesses were built on rights to a territory and particular segments of rights for that territory and particular windows ... Now the Netflix's are going 'Right let's just scrap the territory

model' . . . Multi-territory global buyers are completely changing the landscape . . . It reduces potential revenues. (Zein in Doyle, 2016: 637–8)

In effect, streaming giants are dismantling the classic distribution model, which was based on the distinction between domestic and international rights (Chapter 3). Distributors can no longer maximise revenue by creating competition for content in particular windows and territories (Doyle, 2016: 637–8). As for producers, they need to be content with the money they receive upfront as they will have no further opportunities to monetise their content (Payne, interview 2019).

Content Aggregation

Aggregation consists of *bringing content together under the umbrella of a single brand and marketing it to audiences and/or advertisers.* Aggregators consist of broadcasting organisations and streaming entertainment services. They are the chain's *lead firms* because they have direct access to the advertising and consumer markets, and procure services from *suppliers* located in the other segments. In GVCs, capital always flows in specific directions. In the case of television, it enters the chain from aggregation to then go onto other segments. This is why aggregation is the cornerstone of the TV value chain and where its dominant businesses operate.

Many aggregators have vertically integrated and acquired production and distribution companies upstream, so the question remains: in what sense is aggregation a segment? First, vertical integration does not dissolve *intra-firm* markets and boundaries: only a percentage of the content produced by an integrated TV studio ends up in the aggregation business of the same firm. ITV Studios is a case in point. In 2019, ITV's production division sold £573 million (US$733 million) worth of programming to the broadcaster, and generated £1.25 billion (US$1.6 billion) externally (ITV, 2020: 32). Thus, in terms of revenue, about a third of ITV Studios' output ended up on the broadcaster's channels and DTC platforms. Not everything ITV Studio produces is suitable for ITV audiences, and the broadcaster relies on the open content market for the rest of its programming. The group leans on ITV Studios' revenue not only to generate growth but to diversify and internationalise its revenue streams. While the group's broadcast division is in slight decline (because of the contracting TV advertising market in the United Kingdom), the income from ITV Studios is going up. In 2019, its revenue (£1.25 billion) generated 37.8 percent of the group's total (external) income (£3.3 billion–US$4.2 billion) (ITV, 2020: 30).

The same principle applies to media conglomerates and US networks. Some of the M&A activities they engage in are driven by the strategic aim of securing their content supply chain and expanding libraries. When DTC operations are launched, they know that premium and exclusive content is fundamental to drive subscriber growth. When NBCUniversal and Warner Media did not renew licencing deals with Netflix for *The Office* and *Friends*, it generated headlines (e.g. Alexander, 2019). However, even conglomerates do not have the resources to keep all content in-house and must generate sales on the open market. While they resign themselves to take the financial hit rather than licence content to a direct competitor, thousands of their titles, alongside *The Office* and *Friends*, continue to be licenced to hundreds of broadcasters around the world.

No multinational aggregator produces the breadth of content that matches the needs of its diverse platforms and audiences, and therefore none can do without the open market as a source of programming. This is true of Walt Disney, which acquires content for its non-Disney branded platforms, and Netflix. The latter's relationship with the content market warrants clarification as the label 'Netflix Original' can lead to misunderstandings (Afilipoaie et al., 2021). It simply means that a film or series is exclusive to the platform, independently of whether they have been acquired or commissioned. The streamer acts as a producer (thereby bypassing the content market) only when it commissions a show and covers all the production costs. Netflix, however, remains active in the market and continues to acquire streaming rights for new or existing programmes. Either way, it spent US$15.1 billion adding content to its catalogue in 2020 (Brown, 2021; Chapter 4).

Aggregation requires a specific set of skills and resources. Today, aggregators are first and foremost intellectual property–management companies that protect, exploit, and promote the brands (programmes) they own – when possible – and rent when necessary. They must also devote resources to building a relationship with viewers, which entails understanding them, sourcing the content they want, and finding a way of delivering it on their device of choice. With the return path capabilities of internet delivery, they now have the data to personalise this relationship.

Netflix provides a startling illustration of the focus and skills needed to become a public-facing entertainment destination, and the significance of the two-way relationship in the age of digital entertainment. Netflix's most prized asset is its recommendation engine, which serves a dual purpose. It is a key tool in the platform's battle for attention, and the company estimates that at least 75 per cent of viewing flows from it (Amatriain and Basilico, 2012). The engine also enables the streamer to personalise the search and viewing experience by adapting its recommendations down to every single member. Overall, increased usage and enhanced experience helps retain subscriptions and reduce churn.

The platform's recommendation system is a three-legged stool, according to Todd Yellin, Netflix's vice president of production innovation (Plummer, 2017). First, Netflix 'reverse-engineered Hollywood' by 'meticulously analyz[ing] and tag [ging] every movie and TV show imaginable' (Madrigal, 2014). Trained taggers record every aspect of every minute of the content they watch, following a thirty-six-page instruction manual (Madrigal, 2014). The outcome is an unprecedented data set and a classification of filmed entertainment into 76,897 sub-genres. Categories range from 'mind-bending cult horror movies from the 1980s' to 'critically-acclaimed emotional underdog movies' (Madrigal, 2014).

The second leg consists of user data. One type of data is explicit and consists of viewers' ratings, and the other consists of behavioural metrics and the way people engage with Netflix: 'what people watch, what they watch after, what they watch before, what they watched a year ago, what they've watched recently and what time of day' (Yellin in Plummer, 2017). Behavioural analytics congregate viewers into taste clusters, groups of people who enjoy similar content and share viewing patterns. There are more than 2,000 'taste communities', and every user fits into 3 or 4 clusters (Plummer, 2017).

Personalisation algorithms delve into these two data sets and match up tagged content with taste clusters in order to deliver a customised experience. The outcome is a personalised homepage composed of a series of rows ranked algorithmically in order of relevance, and each 'represents 3 layers of personalization: the choice of genre itself, the subset of titles selected within that genre, and the ranking of those titles' (Amatriain and Basilico, 2012). Netflix does not merely personalise recommendations, it also tailors the artwork that presents the titles. When describing a movie, the algorithms extract and present the metadata according to the theme, mood, cast members, etc. that are most relevant and attractive to a particular user (Chandrashekar et al., 2017).

This proprietary technology does not come cheap, and Netflix spent US$1.5 billion on technology and development in 2019 (Netflix, 2020: 25). However, it gives the streamer a double competitive edge. First, personalisation is an attribute of the Netflix brand. The streamer likes to let its users know that it tailors its service to their tastes, which encourages them to send more feedback, which in turn improves the platform's predictive models of ratings and video consumption (Amatriain and Basilico, 2012).

Second, personalisation increases video consumption by assisting the discovery process. As Netflix engineers explain:

> We want our recommendations to be accurate in that they are relevant to the tastes of our members, but they also need to be diverse so that we can address the spectrum of a member's interests versus only focusing on one.

We want to be able to highlight the depth in the catalog we have in those interests and also the breadth we have across other areas to help our members explore and even find new interests. We want our recommendations to be fresh and responsive to the actions a member takes, such as watching a show, adding to their list, or rating; but we also want some stability so that people are familiar with their homepage and can easily find videos they've been recommended in the recent past. (Alvino and Basilico, 2015)

Nielsen identified no less than 646,152 titles available across all platforms to US viewers in 2019 (Vachhrajani, 2020), so helping members discover new shows and retaining them on-site is essential in the current video ecosystem.

As illustrated by Netflix, modern aggregators' core competencies lie in marketing, in the broadest meaning of the term, which means they strive to build a relationship with their customer base, understand their tastes by way of ratings and data, and acquire and produce the content that best fits. The aim is to build a *branded entertainment destination*; broadcasters used to do it at a national level, leading platforms do so on a global scale. The capital and resources required to achieve this aim are significant, which explains why barriers to entry in the segment are high (even more so at global level), and why rewards are commensurate to the level of risk and investment required.

Conclusion

The TV production sector has been through two decades of radical transformation. Consolidation – multiple small producers joining forces to form larger businesses – has transformed a cottage industry into a sector dominated by global TV studios. Fourteen of these firms were formed by the late 2000s, and further consolidation saw their number reduced to ten a decade later. Vertical integration was another noted trend, and many of these TV studios became part of media conglomerates.

Vertical integration and segmentation are not anti-nomic. Every segment has boundaries and is intersected by a market. The global content market was valued at US$50 billion in 2014 (ITV, 2014: 7), and must have trebled in size since. The role of integrated content divisions is to secure supply lines (and enhance the asset specificity of their owners, Chapter 9), but they remain active in the content market. None of them are 'captive' organisations to their owners: should their programmes not find the best home these would underperform, resulting in negative consequences for all parties involved. In addition, the success of these divisions depends on their ability to retain top creative talent, who would find it unpalatable to supply one sole aggregator (Lambert, interview 2012). No vertically integrated media organisation can seal itself off from the content market. It is for this reason that even the BBC, a public broadcaster, has split its production operations, BBC Studios, from the rest of the organisation in order to serve this market more effectively.[4] Furthermore, while consolidation and integration have undeniably changed the sector, TV production remains diverse and producers of different sizes and capabilities co-exist (Chapter 9).

The same goes for distribution, which remains a distinct segment despite a degree of integration. Integrated distributors acquire and sell third party programming just like their rivals, the numerous specialist and independent firms that still populate the sector. In order to retain credibility in the marketplace (without which independent production companies would not give them content to represent), integrated divisions need to treat all parties with a degree of fairness and integrity. Vertical integration is occurring but in the wider context of segmentation and GVC formation.

The third key trend is international expansion. TV producers, in their pursuit of scale and market power, have embarked on a growth path *within their segment*. Successive waves of M&A activities have led to the formation of ten global TV studios. They have expanded their transnational capabilities and developed their production footprint. They can produce formats in multiple territories, build production hubs, and sell finished programmes on a worldwide basis. In the process, these studios have assimilated themselves into the global TV industry: their internationalisation is an operational requirement in an industry that works as a singular transnational space.

8

Media Delivery

This chapter analyses the media delivery segments of the TV GVC, which is the second leg of the journey that programmes make (Chapter 7). The media delivery supply chain is *the sum of the value-adding tasks necessary to transfer content from source to audience*, which begins when production companies have finished working on the programme and aggregators package it up to reach various audiences. Its segments are publication, transmission, and reception. Building on Chapters 3 and 4, we examine how a mosaic of technologies, provided by a complex web of suppliers, sustains a fast-evolving video ecosystem.

Media delivery analysis is central to the argument about the formation of a TV GVC and the globalisation of the TV industry. Broadcasters were once in charge of the full transmission process, of tasks deemed core to their business, but today media delivery is externalised to the market and devolved to a network of suppliers that collaborate along the value chain. There exist two main classes of supplier. The first consists of *sector-specific* specialist firms that serve the media industries exclusively. The second are *global suppliers*,[1] that is tech giants that have developed deep global capabilities and can leverage an unprecedented infrastructure to deliver content to and from (almost) any location in the world. They gain further leverage by being *multi-sectoral*, serving clients across several industries.

The significance of this evolution lies in the impact of outsourcing on the structure of the television industry. Broadcasters were at the forefront of developments in broadcast engineering. Today, whilst retaining a certain amount of technological expertise, they increasingly outsource media delivery tasks and rely upon the infrastructure of tech giants. Engineering was once part of broadcasters' corporate identity, but traditional broadcasting has had to 'pivot away from what's been an engineering-led activity' (Greenaway, interview 2019), to redefine the contours of these organisations, and of the TV industry as a whole. From a technology standpoint, television used to be a self-reliant engineering ecosystem that was distinct and separate from other industries. Today, it shares technology, transmission infrastructure, and suppliers, with other industries, and the nature and significance of this evolution are analysed in Chapters 9 and 10.

This chapter is set out in the following manner: it compares and contrasts old and new media delivery mechanisms, analysing each segment of the current media delivery chain to provide an overview of the IP-driven video ecosystem. Then, it retraces the moment British broadcasters began to outsource media delivery tasks, examining the reasons motivating their decision. Once the formation of the new production network has been explained, the attention shifts to suppliers. The chapter highlights key trends that can be observed among service providers that are sector-specific, before introducing the concept of global supplier. The notion is applied for the first time in the context of the media industries. This chapter uses the GVC literature in order to introduce it, reasoning that the general characteristics of a global supplier, as identified by GVC researchers, will be relevant to our purpose. It identifies and analyses the key features of those operating in the media delivery chain.

As with Chapter 7, this research relies on fieldwork conducted in the United Kindgom, and uses British broadcasters as a case study. According to Josh Stinehour, a leading specialist, outsourcing in media delivery remains confined 'to certain geographies and high-end customers' (IBC Showcase, 2020). Nonetheless, both sector-specific and multi-sectoral suppliers are active in multiple territories, notably across North America, Europe, and the Middle East. Furthermore, technological progress, and cloud computing in particular, is making the argument for outsourcing evermore compelling and it is forecast that the model will spread to new markets (IBC Showcase, 2020). Thus, while the relevance of this case study is not universal, it is broader than the British Isles, and likely will soon apply to a growing number of countries.

The Past and Present of Media Delivery

Since the origins of sound broadcasting, and for the greater part of the twentieth century, media delivery consisted of the analogue transmission of a signal from a broadcasting facility to listeners' and viewers' radio and TV sets. It was a task broadcasters carried out themselves. In the United Kingdom, the BBC oversaw the entire transmission process and developed its own network of transmitting stations (Briggs, 1995: 225–8, 997). Engineering skills and prowess was at the heart of the corporation's identity, which evolved into a world-leading institution in the field of broadcast engineering. The long list of innovations attributed to the BBC includes the first TV standards converter, the first electronic recording apparatus, and the first transatlantic transmission (BBC, 2017). Between the 1920s and the 1970s, some 350 patents were issued to the BBC that it either used or licenced to manufacturers:

Among the most important, in their time, have been those relating to acoustics and sound absorbers, transmitting aerials (including slot aerials (1949)), receiving aerials, circuits ... transformers, filters and attenuators, several forms of automatic monitor, frequency-dividers and multipliers, measuring equipment, limiters and volume compressors, loudspeakers, microphones ... oscillators, sound recording and reproducing equipment ... video-tape equipment ... television recording on film, band-width compression, several types of television standards converter, pulse-code systems and digital techniques. (Pawley, 1972: 528)

When ITV joined the fray in 1955 it, too, equipped itself with a substantial engineering department in order to surmount the numerous technical challenges the newcomer faced (Stevens, interview 2017; Sendall, 1983: 324–9). In the USA, networks were equally involved in all aspects of media delivery. When the Federal Communications Commission declared CBS's colour TV system as the new standard in October 1950, the network immediately embarked, albeit briefly, into the manufacture of TV sets (Yates and Murphy, 2019: 184–5).

The media delivery these broadcasters established can be characterised by four key attributes. It was *unimodal* because broadcasters dealt with a single (terrestrial) transmission path. It was *proprietary*, as they operated their own hardware-centric infrastructure for the sole purpose of transmitting their channels. Even though the BBC and ITV would eventually share some transmission stations, each operated their own network (Sendall, 1983: 2).

Media delivery was vertically integrated because it was a *task* that broadcasters carried themselves and were equipped to do. Although British broadcasters have always collaborated with equipment suppliers, these arrangements were related to specialised processes and they remained in charge of the entire operation.

The transmission of TV signals was strictly *national*; broadcasters had no business beyond their borders and European countries prohibited foreign TV signals. As a reflection of the national nature of broadcasting, broadcasters' transmission facilities followed the contours of national territory and never ventured beyond (Scannell, 1990).[2]

The Advent of IP Delivery

Media delivery was changing and progressing before the Internet became a vehicle for video distribution. The number of transmission paths increased with the emergence of cable and communications satellites (Chapter 5). Yet, these two means of transmission were to remain on the fringes of the TV industry until a breakthrough in signal compression was achieved through advancements in digital technology (Starks, 2013). With the capability to package more channels in the same bandwidth, pay-TV platforms could offer more choice, which made their product considerably more attractive to consumers. Sky, for instance, Europe's foremost satellite broadcaster, began trading in the United Kingdom in 1989 with four channels transmitted to a few thousand subscribers. Sky Digital, by way of contrast, broadcast hundreds of channels to millions of customers by the 2000s (Horsman, 1997).

Videocassette recorders (VCRs), and later digital video recorders (DVRs), were the first time-shifting technologies. Cable providers invented VoD. They first delivered 'near VoD' by providing content carousels where films started every twenty minutes, and then offered true VoD as capacity increased. Even though IP delivery followed an evolution, it remains a game changer. IP transport not only comprehensively changed media delivery, it transformed business models and brought about a new video ecosystem that far exceeds, both in terms of volume and complexity, the broadcasting ecology of the recent past (Chapters 2 and 4).

This new context makes video delivery more challenging than in the past. VoD is a 24/7 universe where users expect to stream programming anytime and anywhere, regardless of whether in a fixed location or on the move. The devices used to access content are increasingly disparate, ranging from mobile phones and tablets to game consoles and ultra-high-definition 105-inch TV screens. As broadcasters ramp up their VOD operations, they need to run both IP-based and broadcast transmission paths simultaneously. Many broadcasters and streaming platforms are seeking audiences across borders and need delivery services that match their international coverage (Chapters 1 and 2). Transnational TV networks run multiple localised channels, and even national broadcasters, which had one feed per channel in the analogue era, now air multiple regional and sub-regional feeds in order to accommodate local taste and needs.

Media Delivery 2.0

This video environment could not exist without an intricate and efficient media delivery chain, which bears little in common with the old one. The chain consists of three segments. *Publication* involves several stages. Files are first authenticated as coming from the right source (they are no longer delivered by courier) and validated. This consists of a series of quality checks that include automated and human quality controls. Next, files go through a transformation stage to convert them into as many formats as necessary for distribution. In today's ecosystem, a unique TV show or film will need to be versioned in hundreds of formats in order to meet the requirements of a host of distribution platforms. Versions are needed for different transmission paths – terrestrial, cable, satellite, and IP delivery – and for various devices, from mobile phones to connected TV sets. This process is seamless and highly automated: content is prepared in many formats using 'no-touch automation' where pre-programmed rules dictate which formats are needed, and workflow tools orchestrate the creation with no human involvement. The timeline of distribution also matters, and different versions are prepared for compliance managers (to ensure that programmes match the relevant regulatory standards), film classification boards, airlines, cinemas, and broadcasters (Plunkett, interviews 2017).

Content is then stored and readied for transmission, and audience-facing metadata is confirmed. Programme billings are prepared for inclusion in TV listings and electronic programme guides (EPGs), together with programme synopses that describe content to audiences across a range of channels, platforms, and countries. If content goes out to a linear broadcaster, it needs to be scheduled and placed within the context of a detailed media plan that allocates commercials and channel promotions using audience weightings, which can vary from one region to another for the same show. For on-demand platforms, content is catalogued instead of scheduled, then exposed to an application on a smart TV, PC, phone, or tablet. It is essentially made up of metadata comprising programme synopses, promotional images, and genre categories that end users can view to help them decide on the content they choose to watch (Plunkett, interviews, 2017; Smith, interviews, 2017).

Transmission begins when a signal/file is sent out from the playout system. As content leaves the studio, it will go through a series of compression and decompression phases until it reaches the end user. The only place where files are uncompressed is inside the broadcast facility where there is plenty of bandwidth available. But the latter costs money and transmission systems rely on a constant trade-off between quality and bandwidth. Video codecs (Chapter 5) compress down the audio and video to a pre-agreed level to suit available bandwidth in the transmission medium. For instance, if a signal is sent to a satellite, it has to fit in the bandwidth that has been allocated to a particular channel on the satellite's transponder. As a general trend, a signal becomes more compressed the closer it gets to the customer.

The transmission route varies according to type of content and broadcaster. A national TV network may need a multiplicity of signals with different inserts and continuity announcements for each region served. Signals sent to pay-TV platforms and international channels may be delivered through satellite platforms. For entertainment platforms, the content will be sent to CDNs (Chapter 5). Outside broadcast firms may also be part of the process, supplying and operating editing trucks and live transmission facilities for sports events and special ceremonies.

In terms of workflow, publication and transmission are joined at the hip, but they remain distinct from a commercial and technical point of view. The former is more about content management and the latter about content distribution. Several software and hardware infrastructure providers overlap both segments, but most firms tend to gravitate towards one. Media asset management, channel management, and playout specialists do most of their work in the publication segment. Typical transmission firms include infrastructure and media services companies, IP network providers, and satellite operators. In the United Kingdom, Arqiva would be most likely the company a broadcaster would choose for linear distribution. The firm inherited the infrastructure that supported the first BBC TV broadcast in 1936 and operates 1,150 TV transmitter towers across Britain today that can carry a TV signal along various transmission paths (terrestrial, cable, satellite) and distribution platforms (Plunkett, interviews 2017; company sources).

The last segment is *reception*. The complexity at the edge of distribution networks (end device) is far greater today than it once was. In a push-based broadcast environment, the same signal that delivers a piece of content is received by all the devices that tune in, and there is certainty as to its quality. It differs markedly with distribution over the Internet, where the intelligence at the edge is much greater. An IP-driven transmission path includes many intermediary steps from origin server to CDN to local access infrastructure (e.g. Wi-Fi) to end device. Since there is no authority of control between the source and receiving network conditions, the end device has to take responsibility for adapting to different conditions. The industry has decided to optimise performance by placing a lot of the adaptability and decision-making right out at the edge in the end device (Plunkett, interviews 2017).

Attributes of Media Delivery 2.0

The way media delivery is handled today differs vastly from that of the past. The attributes of the new delivery chain contrast with the old ones and help explain the vast changes that are affecting the television industry (Table 8.1). The contemporary media delivery chain is best described as *multimodal*. Broadcasters and media conglomerates that operate both TV channels and on-demand platforms have to deal with two distinct sets of transmission protocols. In a classic broadcast transmission path – or *multicast* – a single piece of content is transmitted over a radio wave; there is only one copy at any time (and frequency), which is shared by

Table 8.1 *Media delivery: past and present*

Former media delivery (1920s – 1990s)	unimodal	proprietary	national	vertically integrated
Media delivery 2.0	multimodal	Open/standardised	global	Segmented/ disintegrated

Source: Chalaby and Plunkett, 2021: 3210.

all the recipients. Even in this configuration, the transmission paths vary between cable, satellite, and terrestrial. The second transmission mechanism – *unicast* – runs over IP and is used by all OTT services. In the unicast model every single stream is a unique copy, and if a million viewers watch the same show, it means that a million copies are being viewed simultaneously. This transmission protocol is a *pull* mechanism, as viewers request their own copy of the material, in opposition to the *push* structure of the broadcast path.

There are two distinct classes of OTT delivery – VoD and live-streaming. On-demand content is watched at the time and place of the viewers choosing and consists of catalogues of movies and TV shows such as those made available through major subscription services, or 'catch-up' content with shorter rights windows on traditional broadcaster platforms (e.g. BBC's iPlayer).

Live streaming content is event-driven programming such as live sports and news. While both on-demand and live streaming content is carried across OTT networks, the live streaming use case has particularly stringent latency requirements. Audiences expect live action content to be delivered in near or real time so the content publication and transmission paths must be optimised to make this possible. Live streaming content of the most popular events presents another challenge – that of concurrency and scale. This results in significantly different approaches to encoding and transport optimisation of OTT content depending on whether it is VoD or live streaming. However, as live streamed content is often tomorrow's on-demand (as when a sports event becomes available on the catch-up service), there is often an additional live-to-VoD phase where content encoding and packaging is converted from one use case to the other.

Broadcast networks were at one time *proprietary* in the sense that they were owned by a single operator that used them for the sole purpose of transmitting TV channels. As a consequence, broadcasting developed as a separate ecosystem akin to the Galàpagos Islands: the industry developed its own infrastructure for connectivity and transport with its own cables, ports, and switches, together with its own vocabulary and set of terminologies. With the transition to IP delivery, broadcasting is embracing the common IT stack and sharing technologies and equipment with other industries. When broadcast engineers procure equipment, they purchase only the upper level broadcast–specific application, not the entire physical device. Apart from specialist applications, hardware, operating systems, and the rest of the IT stack are all generic.

Third, the geographical scope of media delivery has changed. Transmission networks covered entire national geographies to ensure the whole population had access to the same programmes – and only those. Today, media conglomerates, online platforms, and most other video aggregators aim to reach audiences across borders (Chapters 1 and 2).

Finally, media delivery is no longer a task that broadcasters do themselves but a value chain that involves a network of collaborating firms. Broadcast vendors have long existed, but broadcasters assumed the bulk of the work and remained in charge of the whole operation. Today, the trend is towards outsourcing.

The Origins of Outsourcing in Media Delivery: The Case of British Broadcasters

British broadcasters began to outsource media delivery tasks in the 2000s. By the end of the decade they outsourced most, if not all of these tasks (Table 8.2).

The specific circumstances that led to outsourcing vary between broadcasters, but the fact that they nearly all reached the same conclusion at the same time is an indication of the strength of the drivers that underpin the strategy. Outsourcing in media delivery is driven by two factors. As always, costs come into the picture because broadcasters, like any other firm, are under constant pressure to deliver

Table 8.2 *Outsourcing by British broadcasters in media delivery*

	Publication (playout and media management)	Linear transmission (multicast)	Nonlinear (on-demand) distribution (unicast)
BBC	Red Bee Media	Arqiva	BBC
ITV	Deluxe/ Red Bee Media	Arqiva	BT
Channel 4	Red Bee Media	Arqiva	Red Bee Media
Channel 5	Red Bee Media	Arqiva	Red Bee Media
Sky	Sky	Société Européenne des Satellites	Sky
BT Sport	Arqiva/ Red Bee Media	BT Media & Broadcast	BT

Source: author

more for less. The BBC, ITV, and Channel 4 all outsourced at times of financial strain and the decision involved their respective chief financial officers (CFO). But the choice to outsource was also prompted by the rapid pace of technological change. For ITV and Channel 4, it was the investment required to upgrade to HD (high definition) that prompted a rethink of their media delivery chain arrangements (Stevens, interview 2017). Shane Tucker, Channel 4's broadcast engineering officer, recalls:

> I think our CFO made the decision at the time and it was purely based on cost and efficiencies. Channel 4 was about to launch a HD channel when we were negotiating and that was basically one of the drivers. All the investment to upgrade our entire infrastructure to be HD would cost us x amount and then they thought, actually we could outsource the entire operation, and that was probably the driving force really. (Tucker, interview 2017)

At the BBC, outsourcing was the conclusion of a process that had begun with the rapid growth of its public service and commercial channels. The department that was originally responsible for BBC TV channel playout, broadcasting and promotion, grew significantly during the 1990s, but did so in an organic rather than strategic way as an increasing amount of demands were placed on it. Towards the end of the decade, the need to refresh its playout infrastructure created an opportunity to approach the whole operation in a more strategic way, utilising the latest technology and introducing economies of scale to help drive down capital and operational costs. This led to the commissioning of a new building close to Television Centre in West London. The expense was such, however, that Director General Greg Dyke and Finance Director John Smith approved the incorporation of the department in order to create a limited company, with the aim of providing broadcast services to other organisations and thereby recouping some of the investment. BBC Broadcast Ltd was created in 2002 and, after limited success as a wholly owned subsidiary of the BBC, was put up for sale following a review launched by the subsequent Director General, Mark Thompson. It was purchased in 2005 by Macquarie, the Australian investment bank. The fledgling group expanded in several markets through acquisitions in Australia, Spain, and Germany, and delivered impressive growth with its Access Services offer: multilingual subtitling, signing, and audio description. In 2014, Red Bee Media, as it was rebranded, was bought by Ericsson in a further consolidation of the UK broadcast services market (company sources; Smith, interview 2017).

Sky has the least outsourced media delivery chain, because it has not faced the same financial pressures experienced by terrestrial broadcasters. It also has a very distinctive transmission path, using DTH satellite distribution in order to reach its UK customers (Chapter 5). Likewise, the BBC still runs its own nonlinear on-demand operation because of its long heritage of technical innovation and, with BBC iPlayer, the corporation has a world-leading product that can be developed economically in-house (Smith, interview 2017).

By way of contrast, ITV, Channel 4, Channel 5, and BT Sport have fully embraced the outsourcing model (even though the latter uses the transmission facilities of its parent company). Launched in August 2013, BT Sport built a TV studio in eighteen weeks (a job that can take up to four years) and launched its first channel in nine months. It was the first in Britain to broadcast in 4K and to run a fully digital (tapeless) operation. As Jamie Hindhaugh, the COO of BT Sport and BT TV, explains, none of this would have been possible without outsourcing. He describes the company as an 'umbrella', 'a creative village in a centre of excellence' that mixes internal experts with external partners (Hindhaugh, interview 2017).

Outsourcing enables broadcasters to handle the complexity of modern media delivery chains while remaining agile at a time of rapid technological change. When all regions and sub-regions are taken into account, ITV has fifty-two channels playing out on linear streams alone. Similarly, at the BBC, commitments to serving audiences in Scotland, Wales, and Northern Ireland on BBC One and Two (and BBC Alba in Scotland), in addition to the fifteen English regions and sub-regions, means the total number of broadcast linear streams is, in practice, much greater than the channel portfolio suggests. The schedule reactivity of channels like ITV1 and BBC One necessitates playout and distribution operations that are particularly complex (Stevens, interview 2017; Smith, interviews 2017).

Recent evolutions in the media delivery chain make outsourcing the only viable option for broadcasters. Consumer demand for anytime/anywhere programming and mobile-centric viewing means they must deliver content via a multitude of platforms and formats. Sinead Greenaway, UKTV's chief technology officer, remembers: 'every time a new platform arrived we'd just build another workflow, so it's completely inefficient' (Greenaway, interview 2019). Multiple transmission pathways necessitate an amount of investment and expertise that is difficult to sustain for most organisations, but without technical support, they run the risk of operating TV services with a high level of unreliability and multiplying the number of 'irregs' (outages or failures/issues that can happen to a linear stream) (Stevens, interview 2017).

Technology can deliver considerable cost savings through economies of scale, especially when shared across companies and even industries. In the past, when video was exclusively distributed within a broadcast facility, it was sent across a proprietary infrastructure. That is, broadcasters owned and operated their own hardware-centric infrastructure for the sole purpose of transmitting its channels.

With the growth and globalisation of IP delivery, things have changed on several counts. First, using IP-transport and files rather than tapes, television is migrating to the same technology components that other industries are currently using, thus tapping into significant economies of scale. With cloud computing, media files can now be hosted in the same high-density server infrastructure used by companies in any field of activity. All the companies that manage, store, and transfer files provide IP-transport and connectivity for broadcasters and have clients across many industries, from medical imaging to seismic exploration.

For those service providers that are sector-specific and use cloud computing privately or publicly, they can reuse and repurpose their infrastructure across their entire service line, as a playout server can become a transcoder, which can become a multi-viewer, etc. No longer having to invest in single-purpose dedicated boxes enables them to limit depreciation and lower amortisation costs (Alexandre Dubiez, Head of Global Playout and Studio Solutions, Red Bee Media, in IBC Showcase, 2020).

Costs can also be reduced further down the line. When broadcasters bought specialist equipment from a small group of industry suppliers there was little scope for economies of scale. But these are increasingly achievable when purchasing generic IP infrastructure that is used across industries. Further savings are to be made when procurement is driven by a media delivery and management specialist that deals with the same vendors for its entire portfolio of clients.

When physical tapes were being wheeled around by people in local facilities, and distributed across private connectivity systems, the ability to automate was restricted. Today, with software-based systems and generic IP–type infrastructure, many tasks once performed by a human workforce are now being automated, further reducing costs (Plunkett, interviews 2017).

Sector-Specific Suppliers

The evolution of the media delivery supply chain echoes that of content production in many respects. The media tech sector – valued at US$51 billion – has gone through intense rounds of M&A in recent years, sharply reducing the number of businesses operating (Devoncroft, 2017: 16–17). These firms consolidate in order to become the leader in their chosen segment, generate economies of scale, acquire proprietary technology and expertise, and expand their geographical footprint – a prerequisite to serving the sector's lead firms. Consolidation is accentuated by their preference to run lean supply chains; new media technology projects tend to involve two to three suppliers only (Devoncroft, 2017: 39).

Ericsson offers a case in point. In order to build a presence in the publication (playout and media services) segment, the Stockholm-based telecom company has acquired forty-five companies in IPTV and media management (full ownership only, excluding minority stakes and calls for capital from partly owned businesses). Table 8.3 lists Ericsson's most recent transactions and highlights the company's strategy in the segment.

Building an international presence was among Ericsson's objectives. Its media and broadcast division originates more than 500 TV channels and distributes over 2.7 million hours of programming each year through eight media hubs located in Abu Dhabi, Britain (multiple locations), Finland, France, Sweden, and the USA. The process of acquiring international scale is facilitated by the borderless nature of IP technology: while in the past the operational teams and the equipment would need to be co-located, today's technology enables TV channels to be operated remotely (IBC Showcase, 2020; Plunkett, interviews 2017).

All of the chain's software and hardware vendors have similar capabilities. Aspera, an example among hundreds, is an IBM-owned company specialising in high-speed data transfer using patented technology and has more than 3,000 customers worldwide (company source).

To a much lesser extent than TV production, vertical integration is also occurring in media delivery, as some media conglomerates have made targeted investments into the segment. BAMTech, which specialises in services to the streaming industry; AppNexus (ad-tech); Metrological, which integrates OTT platforms to the viewing experience; and Nevion, a cloud–based production solutions provider, are among the tech firms recently acquired by Disney, AT&T, Comcast, and Sony, respectively. The segment, however, is characterised by the emergence of even larger suppliers that operate across multiple industries.

GVCs and the Rise of Global Suppliers

The advent of IP transport has brought a new class of suppliers to the TV industry: tech giants. This section introduces the concept of global supplier, before examining those operating in the TV industry. As outsourcing spreads, GVCs grow, and so too the suppliers. GVC researchers have observed 'the rise of a *global supply base* populated by large, international, highly capable suppliers, contract manufacturers, intermediaries, and service providers, something unique in the history of the world economy' (Sturgeon et al., 2011: 232). 'A new class of huge global suppliers' has emerged, they argue, made of manufacturing and trading companies 'that no one has ever heard of' but which have developed deep global capabilities (Sturgeon et al., 2011: 235, 236).

Such suppliers currently operate in the media delivery chain. What makes them distinctive from other international suppliers, and what are their key

Table 8.3 *Ericsson's key acquisitions in the media delivery chain*

Date of transaction	Acquired company	Description	Country of registration	Value of transaction
27/10/2016	Envivio	IP video processing and distribution software developer	USA	111.2 M €
02/02/2015	twofour54's playout business	Playout	United Arab Emirates	n.a.
31/12/2014	Fabrix Systems	Cloud storage and computing platform operator	Israel	78.2 M €
12/05/2104	Creative Broadcast Services (alias Red Bee Media)	Playout and online video content broadcasting services	United Kingdom	n.a.
05/09/2013	Microsoft Mediaroom	IPTV platform operator	USA	n.a.
03/07/2012	Technicolor's broadcasting services division	Media broadcasting services	France, Netherlands and United Kingdom	28.0 M €
20/12/2007	HyC	Digital TV and broadband consultancy firm	Spain	n.a.
14/06/2007	Tandberg Television	IPTV technology	Norway	929.2 M €

Source: data from Zephyr database, accessed 15 March 2017

characteristics? GVC scholars have identified such suppliers in three industries: fashion (e.g. Li and Fung), electronics (e.g. Flex), and automotive (e.g. Valeo).[3] They have a *global footprint* in terms of production and distribution coverage. For instance, Flex (formerly Flextronics), which is among the world's largest electronic manufacturing service (EMS) companies, is supplier to many of the world's most famous consumer electronics brands. It operates 137 centres for logistics, manufacturing or research, across 27 countries (Flex, 2018; Sturgeon and Kawakami, 2010). Li and Fung's extensive network of supply chains involves 17,000 staff spread across 230 locations in 40 different territories (Li and Fung, 2019).

These firms are no longer mere 'captive' but fully fledged *turnkey suppliers* (Sturgeon and Lee, 2005: 41). They orchestrate entire supply chains, starting with product design, carrying on to sourcing, manufacturing, and packaging, and ending with global logistics and retail management (Sturgeon et al., 2011: 253). They coordinate and 'have power over a vast number of upstream or lower-tier suppliers' (Raj-Reichert, 2019: 359).

Global suppliers are *multi-sectoral* operating across several industrial sectors. Flex, for instance, has clients in thirteen different industries from aerospace and defense to healthcare and consumer electronics (Flex, 2018).

Global suppliers derive a competitive advantage from their scale and capabilities. To start with, only they can provide worldwide support to their clients. The lead firms they serve invariably operate in multiple markets and need manufacturing or logistics support irrespective of geography. For example, in the automotive industry, a braking system manufacturer is expected to install equipment in all the plants that its clients operate. As an automotive supplier explains:

> Today it is a requirement to serve platforms – it is part of the bid. If a supplier doesn't have a global strategy, it can't bid. New projects are no longer seen as an opportunity to expand globally – instead, a supplier must have a global base in place to even make a bid. (in Sturgeon and Florida, 2004: 69–70)

Global suppliers generate economies of scope, which they achieve by buying raw materials in bulk, manufacturing the same component on an unprecedented scale, or saving costs by switching production from one client or component to another in the same facilities (Sturgeon and Florida, 2004: 69). Substantial economies of scale are obtained by deploying *generic assets* and *processes* in manufacturing or logistics across their customer base (Sturgeon and Lee, 2005: 39–40).

Contrary to expectations, global suppliers are agile and have the flexibility in their network of facilities to shift production between regions to adjust to changing tax regimes and trade policies. For example, they can shift from global to local sourcing by moving production from Asia to North America should an

American car manufacturer need to adapt to evolving US regulations (Sturgeon and Florida, 2004: 68).

Finally, multi-sectoral suppliers are in the unique and privileged position of being able to *transfer knowledge* across markets, clients, and industries. Like Li and Fung, Flex operates across more than 1,000 supply chains, dealing with 30,000 suppliers in thirty-five countries. As it solves issues that are specific to one sector, it gains knowledge that can be applied across others. The spread of these activities generates a wealth of data and feedback that give the business unique insights into trends ahead of industries and markets (Flex, 2018). This research will now argue that a similar type of supplier has emerged in media delivery.

Standing on the Shoulders of Tech Giants: Global Suppliers in Media Delivery

Neither nineteenth-century telegraph companies nor early twentieth-century wireless operators (e.g. Marconi) matched the capabilities of today's global and multi-sectoral suppliers (Raboy, 2016). The ability to operate an infrastructure on a global scale and deliver content anytime/anywhere on the planet came later. As TV networks began to internationalise they turned to the satellite industry for distribution (Chapters 1 and 3). Satellite operators as suppliers with deep global capabilities were the precursors of a trend that has become prevalent. The growing preponderance of an IP-driven video transport environment has facilitated the emergence of global suppliers in two other areas of media delivery: CDNs and cloud computing.

Communications Satellite Operators

The first communications satellites launched in the 1960s and most satellite operators had a national or regional remit (Chapter 5). Intelsat was the exception, and the Washington-based organisation was the first to achieve global coverage (for telephony) in 1969. Once private satellite operators were given freer rein by many governments, the industry went through several decades of growth and consolidation (Labrador and Galace, 2005; Thussu, 2002), to leave three operators that fit the global supplier label for video services: Intelsat, Eutelsat, and the Société Européenne des Satellites (SES). As shown in Table 8.4, their satellite fleets, orbital positions, premium video neighbourhoods, and ground facilities cover six continents and allow them to deliver content and bandwidth to and from virtually any location on the globe. SES for instance, has achieved

Table 8.4 *Communications satellite operators with global capabilities, 2021*

Operator	1st satellite (year launched)	Headquarters	Full-year 2019 Revenue (US$ billion)	Full-year 2020 Revenue (US$ billion)	Satellite fleet (number of spacecraft)	Number of video neighbour-hoods	Number of TV channels transmitted
SES	1988	Luxembourg	2.2	2.1	55	40	8,300
Intelsat	1965	Luxembourg	2.1	1.9	54	37	5,087
Eutelsat	1983	Paris	1.5[1]	1.4[1]	39	19	6,788

Source: updated from Chalaby and Plunkett, 2021: 3215. Exchange rate EUR–USD as of average closing price in 2019 and 2020 (www.macrotrends.net).

Note[1] Eutelsat's fiscal year runs from 1 July to 30 June.

Table 8.5 *Intelsat's customer set, 2019–20*

Customer set	Representative customers	Annual revenue 2019 (US$ million)	Annual revenue 2020 (US$ million)	Per cent of total revenue (2020)
Media	AT&T, MultiChoice, The Walt Disney Company, Discovery Communications, Telefonica, Corporacion de Radio Television del Norte	883	813	47%
Network Services	Marlink KVH Industries, Speedcast, Global Eagel, Gogo, Verizon, SoftBank, Orange, Telecom Italia	770	677	37%
Government	Australian Defence Force, US Department of Defense, US Department of State, Leonardo	378	393	18%

Source: Intelsat, 2020: 9; Intelsat, 2021: 12.

99 per cent coverage of the earth and operates satellites from Europe to the South Pacific region.

Satellite operators serve the TV industry in various ways, such as the transmission of TV channels, the distribution of live content from sports events and music festivals, and the delivery of broadband and mobile connectivity to rural areas. However, their list of clients spans several industries, Intelsat being a case in point (Table 8.5).

The CDN Industry

The internet backbone would not be able to cope with the current level of demand for video distribution, thus CDNs have been built to carry the bulk of this traffic (Chapter 5). They currently transport 56 per cent of total internet traffic, and this percentage is forecast to reach 72 per cent by 2022 (Cisco, 2018: 3).

Telefónica in Spain and Latin America, Globo in Brazil, and the BBC in the United Kingdom, are among the content providers that run their own private

CDNs, which they deploy at national or regional levels (IBC365 Webinar, 2020). Global proprietary CDN infrastructures are rare. Apple has built its own distribution network, and so has Netflix, whose Open Connect is deemed the world's largest private CDN. The streaming service has developed a network of server appliances that are connected to ISPs in hundreds of locations worldwide.[4] However, even when they do so, content providers would rather not have to invest in their own distribution infrastructure. As Adriaan Bloem, Shahid head of digital infrastructure (a Dubai-based media platform), explained:

> Nobody wants to build their own CDN unless you are a CDN provider. We are a broadcaster, this is not our core speciality, and this is not what our users are going to be particularly interested in. To our users, it just has to look like magic, right? You click play and it has to start streaming, and we have to make it work in a way that they have ... no idea of what's going on behind the scenes. (IBC365 Webinar, 2021)

Outsourcing delivers multiple benefits. When CDN deployment is needed on a global scale, streamers have three options. The largest CDNs have the scale to sustain global deployment, and some content owners happily rely on a single CDN. However, it is unlikely that even these networks can offer the optimal solution and cost optimisation in every target region (Medianova, 2020). Some media firms need to ensure optimal performance and resilience wherever they stream, and they seek solutions that offer greater capacity and the ability to balance traffic load when necessary. They opt either for a multi-CDN strategy that combines several third-party services, or a hybrid CDN combination that brings together proprietary and multiple third-party networks. For instance, Disney+ contracts six third-party CDN providers to access multiple markets, and Netflix complements its own Open Connect with other CDNs. Even Amazon Prime Video, which can rely on the infrastructure of a parent company's AWS, needs six networks to reach its customers (Kilpatrick, interview 2019). Thus, all major video originators, even those with access to a proprietary infrastructure, have recourse to third-party CDNs.

The largest CDNs have reached a global scale and have Points of Presence (PoPs) in 100+ territories (Table 8.6). While the geographical distribution of these PoPs is inevitably unequal and depends on viable markets, they nonetheless span the globe, and are expanding fast. Microsoft Azure CDN's geographical distribution, for instance, crosses every world region.[5]

The six CDN providers listed in Table 8.6 control between half and three quarters of the market in the media and entertainment sector. In addition, they often serve customers in financial services, the travel and hospitality industry, public sector, retail, and software and technology. The CDN industry is highly

Table 8.6 *Global CDNs for the media and entertainment sector, 2021*

Company	Number of PoPs or servers	Key media clients	Notes
Akamai Technologies	285,000 servers, 1,400+ networks, 133 countries	Used by '29 of the top media and entertainment companies'	Industry pioneer; acknowledged as the largest CDN
CloudFront (AWS)	150+ PoPs (24 regions, 61 availability zones)	Amazon Prime Video, Condé Nast Italia, Digital De Agostini (Italy), Discovery Communications, Hulu, M6 (France), PBS, Spotify, Seven Networks (Australia), Sony DADC, Spuul, TVNZ (New Zealand)	Leveraging its parent company's (Amazon) large infrastructure
Limelight Networks	100+ PoPs	BBC, Channel 4 (UK), Channel 5 (UK), Daily Motion, DirecTV, Echostar, Lionsgate, Marvel, Pluto TV, Pokémon, SKY	Industry pioneer
Verizon Digital Media Services	130+ PoPs	ABC, Al Jazeera, BBC, Canal +, CBS, Discovery, Disney, ESPN, HBO, MTV, NBC, Viacom, Warner Bros. Pictures	Formerly EdgeCast Networks, acquired by Verizon in 2013, see Table 3.4
Google Cloud CDN	140 PoPs, 22 regional caches, 200+ countries	*Cloud* clients that may use CDN: 20th Century Fox, Bloomberg, King, Sky, Sony Music, Vimeo	Powering YouTube
Microsoft Azure CDN	129 PoPs, 54 regions, 140 countries	NBC Sports	Recently launched, running at the edge of Microsoft's global network

Source: updated from Chalaby and Plunkett, 2021: 3217

concentrated because the need for scale – and the benefits that brings – creates high entry barriers to market. Although smaller CDNs can deploy mitigating strategies,[6] those with global scope have an in-built commercial and technological advantage. Some content owners can request global coverage from their CDN partner(s). Yves Boudreau, VP of Partnerships and Ecosystem Strategy at Ericsson, explains: 'When Fox goes and pays a global CDN to deliver its content, it pays a global CDN to deliver globally' (Boudreau, 2017). Zee5, Zee Entertainment's SVoD platform, relies solely on Microsoft Azure to stream 100,000+ hours of on-demand content and 90+ live TV channels to more than 190 territories. Similar to automotive firms, media conglomerates operate across geographies and demand adequate support from their suppliers, who need global capabilities to be in the market.

A second advantage of global CDNs is their *elasticity*, because of the 'upside flexibility' it allows (Sturgeon, 2002: 458): large providers can scale up capacity at short notice, ensuring they are able to fulfil any streaming demand, no matter how large. For AWS, this includes European-wide streaming of the Six Nations Championship (rugby) and continent-wide coverage of the Indian Premier League (IPL, cricket). For the IPL, the Amazon subsidiary needs to cope with more than 10 million concurrent streams each night (Kilpatrick, interview 2019).

This upside flexibility provides yet another incentive for media owners to contract out CDN deployment: they can upscale without capital investment because expenditure increases only as needs expand. And for the CDN providers spreading their own investment and cost across thousands of users, this expenditure represents a fraction of what is involved in running a proprietary CDN. Being able to leverage scale, large CDN providers like Akamai are profitable, and the regional or national players (such as the telcos), can do well by bundling CDN services into their wider service portfolio.

Furthermore, 'distributing CDN servers over a wide geographic area expands the range of options for serving content from a server that is geographically close to the end-user' (Stocker et al., 2017:11). These options not only bring down latency but also increase resilience as traffic can be rerouted in case of technical issues (outage, etc.), which might take a data centre out of action (Kilpatrick, interview 2019).

The ability to leverage scale brings economic benefits. Essentially, CDN providers sell a commodity – bandwidth - whose price, like oil, varies little globally. First and foremost, buyers consider cost per gigabyte, and global providers can leverage significant economies of scale. Because of the high volumes they are dealing with, they can lower the average costs on delivering data to reach a point beyond the *minimum efficient scale* of the long-run average cost curve, which smaller firms cannot do (Sloman et al., 2016: 155–7). In addition, as the ratio of fixed costs/variable costs is very high in the CDN industry, once the largest suppliers have invested in infrastructure, the costs of adding features and clients is marginal, and having large numbers of clients brings costs down further. For instance, AWS was able to reduce prices more than sixty times in the past five years (Darnell, interview 2019; Google executive, interview 2019; Kilpatrick, interview 2019).

Cloud Computing

Some media firms are investing in their own private cloud facilities but do-it-yourself data centres have a low utilisation rate (circa 20 per cent), which has negative implications in terms of amortisation and depreciation (Kilpatrick, interview 2019). As the industry's leading survey shows (100,000 + responses worldwide), the favourite option is to externalise computing services and migrate workflows to the public cloud (Devoncroft, 2018). Most broadcasters in Europe and the USA are in the process of moving workflow to the cloud. In the United Kingdom, those broadcasters moving their streaming platforms include BBC (iPlayer), Channel 4 (All 4), and UKTV, as have Turner, Fox, and Comcast in the USA. As seen in Chapter 5, Discovery Networks has closed its own VoD operations and moved 300 TV channels onto cloud, streaming them globally from Northern Virginia. Netflix has deployed Open Connect, but for everything else (metadata systems, customer information, storage, algorithms, etc.), it is AWS. Netflix shut its last data centre in 2016, and 'almost one hundred percent of everything they do is on AWS' (Kilpatrick, interview 2019).

As with CDNs, the upside flexibility and consumption-based pricing of cloud services enable media owners to scale up without capital investment. These services' overall performance and resilience further tilt the balance in their favour. Microsoft Azure's network, for instance, is split into fifty-four regions worldwide (e.g. Norway West, US Gov Arizona, Japan East), each region is divided into geographical availability zones, and each zone consists of multiple data centres and thousands of servers that themselves sit on different power supplies. Microsoft has built the resilience of its network to the point where it can lose an entire availability zone to a catastrophic failure without any loss of performance (Darnell, interview 2019).

Resilience is among the reasons why media owners migrate to the cloud. A&E Networks cumulatively reaches 335 million viewers in more than 200 territories and has more than 500 million digital users. The company was struggling with the cost and complexity of maintaining its own infrastructure. The capital expenditure (capex) was substantial, and the system was not efficient. For instance, it was taking two weeks for the programme sales team to know whether the rights of a particular title were available. But it is only when the firm realised that its data centres were standing right in the path of Hurricane Sandy (a destructive storm that affected twenty-four US states in 2012), that it decided to shift its entire operations to the cloud. Outsourcing media delivery operations to AWS has reduced costs for A&E Networks, and made the whole operation more secure (McGrath and Vachhrajani, 2020).

When Netflix launched in April 1998, the online DVD rental store was beset by technical difficulties and a website that crashed continuously. The Santa Cruz-based start-up had no choice but to spend the little money it had on extra servers (Randoph, 2019: 112–16). The cost of financing and the complexity of running Netflix's data centres was growing exponentially, not least when Netflix pivoted to streaming in 2007. Despite huge investment, the platform was not immune to problems. In 2008, a data centre failure shut its entire operation for three days, and management was standing at a crossroads: 'turn Netflix into a world-class data centre operations company or move the service to the public cloud' (Macaulay, 2018). The streamer realised that the amount of investment needed to improve the resilience of its service was significant, and decided to turn to a major cloud services provider for media delivery and save its cash for content.

Cloud computing is a highly concentrated industry. Worldwide, the sector is dominated by five global suppliers: AWS, Microsoft Azure, Google Cloud, Alibaba, and IBM (Synergy, 2018). In addition to the benefits of consumption-based pricing, the elasticity, scalability, and overall performance of cloud services increasingly tilt the balance in their favour.

AWS alone controls one third of the market, and the top three providers hold more than half the market in their hands (Panettieri, 2018). Furthermore, the growth rate of the top four providers exceeds that of the 'small-to-medium sized cloud operators who collectively have seen their market share diminish' (Synergy, 2018). In the media and entertainment sector, the market leader is undoubtedly AWS. In EMEA alone, it serves in excess of 5,000 clients, including broadcasters, publishers, TV production and post-production companies, visual effect houses, storage firms, analytics companies, digital distributors, digital advertisers, and advertising agencies (Atkinson, 2017; Kilpatrick, interview 2019).

Concentration stems from the strong economies of scale that prevail in the cloud computing industry. Developing cloud infrastructure is capital intensive, and an availability zone alone can cost up US$4 billion (industry source). Once in place, this infrastructure needs to be amortised with the largest possible number of clients. Thus, large cloud providers are multi-sectoral and serve clients across industrial sectors. AWS, Google Cloud, and Microsoft Azure have adopted a similar structure, whereby centralised product teams develop the applications that are used across the 'verticals': the client-facing teams that take care, among others, of media and entertainment, gaming, social media networks, web hosting, e-commerce, financial services, healthcare, education, and policing. Whilst some features vary, the underlying assets remain the same: the discs and servers, the data centres and fibre optic cables, the field enablement portals, and most platforms are standardised across all verticals. For instance, AWS has 120 product teams whose work and research is leveraged across all sectors (Kilpatrick, interview 2019).

In addition, size benefits global cloud providers because the technology they deploy is essentially borderless. Computing processes are today assisted by artificial intelligence and machine learning (AI/ML), which are applied in multiple ways to automate operations along the media delivery chain. AI/ML technology is used in asset management systems to tag content, search assets, and add metadata. AWS' AI/ML applications include automated picture selection, transcription and translation, and face recognition, a feature first tested by Sky during its coverage of the wedding of Prince Harry and Meghan Markle in May 2018 (Kilpatrick, interview 2019). In transmission, AI/ML is used to optimise CDN performance and scale up resources by predicting usage peaks, for instance in the occurrence of live sports events and new releases (Zanni, 2019). Google works with DeepMind, its AI/ML division, to control electricity flows in its data centres (Google executive, interview 2019). Cognitive technology drives personalisation and plays a key role in the recommendation engines of broadcasters and platforms alike (Atkinson, 2017).

Like all multi-sectoral suppliers, cloud providers – and their clients – reap the benefits of knowledge transfers and cross-fertilisation: Microsoft Azure has made advances in latency – crucial for the media and entertainment sector – after lessons learned from clients in finance, and Google Cloud from its involvement in gaming. Google has changed its recommendation algorithms based on its experience with retail customers. Conversely, AWS transcoding engines for video streaming, which are primarily used in media and entertainment, are also deployed in health and policing (Darnell, interview 2019; Google executive, interview 2019; Kilpatrick, interview 2019).

In summary, faced with the mounting cost of upgrading technology, the need to access a complex video ecosystem and to serve audiences across borders, broadcasters began to outsource media delivery in the 2000s. This evolution gathered pace with the advent of IP-based transport facilitating the collaboration of firms in media delivery and the formation of multi-sectoral suppliers capable of significant economies of scale. Chapter 9 examines the implications of this evolution for the TV industry and analyses its chain governance as a whole, that is, the nature of the relationships between lead firms and sector-specific and multi-sectoral suppliers.

Digital Disruption, Firm Behaviour, and Industry Structure

This chapter is analytical in scope and examines the behaviour of various types of corporate actors, and their linkages, in the context of a fast-changing GVC. The restructuring of the TV industry around transnational production networks has created two types of companies (lead firms and suppliers), and two classes of suppliers (sector-specific and multi-sectoral). Using Schumpeter's notion of creative destruction, the first section reflects on the impact of the digital revolution on lead firms and sector-specific suppliers. The second section focuses on the *relationships* between the different sets of actors and examines the modes of governance that prevail in the TV GVC. The thrust of corporate strategies, it argues, is strongly influenced by businesses' positions in the GVC, and the *power asymmetries* between lead firms and suppliers are leading them to divergent approaches to integration. The final section demonstrates how the rise of the global suppliers (the tech giants) in the TV industry is furthering the global integration of the sector, and facilitating industry co-evolution through the formation of a supply base that is shared across several industries. Furthermore, the *size asymmetry* between media firms and the new class of suppliers makes it difficult – if not impossible – for the former to grow and compete effectively with those tech giants that have entered the video market.

Streaming Killed the Rental Video Star: Creative Destruction across the TV GVC

Streaming is revolutionising the TV industry but does not have the same impact on every segment. Aggregation is most directly affected as streamers chase the same sources of revenue (advertising and subscription) as broadcasters and pay-TV platforms. While some aggregators are simply swept away by the 'gale of creative destruction' (Schumpeter, 1947: 87), those that buckle down retain more strategic freedom to alter the perimeter of their business and sources of revenue than their suppliers. Regarding the latter, streaming is a boon for TV producers of all sizes, but more of an issue for those in media delivery. However, across the chain, the strategic response of most suppliers remains similar and consists of seeking growth by internationalising activities while remaining within their segments.

Like Wallerstein (Chapter 1), Joseph Schumpeter underlined the historical nature of capitalism: 'The essential point to grasp is that in dealing with capitalism we are dealing with an evolutionary process' (Schumpeter, 1947: 82). Capitalism is a system in perpetual motion, constantly opening new markets, generating new consumer goods, and new ways of manufacturing and transporting them:

> Industrial mutation … incessantly revolutionizes the economic structure from *within*, incessantly destroying the old one, incessantly creating a new one. This process of Creative Destruction is the essential fact about capitalism. It is what capitalism consists in and what every capitalist concern has got to live in. (Schumpeter, 1947: 83)

The advent of streaming constitutes a case in point. At the turn of the millennium, the burst of the internet bubble was beginning to bite and Netflix – still a DVD-renting online store – was bleeding cash. Aware that fresh capital would not come from another financing round, Reed Hastings, the CEO, imagined the only alternative solution: find a buyer. For that purpose, he and Marc Randolph, Netlix's other co-founder, flew to Dallas in September 2000 with the hope of sealing a deal with Blockbuster. The video-rental chain was close to its peak when it operated around 9,000 stores across the USA and several other territories, employed in excess of 80,000 staff, served 65 million registered customers, and had annual sales approaching US\$6 billion. Hastings' plan was for Netflix to become part of Blockbuster and take care of its online sales, at a selling price of US\$50 million. John Antioco, Blockbuster CEO, declined, 'struggling not to laugh' (Randolph, 2019: 242; see also Hastings and Meyer, 2020: xi–xiii).

Blockbuster subsequently endeavoured to catch up with the streaming revolution but committed the mistake of trying to leverage its brick-and-mortar stores with every online initiative it launched (such as one where customers could order online and collect in store). Streaming delivery, however, was making the company redundant. It filed for bankruptcy in 2010 when Netflix's market capitalisation was approaching US\$10 billion.

Most incumbent businesses are guilty of engaging in monopolistic practices that aim at maximising profit accrued from existing market structures. However, when new technologies and competition are reshaping industries, these practices become meaningless (Schumpeter, 1947: 87). Clinging on to a market that is being swept away from under its feet was the cardinal sin of Blockbuster, alongside others unwilling or unable to engage with change.

Most media and entertainment businesses, however, are making strategic adjustments. They have embraced streaming, investing considerable resources into their DTC operations (Chapters 2 and 7). In addition, they have reinforced their presence in TV content production and, to a lesser degree, media technology. Nine of the ten major TV studios are vertically integrated (Table 7.1). Some diagonal M&A activities, such as Disney's acquisition of Fox, were equally motivated by the need to grab additional content and production capabilities. Smaller aggregators, such as European broadcasters, have also made acquisitions in the TV production segment (Chapter 7).

While lead firms' investments into media tech have been selective and the overall trend is towards outsourcing tasks and infrastructure (Chapter 8), their interest in TV production has been sustained. This upstream move in the TV GVC is logical as they seek to achieve a higher degree of *asset specificity*. IP-transport and connectivity is reducing the specificity of the media delivery infrastructure since the new transmission paths increasingly work with technologies and facilities that are repurposed across several industrial sectors. By way of contrast, a TV series whose rights are controlled by an aggregator is a specific and proprietary asset. Furthermore, these assets generate rent when licensed to third parties. Economists agree that the optimal solution for firms is to devolve tasks that are non-specific and best left to the market, and integrate those that are specific (e.g. Langlois, 2003; Milberg and Winkler, 2013: 141–7, Ruzzier, 2012).

The reasoning is clearly laid bare by Netflix. The streamer's objective in the global battle for attention is to win 'moments of truth' with customers by owning or licensing engaging and compelling content (Hahn, 2015). The streamer also decided that 'becoming an excellent data centre operations company does not necessarily help us meet the goal of winning these moments of truth' (Hahn, 2015); hence the large content budget, and the outsourcing to AWS.

For sector-specific suppliers, the impact of the streaming revolution varies across the TV GVC. Streaming is a boon for TV producers: it is a new set of rights and a new set of clients. Even the smaller TV producers can develop shows (at least up to a certain budget) for a wide array of broadcasters and streamers. According to the founder of Youngest Media, the variety of clients is liberating:

> you need to think creatively about the company in a different way and what we've found is that by having this structure where we can pitch in any territory and on any platform it's an incredible creative liberation for our young development people, because suddenly their ideas are freed up from

the constraints of linear slots and the idea that if it doesn't sustain a commercial hour we can't sell this show. These things are very artificial constraints on ideas and suddenly being able to say, well, a brilliant five to ten minute idea could be perfect for Quibi[1] or indeed a two-hour show could be perfect for the German market is incredibly liberating for our creatives. And that ability to service all different levels which I think is something unusual because we've been able to from day one, is a real creative and commercial advantage. (Flynn, interview 2019)

The impact of streaming is less positive in the media delivery segments, at least for the suppliers that are specific to the TV industry. As it is using generic tech, lead firms are no longer purchasing hardware from specialist suppliers, just the broadcast-specific applications (Chapter 8). Some suppliers have seen their skill set and technology become redundant, and closures have been frequent in the sector in recent years (IBC Showcase, 2020).

Creative Destruction and Globalisation: Sector-Specific Suppliers

In times of change, suppliers do not enjoy as much strategic freedom as lead firms. As seen, the latter can choose which tasks to perform and which tasks to trade, and cherry-pick firms they want to acquire in other segments. For suppliers, the source of their competitive advantage is their specialism: to remain relevant in the TV GVC, they must deliver a service to lead firms. As Porter argues, occupying a clear position in a value chain helps a firm to differentiate itself from its competitors by developing a unique selling proposition (Porter, 2004: 120). If a business has already assigned facilities to specific tasks, staying in the same segment enables it to further exploit these assets and solidify its cost position (Porter, 2004: 65–7). The expertise and reputation a business accumulates are sector-specific: as a firm operates in a chain, it expands its set of relationships (relational capital) and gains the trust of its customers (reputational capital) (Capello and Faggian, 2005). For managers, the question becomes: how to grow and expand the firm within a segment?

Thus, suppliers' best option for growth is to combine with other firms in the same segment, and horizontal integration is prevalent across the TV GVC (Chapters 7 and 8). Suppliers' position in the GVC constrains their room for manoeuvre, and this constraint is one of the drivers of the TV industry's deep global integration. Banijay and Ericsson's media and broadcast division are a product of the same conclusion: accessing new markets by internationalising is the best solution to expand within a segment. The horizontal combination of firms located in different geographies creates businesses with international capabilities and internationalises the chain's value-adding sequences. Once segment leaders reach a certain scale, it constitutes a new benchmark for the rest of the suppliers that may need the same amount of synergies and multinational coverage to compete efficiently. In turn, the internationalisation of value-adding sequences creates an industry that is structured by global networks of production populated by mutually interdependent transnational firms.

Mode of Governances in the TV GVC

This section examines the modes of governance that prevail in the television GVC. They are plural and vary according to the type of suppliers and segments.

TV Production

How is the TV content value chain coordinated? Who drives the chain, and how are risks and profits distributed? The examination of the chain's governance structure sheds light on these issues. Following the typology outlined in Chapter 1, the prevailing type of governance between aggregators and their content suppliers is both *relational* and *captive* in character. A TV programme cannot be easily codified (although a TV genre is a type of codification); transactions between commissioners and producers are fairly complex and frequent, often necessitating spatial proximity; and the capabilities of TV producers creating and developing TV shows is high. In addition, as ratings are always uncertain and commercial risk can be considerable (although mitigation strategies are available; Chalaby, 2018), reputation and trust play an important role between TV executives who commission content and the producers who supply it.

Vertical integration does not alter the mode of governance from relational to hierarchical, because of the nature of TV content production and the skills of TV producers. Integrated producers do not work exclusively for their parent firm and instead act as suppliers in the wider TV content market (Chapter 7). Furthermore, in order to perform efficiently in the content market, integrated producers need to retain top creative talent that are highly qualified and mobile. Managing creative staff is a balancing act that requires the right amount of objectives and incentives. By necessity, most integrated TV studios, such as All3Media, adopt a devolved managerial structure that grants a fair amount of autonomy to their production labels (Lambert, interview 2012). Integrating TV production companies grant media firms *access* to programming and talent without handing over *control* of them (Lampel and Shamsie, 2006: 279).

It remains, however, that a great deal of power asymmetry exists between commissioning organisations and content suppliers in virtue of differences in size and number. Aggregators have higher revenues than TV producers. In any given territory, they have access to markets (advertising or consumer) that are larger than those of programming and media services. In addition, the aggregation segment is often oligopolistic: while streaming services add competition, a handful of TV networks still dominate both audience share and the TV advertising market in most countries (Noam, 2016). Once established as news and entertainment brands, they are able to derive an economic rent from their position, making aggregation an activity with higher entry barriers than any other.

Size and rent generation give lead firms exceptional access to economic capital. Financial markets recognise the advantages of their position and their capitalisation far exceeds those of sector-specific suppliers. While independent content producers are generally in private hands (including Banijay, the largest), lead firms have annual revenues and market capitalisations in the US\$ multi-billion range, even though there is a significant gap between Europe and US-based conglomerates (Table 9.1). Equally, the price to earnings (P/E) ratios varies according to the scale and novelty of their business model, ranging from an average of US\$15.01 for the three European broadcasters to US\$53.85 for Netflix.

A further sign of lead firms' access to capital is the amount of debt some of them carry. AT&T and Comcast are among the most indebted US businesses, with total debts standing at US\$157.2 billion and US\$103.8 billion, respectively; Netflix total debt obligations amount to US\$21.9 billion as of 31 December 2021 (AT&T, 2021: 27; Comcast, 2021: 61; Netflix, 2021: 56).

By way of contrast, the revenue of the largest TV studios is far smaller (Table 7.1). The TV production sector remains fragmented and is characterised by relatively low barriers to entry. In the United Kingdom, well over half the producers have revenues below £10 million (Figure 9.1).

Regarding numbers, there are far fewer commissioning aggregators than there are TV producers, and as a result the typical aggregator deals with hundreds of content suppliers. The resulting power differential manifests itself in several ways. Producers have multiple grievances against commissioners, from late payments to impossible deadlines and unwelcome interferences in production (e.g. Chalaby, 2016: 76–80; Khalsa, 2013). Pitting producers against one another, commissioners are in a position to demand the highest amount of labour for the lowest fee. Production margins are always tight and do not leave much room for error (Curtis, 2014; Khalsa, 2013).

The advent of streaming is great news for TV producers: demand for content has never been so high and digital commissions, in the United Kingdom at least, represent a growing percentage of producers' revenue (Oliver and Ohlbaum, 2019: 11).

Table 9.1 *Lead firms' revenue and market capitalisation, 2019–21*

Company name	2019 total revenues (in US$ bn)	2020 total revenues (in US$ bn)	2021 Market capitalisation (in US$ bn)	2021 Price to earnings ratio (in US$)	Credit rating (Moody's)
AT&T	163.5	171.8	182.0	215.0	Baa2
Comcast	108.9	103.5	248.9	20.3	A3
Walt Disney	69.6	65.4	307.9	277.0	A2
Netflix	20.2	25.0	294.5	59.9	Ba1
RTL	7.9	7.1	9.0	7.1	Withdrawn, low level of debt
ProSienbenSat.1	4.8	4.7	4.0	8.3	Withdrawn
ITV	4.6	3.9	5.8	15.8	Baa3

Source: annual reports, Google Finance, Moody's. All prices and exchange rates on 23 October 2021.

Figure 9.1 Structure of the UK independent production sector, by turnover bracket, 2021

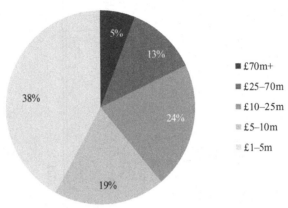

Source: Oliver and Ohlbaum, 2021: 12

However, the power asymmetry between TV producers and global streaming services is exacerbated, not merely because of the latter's size and budget. A streamer registered overseas is not subject to regulations aimed at protecting local content suppliers.[2] Thus, streamers can dictate the terms of trade and their rights position is notoriously exacting (Chapters 2 and 7). When they manage to retain all rights, producers lose access to their own intellectual property and can no longer use it to build their assets. On the finances front, while streaming services have a reputation of paying correct fees, some have instigated a staggered payment system. Netflix pays its production fees in installments and 'drip-feeds a total of [US]$19.3bn to producers', forcing them to bridge the gap with US$ multi-million loans with interest that eats further into the production margins (Nicolaou and Rennison, 2019).

The power imbalance between the two parties is underscored by streamers' frequent failure – despite assurances to the contrary – to clearly label the origin of the content they acquire. In the United Kingdom, a House of Commons committee noticed that some BBC content was not properly branded by Amazon Prime Video (Digital, Culture, Media and Sport Committee, 2021: 28). Furthermore, streamers do not share ratings data with their suppliers, keeping hold of a valuable tool in the digital economy and a precious source of information for future investments (Turton and Opie, 2019; UNCTAD, 2017: 179).

Governance in the TV content production network falls under the relational and captive categories. Producers have a high degree of competence and hold assets that may be difficult to duplicate. Programmes are not easily codified and their development requires a close relationship between all parties involved. There are a few instances of producers in a particularly good position due to the elevated status of TV brands they own (such as a hit show or global format), their track record, and the reputation of their creative staff. None of these factors is enough to shift the balance of power between lead firms – particularly global streamers – and suppliers. Clawing back power is one of the avowed goals of the sector's horizontal consolidation. Scale, however, does not solve TV production's most fundamental issue whereby producers depend upon one (small) set of clients and, collectively, remain captive to the chain's lead firms.

Media Delivery

Modes of governance in the media delivery chain are either relational or modular (Chapter 1). It is relational when suppliers provide a range of bespoke services for a broadcaster in playout or media asset management (publication segment). In such cases, companies enter a long-term relationship and their staff interact on a daily basis, sometimes working in the same space. Governance is modular when the interaction between lead firms and suppliers is at arm's length, based on codified specifications and agreed standards. The relationship between buyers and sellers is kept relatively straightforward and flexible despite dealing with sophisticated technology. In such a configuration, coordination and capabilities are equally distributed along the chain. Standards also enhance the modularity of the media delivery chain, enabling multiple manufacturers, vendors, and solution providers, to collaborate and provide solutions across segments. They ensure the interoperability of the multiple components and systems that data packets need to cross for a successful journey to destination.

In media delivery, lead firms deal with businesses that have a high level of expertise and operate in a sector with higher barriers of entry, giving them an amount of 'competence power' (Sturgeon, 2009: 129). Aggregators have responded to the situation by creating complex procurement processes that can stretch over several years.

British broadcasters' procurement processes vary, not least because public service organisations must abide by public procurement rules, which remain closely aligned to European Procurement Directives even after Brexit (Achilles, 2021). In principle, however, three stages can be distinguished. First a planning team is assembled to arrange requirements, including the publication of a core contract that is open for debate with the bidders. The competitive dialogue commences, whereby suppliers are asked to register their interest and fill out a pre-qualification questionnaire (the RFI phase – request for information). On the basis of information collected from potential vendors, a shortlist is drawn up of suppliers that have the scale, capacity, and expertise to deliver the services under contract. These companies are invited to bid for the next series of competitive rounds (the RFQ phase – request for quotation), lasting until potential suppliers have been whiffled down to the winner. Throughout, broadcasters make a strenuous effort to even out the playing field in order to ensure that the incumbent does not have an unfair advantage (Smith, interview, 2017; Stevens, interview, 2017; Tucker, interview, 2017).

During the course of the contract, broadcasters have different mechanisms for ensuring that standards are maintained and suppliers deliver on promises, and that 'best in class' is rewarded while applying penalties for drops in performance (Hindhaugh, interview, 2017; Smith, interview, 2017). With such a process, contracts are tight, and so are the margins.

The use of the common IT stack for media delivery purposes, and cloud computing in particular, has brought to the fore a new class of suppliers: tech giants (Chapter 8). While the relationship between lead firms and big tech remains modular, the latter's size and scope of activities has implications for the former and the TV industry in general.

From Global Suppliers to a Shared Supply Base

IP-based technologies have enabled the formation of a task network because the conversion of media files into bytes – a highly standardised commodity – has greatly increased the interoperability and modularity of the media delivery GVC (Sturgeon and Kawakami, 2010: 10). IP standards being known and agreed upon, it is easier for suppliers to enter the chain at a specific point, and specialise in a task or segment of their choice. Standards minimise the amount of knowledge firms need to exchange in order to interact, thereby lowering transaction costs among firms involved in the network. Low-cost transactions can now occur at *thin crossing points* located between the chain's segments (Baldwin, 2008).

How is specialisation in a task or segment a viable business model? Media files have become data packets like any other, thus it makes no difference to a server or a router if the file it transports is a surveillance video or a reality TV show. This has made it possible for suppliers to serve the broadcasting sector with the same common IT stack and general-purpose equipment they use in other industries, allowing them to support a cross-sectoral customer base with the same underlying and generic assets (Chapter 8).

In order to comprehend the relationship between lead firms and the tech giants that act as multi-sectoral suppliers, the chain governance must be examined at the macro-level, above and beyond the linkage mechanisms and power relations among its actors. Who drives the chain, and who determines its trajectory? Ponte and Sturgeon attempt to answer these questions by distinguishing between uni-polar, bipolar, and multipolar chains. The first is driven and shaped by a single powerful actor; the second 'involves two different types of actors ... exercising similar degrees of control over different functions in the chain'; and the third is not driven as purposefully, exhibiting 'multiple foci of power' and actors that 'have control and influence over different functions in the chain' (Ponte and Sturgeon, 2014: 215; Raj-Reichert, 2019: 357). The media delivery chain shows signs of bipolarity since its trajectory is co-defined by lead firms and tech giants. The rise to power of tech companies that co-drive this chain is remarkable.

Broadcasters are no longer the innovation centres they once were and struggle to recruit high-calibre engineers who do not regard them as tech companies (Stevens, interview 2017). Much of the capabilities, skill set, and innovation drive that determine the shape of the chain now rests in the hands of the latter. The suppliers' rise to prominence is underlined by the strategy of the tech giants (e.g. YouTube, Amazon Video Prime) who have launched content arms that compete directly with their own media customers.

The rise of global suppliers has three major implications: *further consolidation*, *further global integration*, and *industry co-evolution*. The media technology sector has gone through intense rounds of M&A activities in recent years, sharply reducing the number of operating firms (Chapter 8). Although there is no indication that the supply market in media delivery is oligopolistic, the presence of global suppliers raises the barriers to entry and makes it more difficult for small suppliers to find economies of scale and compete in the market. Their only option is to find an innovative niche or enter the bespoke market by tailoring off-the-shelf tech for their clients.

Global integration has a double meaning. It refers to the scale of the companies involved. With the consolidation of the media technology sector, media delivery has become a chain where lead firms and their suppliers have an equally large footprint in a multinational-to-multinational operation. Further, media delivery has become a *global-scale production system*, in the sense that the firms involved have developed the capability to deliver content to and from any location in the world on a 24/7 basis. The key beneficiaries are the leading OTT platforms that need to operate at scale and use this system to route content to users irrespective of distance (unless prevented by local regulations). Audiences benefit too as the amount and diversity of content they can watch is unprecedented in history.

The television industry now *shares a supply base* with other sectors, leading to the phenomenon of *industry co-evolution*, which occurs when lead firms across different industrial sectors 'interact with broadly shared supply bases to drive the evolution of entire industries' (Sturgeon and Lee, 2005: 35). This shared supply base is triggering a self-reinforcing mechanism that strengthens the necessity of outsourcing and the strategic pre-eminence of global suppliers:

> Shared supply bases, as in the modular production network, tend to generate a self-reinforcing dynamic – a classic network effect – because pooling effects create large external economies of scale and scope and powerful learning effects. These learning effects induce an increasing number of lead firms to tap the network, which in turn further enhances the competence, scale, and scope of the turnkey supply base and induces more firms to participate. Thus a historical process is unleashed, where the development of an external supply base through outsourcing encourages further outsourcing, and so on.
>
> (Sturgeon and Lee, 2005: 45)

For the television industry, the immediate implications of a shared supply base are double-edged. Media firms benefit from cross-sectoral research and development that brings costs down, allowing them to deliver more content for less. However, they have lost a certain amount of control with evolving technology and must rely on third party infrastructure to deliver content.

Life with Tech Giants: Implications for Television

In the long term, the presence of tech giants in the media delivery GVC raises the issue of the TV industry's future structure and perimeter. If, as just argued, the media delivery chain is bipolar, then it is co-driven by lead firms and tech giants. The balance of power between the two parties will hinge on a series of factors. For the first time, lead firms face businesses far larger than themselves, and the *size asymmetry* that exists between them is now in favour of the tech giants (Table 9.2).

In the same way size has played in favour of lead firms in terms of access to capital and investment capabilities, the same applies to tech giants. In a globally integrated industry, the benefit that scale brings cannot be underestimated, as argued throughout this book. Tech giants also derive power from the influence they bear on the new breed of 'hybrid' standard-setting bodies (Chapter 4; Graz, 2019). Further, these tech giants having realised the edge that global infrastructure gives them, have gone on to develop their own streaming services. In many markets, they are part of the services that are winning the battle for attention among the younger generations. In the United Kingdom, the daily viewing minutes of young adults (eighteen- to thirty-four-year-olds) in 2020 were as follows: SVoD (essentially Amazon Prime Video, Disney+, and Netflix), 91; YouTube, 72; broadcaster content (BVoD, live TV, and recorded playback),

Table 9.2 *Tech giants active in media delivery or streaming, by annual revenue, 2020*

Company	2020 annual revenue (in US$ bn)	Market capitalisation (in US$ bn)	Presence in media delivery market	Streaming services
Amazon	386.1	1,770	Yes	- Amazon Video Prime - IMDb TV - Twitch
Apple	274.5	2,470	No	Apple TV+
Alphabet (Google)	182.5	1,980	Yes	YouTube
Microsoft	143.0	2,530	Yes	/
Meta Platforms (Facebook)	84.2	942	No	Facebook Watch

Source: annual reports and financial statements. Market capitalisation on 11 November 2021.

Table 9.3 *Facebook's and Google's advertising revenue, 2017–20*

Company/platform	Advertising revenue (in US$ bn)			
	2017	2018	2019	2020
Facebook	39.9	55.0	69.7	84.2
YouTube ads	8.2	11.2	15.1	19.8
Google Advertising (total)[1]	95.6	116.5	134.8	146.9

Source: annual reports and financial statements.
Note[1]: includes Google Search, YouTube ads and Google Network Members' properties.

102 (Ofcom, 2021: 22). These platforms post strong growth year after year. By way of contrast, many broadcasters primarily operate in national markets, and their potential for growth is virtually non-existent.

Two of the tech giants have adopted business models based on advertising, the traditional lifeblood of commercial broadcasters. They are attracting an ever-growing portion of the pie, and broadcasters are acutely aware of their presence in this market (Table 9.3).

These factors may combine to tip the balance of power in favour of the tech giants. A possible scenario is that television disappears as an autonomous industry and is replaced by a video system dominated by the tech giants whose primary interest may not lie in television.

However, the future of the industry will not entirely be determined by commercial and technological factors. As Cunningham and Craig state, tech giants have so far benefitted from a lax and lenient regulatory environment worldwide (Cunningham and Craig, 2019: 266). A new regulatory era is taking shape as governments are waking to the vast influence being brought to bear on societies and economies. In the USA, the big tech firms have been subject to ongoing inquiries as their scale and market power attract increasing attention from lawmakers. Alphabet itself acknowledges in its latest report that 'we are subject to increasing regulatory scrutiny as well as changes in public policies governing a wide range of topics that may negatively affect our business' (Alphabet, 2020: 15). The US Congress, various regulatory agencies, and several attorneys have launched investigations questioning aspects of their business practices, from the way they handle data to potential antitrust violations (Del Rey, 2020; Nicas et al., 2019; Swartz, 2020).

In Europe, the French government will be the first to tax local revenues of global tech firms, and a French minister has warned that the new tax is 'just the tip of the iceberg in terms of new regulations that must be introduced internationally to deal with the powerful tech giants' (Chrisafis, 2020).

The European Commission has begun to draft a comprehensive digital strategy that aims to harness digital technologies in a way that protects Europe's open societies, reflects their values, and benefits their businesses. It is an assertive policy drive that involves regulating an array of technologies (e.g. artificial intelligence, online platforms), placing digital transformation at the heart of the foreign policy agenda, and building up Europe's digital capabilities. Overall, the EU is seeking to retain (or regain) its 'technological sovereignty' by building its own 'key capacities' and reducing its 'dependency on other parts of the globe' (European Commission, 2020: 3).

It is an ambitious policy project that, if completed, may redraw the geographic boundaries of some GVCs, including media delivery. But even Ursula von der Leyen, the president of the European Commission, sounds a note of caution. While she states her aim to achieve technological sovereignty, she acknowledges that 'it may be too late to replicate hyperscalers' (von der Leyen, 2019: 13). The merit of the EU policy, however, is to recognise the power that scale brings in the digital economy, and to carry the debate into the diplomatic arena.

Conclusion

Among the multiple trends that are reshaping the TV industry (Chapter 2), vertical disintegration has not received the attention it deserves. Today, a piece of content, from conception to consumption, goes through a long odyssey, crossing the path of many firms and territories. The making of a programme has become a collaborative effort among many businesses contracted to perform a specific role along the chain. Lead firms outsource for multiple reasons. They want to achieve a higher degree of asset specificity and focus on their core activities. Under pressure to invest in content and increase returns to shareholders, they save resources by externalising tasks to suppliers that have the scale and expertise to perform them more efficiently. Lead firms have also narrowed their mission and wish to present a coherent and compelling narrative to stakeholders. The tasks involved in the making and distribution of a TV programme have become more complex, and a sole company cannot possess the full range of necessary skills.

The GVC analysis offers a deeper understanding of globalisation of the TV industry. The bird's-eye view reveals an industry that increasingly works as a single transnational space. The segment-by-segment analysis unveils the complexity of this three-dimensional puzzle, where parts moving in one corner of the puzzle shift elements elsewhere. Different types of firms need to be distinguished (lead firms versus suppliers), as well as different classes of suppliers (sector-specific versus multi-sectoral). How firms behave depends on their classification and segment. Certain trends, such as convergence, affect some businesses more than others: while the advent of streamers is a boon for TV producers, it presents an existential threat for some aggregators. Lead firms, however, have more freedom and a wider array of options to counter any threat than suppliers.

Supplier have been ignored far too long by the literature, yet their behaviour has an influence on the entire TV GVC. Sector-specific suppliers have little room to manoeuvre and do not have the luxury of choosing between tasks to perform and ones to trade. While lead firms can invest downstream or upstream, suppliers tend to congregate horizontally and internationally in search of scale and new markets within their segment. Consequently, by internationalising the chain's value-adding sequences, they participate fully in the globalisation of the TV industry. As for global suppliers, their influence on the sector is even deeper. While media conglomerates were formerly the sole dominant force in the TV GVC, the size asymmetry between them and tech giants mean they are no longer in full control of the chain. The presence of tech firms, while further globalising the industry, is also shifting its perimeter.

In sum, the understanding of transnational production networks requires a holistic perspective and a structural analysis of each value-adding sequence. The transnational relationships among the segments and the firms that populate them create an integrated system on a global scale.

10

The Transnational Media Firm

The chapter delves into the transnational dimension of the global TV system. Transnational denotes the crossing of national borders while acknowledging their continued relevance and is a process that designates the imbrication of several spatial dimensions within one artefact or phenomenon (Introduction).

As media globalisation has progressed, transnational media have evolved, and this chapter contends that a new generation has emerged. The first, which developed in the later part of the twentieth century, consists of cross-border TV networks and formats (Chapter 3). The second is the rise of streaming platforms (Chapter 4). During the first generation, the transnational remained a *professional practice* out of viewers reach. These media are transnational because they are professionally adapted for local audiences as they cross borders. With the arrival of the second generation, the transnational has become *an everyday mode of media consumption and interaction*. Online entertainment services have altered the status of the transnational within TV culture, and what was once at the margins now sits at the core. This chapter demonstrates how transnational consumption makes SVoD platforms more cosmopolitan than cross-border TV networks. Turning to video-sharing platforms – YouTube in particular – it argues that in the history of TV culture this constitutes a shift in status of the transnational by turning a professional practice into a popular one performed by millions.

The chapter's second purpose is to examine the key organisational characteristics of the transnational media firm. It compares four types of organisational configuration (multinational, global, international, and transnational), and analyses the latter in depth. It connects organisational theory to the GVC framework, demonstrating how the nature of a firm's activities and position in the value chain play a determining role in the type of organisational structure it is most likely to adopt.

Transnational Pioneers

As broadcasters expanded across frontiers they learned to cope in a multinational universe and adapt their channels to local tastes. Broadcasters progressively broke up pan-regional satellite feeds and turned them into *transnational networks of local channels* (Chapter 3). These channels share a concept, a brand, resources and infrastructure, and much of the programming, but develop according to their respective environment. Employing a small amount of local staff, they register with local regulatory bodies and set up their own schedule, mixing shared network content with their own programming. Brands like Cartoon Network, Discovery, Disney, MTV, or National Geographic applied this recipe in the 1990s and are still operating successfully today.

Music television brand MTV pioneered the technique and built the most accomplished transnational TV network. When the US cable channel began to internationalise, it operated under the naive assumption that musical tastes were similar everywhere. Adopting the mantra 'One World – One Music' the playlist of the unique international feed was heavily dominated by Anglo-American acts. Local competition slowly built up until management realised that viewers were not connecting with the channel because it did not speak to their culture. From 1997 onwards, MTV split its multi-territory satellite feed and proceeded to localise. By the end of the next decade, the music network had launched hundreds of localised channels operating under various brands (MTV Classic, MTV Dance, MTV Live, etc.) covering in excess of forty markets (in addition to the remaining pan-regional feeds). Every channel acquired a strong local component: 70 per cent of the music was of local origin on MTV China or MTV Japan, and up to 90 per cent in India (Chalaby, 2009: 233). Today, while the MTV brand has lost its lustre, its network of channels and digital platforms still operates on this basis.[1]

Before the advent of streaming services, transnational TV networks constituted the most elaborate answer to the difficulties of operating TV channels across frontiers, bringing together global resources with sensitivity to local differences. Localised channels share resources, creative projects, ideas, knowledge, and an administrative and technical infrastructure, enabling networks to generate economies of scale and amortise cost over more than one market. Localised channels also benefit from the brand, marketing, and library of content. At the same time, they adapt to local markets by developing their own schedule and positioning, and generally espousing the local culture.

The next expansion in transnational media came from the TV format trade, whose sharp growth in the late 1990s constitutes a key element of television's global shift (Chapter 3). Formats are transnational because they combine a kernel of rules and principles that are immutable (some formats are more flexible than others) and elements that are adaptable as they travel. Formatted shows follow rules that are applied across borders but that are combined with local ingredients to weave narratives designed for specific cultures. A format such as *Got Talent* is a global platform designed to generate local heroes and stories. Thus, at the heart of the TV format trade lies a transnational paradox: for the structure of a show to circulate internationally its adaptations must resonate with audiences in each market in which it airs. The creative processes that sustain new formats are often transnational in scope: some formats are created by multi-territory teams, and their production bible is enriched as they travel. For audiences, however, formats are local shows and most viewers are unaware of their transnational mechanisms and foreign origin.

The SVoD Space: Transnationalism and Cosmopolitanism

Streaming is changing television culture by bringing the transnational to its fore, and SVoD and video-sharing platforms are making distinct contributions to the phenomenon. This section examines the former and the next will focus on the latter.

The programming of cross-border TV networks and the catalogue of streaming platforms are both transnational in scope. Both invest in content of diverse origin in order to resonate with different cultures. Netflix, for instance, is aware of the 'strong relationship between the degree to which SVoD catalogues have been localised and overall subscriber uptake' (Bisson, 2017: 9). Three years ago, almost half (48 per cent) of Netflix's commissions and productions came from outside the USA, and it rose to 63 per cent in 2020 (Bisson, 2017: 13; Gamerman, 2020). The quantity of non-US originals stands at 43 per cent on Amazon Prime Video, and 18 per cent on Apple TV+ and Disney+ (Gamerman, 2020). In 2020, Netflix commissioned originals from thirty-two countries: thirteen from India, Korea, and Spain (each); eight from Mexico and the United Kingdom; seven from Germany and Italy; six from Japan; five from Canada, Finland, France, and Taiwan; and four from Brazil and Belgium (Wescott, 2021).

There is, however, a key difference between platforms and networks. Cross-border TV networks are not transnational at the point of consumption. Once they reach their destination, the offering is an adapted selection of programmes to local viewers that is set up to mimic national television and reinforce the binds between nation, language, and culture (Waisbord, 2004: 373).

Streaming platforms work differently: their investment in international content is driven by the same marketing imperative, but the entire catalogue can be accessed by audiences everywhere. Some of Netflix's most popular series, such as *Emily in Paris*, *Narcos: Mexico*, and *The Witcher* were in the week's top-ten programmes in up to ninety countries in 2021 (see Netflix, 2022). Non–English language content travels increasingly well. Some of those on Netflix have garnered far larger audiences abroad than at home and global hits come with increasing regularity: *Dark* (Germany), *Elite* (Spain), *Kingdom* (South Korea), *Money Heist*

(Spain), *Shtisel* (Israel), and *Squid Game* (South Korea). Between 8 and 14 November 2021, the most popular English titles amassed 258.6 million viewing hours versus 134 million for non-English titles, and *Squid Game* was in the top ten in ninety-three countries (Netflix, 2022). Non-English drama is increasingly popular with Western audiences: *Barbarians* (Germany), *The Rain* (Denmark), and *Money Heist* (Spain) were among those that attracted the interest of US audiences in 2020 (Gamerman, 2020). During four weeks in September and October 2021, *Squid Game* was the platform's most popular show in the USA (Netflix, 2022).

Furthermore, if inclined, households can pick streaming services that specialise in international drama. In the USA, customers have access to platforms such as Acorn TV (British-style shows), Viki (Asian content), Britbox (British drama), or Walter Presents (non-English TV series). There are a fair number of international shows on Sundance Now, AMC Networks' indie platform. Britbox alone had one million American subscribers in 2020 and Viki is growing fast (Klinge, 2020; White, 2020). These are niche platforms whose subscription numbers remain modest, but nonetheless they make foreign drama more accessible.

Choice expanded in the broadcasting era but streaming has entrenched it. Transnational consumption makes SVoD platforms more cosmopolitan than cross-border TV networks because they open up Western TV cultures and contribute to the loosening of ties between nation, territory, and culture (Beck and Grande, 2010: 412).

YouTube: Towards Transnational Intertextuality

The academic literature on YouTube is growing apace, but the AVoD platform's transnational dimension has yet to be analysed in depth. This section argues that it is the streamer's most distinctive feature. As seen in Chapter 4, YouTube operates at scale and displays some unique metrics: it has more than 2 billion logged-in visits each month, stores over 10 billion videos, and is available in 80 languages.

YouTube rests on the world's largest proprietary communications infrastructure, which consists of 21 data centres (including some hyperscalers), 22 cloud regions, 140 points of presence, multiple investments in subsea cable networks, and availability in more than 200 territories (Chapters 4 and 8). Such an infrastructure is expensive to build and maintain, and requires significant capital expenditure; engineers are also necessary to develop the software technology that runs on top. In brief, YouTube is a global platform designed to work at scale. For the first time, '*anyone* in the world [can] share a video with *everyone* in the world' (Kyncl and Peyvan, 2017: x).

Users, by way of contrast, are rooted in one location. The juxtaposition of the local and the global is a fact that Cécile Frot-Coutaz, the platform head of content, is well aware of:

> Obviously it's a global platform and it's a tech platform and tech has to scale ... However, when it comes to the content that's hyperlocal, users are Russian, French, German, Egyptian, Swedish, Norwegian, etc., and the advertisers are also Norwegian, French, Egyptian, etc., so the business piece is very, very local and the creators are local and the content partners are local ... So what we have to do as a company is straddle the two, straddle the very global nature of the tech platform and the hyperlocal nature of the business.
>
> (Frot-Coutaz, interview 2020)

Content originates locally and much of it stays local. However, without any obstacle to cross-border distribution, anyone can search or stumble on a video, hence contributing to its circulation. Many YouTubers are active users that like, share, comment, and sometimes react and transform videos (Oh, 2017). These exchanges create cross-frontier conversations, making YouTube's participatory culture imminently transnational.

In terms of participation, videos can be divided into two main categories, virals and memes. A viral video is 'a clip that spreads to the masses via digital word-of-mouth mechanisms without significant change' (Shifman, 2011: 190). Most viral videos may be mundane, but some generate significant cultural trends. Korean artist Park Jae-Sang's *Gangnam Style*, posted in July 2012, was the first to break the billion-view mark, eventually reaching nearly 4 billion views at the time of writing. The video propelled the song to the top of numerous music charts and, in the process, contributed to the popularisation of K-pop. In its wake the 'global viewership of Korean artists tripled ... with 91 percent of the views coming from outside Korea' (Allocca, 2018: 18). Luis Fonsi's *Despacito* is among YouTube's most popular videos; posted in January 2017, it has passed 7.6 billion views. The song topped the charts in forty-seven territories and helped establish Latin pop on the international music scene.

The second type of video is the meme, defined 'as a popular clip that lures extensive creative user engagement in the form of parody, pastiche, mash-ups or other derivative work' (Shifman, 2011: 190). The two key mechanisms used by memetic videos are remixing and imitation (Shifman, 2011: 190). Remixing consists of any combination of several possible operations, including 'the selecting, manipulating, recombining, and restructuring of existing media', in order to create an original contribution (Allocca, 2018: 55). Millions of memetic videos have been posted on YouTube, inspired by iconic cultural or political moments, classic media texts, or original YouTube videos. Memes of Nyan Cat, Hitler's outrage in *Downfall*, or the Harlem Shake, count among the most widespread (Allocca, 2018: 51–4, 70–1, 95–8). Pinkfong's *Baby Shark Dance*, a video that has amassed 9.7 billion views at the time of writing, has inspired thousands of memes. Popular songs, movies, and brands all feature in countless remixes. For instance, *The Empire Strikes Back Uncut* is a fan-made two-hour-long shot-for-shot recreation of the movie, which has required significant crowdsourcing and editing skills.

Memetic videos refer to another pre-existing text and do not make sense by themselves. For the viewer to appreciate a meme, she needs to be aware of the original text it refers to. The textual reference constitutes the essence of memes, conferring them an intertextual quality (Riffaterre, 1984: 91). Memes on any popular theme travel to and from multiple countries, creating instances of *transnational intertextuality*.

YouTube could not have sustained its growth on viral videos alone and shifted emphasis from videos to channels (Burgess and Green, 2018: 87–93). Users can tag any channel and turn on notifications, which then appear on their home feed. This system of free subscription enables creators to measure their popularity and YouTube to gauge their success. In 2018, the platform added a new product – channel membership – which needs to be paid for. For a fee, members can get content earlier and receive any additional benefit creators wish to offer them. Channel memberships add a new tool to creators' digital monetisation strategy, complementing revenue from advertising, sponsorship, and donations.

YouTube's imbrication of the local and the global is manifest in its channel economy. The platform's usage varies from one territory to another and, in any given country, the most subscribed channels are invariably local (noxinfluencer.com, 2021a). The platform's localised features, its look, feel, and content, differ sharply across markets. Local cultures are equally reflected in the scope and nature of YouTubers' output. For instance, 'agri-tubers' (pertaining to agriculture) are popular in France, as are those channels that help students revise for the *baccalauréat*, the national exam that gives access to higher education (Frot-Coutaz, interview 2020).

However, channels travel unfettered on YouTube, and many have subscribers in multiple territories. Some of the platform's largest channels are based in India, all uploading content related to local culture and entertainment. T-Series, SET India, Zee Music Company, Zee TV, and Goldmines totalled 506.1 million subscribers at the time of writing. On average, their domestic viewers represent 36.6 per cent of their total audience (Table 10.1). While the geographical dispersion of their audiences certainly reflects the spread of the Indian diaspora, interest from other cultures should not be excluded.

On YouTube, creators have access to an international audience at the start of their streaming journey. London-based entrepreneur Jamal Edwards founded

Table 10.1 *International audience for India's five top YouTube channels, by geographical location, October 2021*

Genre	T-Series	SET India	Zee Music Company	Zee TV	Goldmines
	Music	Entertainment	Music	Entertainment	Films
Total number of subscribers (in millions)	194	116	77.4	59.4	59.3
India (% of viewers)	37	38	39	26	43
USA (% of viewers)	20	23	19	14	19
UK (% of viewers)	5	6	4	3	5
Spain (% of viewers)	5	5	5	3	5
Kenya (% of viewers)	4	3	3	13	3
Canada (% of viewers)	3	4	3	2	3
Taiwan (% of viewers)	3	4	3	/	2
Australia (% of viewers)	2	2	2	/	2
Indonesia (% of viewers)	2	2	2	7	3
Malaysia (% of viewers)	/	/	/	4	/
RoW (% of viewers)	19	13	20	28	15
Total (% of viewers)	100	100	100	100	100

Source: compiled from noxinfluencer.com, 2021b.

SBTV: Music in November 2006. Four years later, he met an artist looking to break into the underground music scene and helped him to create the video that would go on to launch his career; the musician was Ed Sheeran. Today, *SBTV* has 1.18 million subscribers, and 36 per cent of its viewers are located in the United Kingdom; the others being USA (28 per cent); India (15 per cent); Canada (5 per cent); and other countries. *SBTV*'s cross-border reach contributes to the channel's advertising revenue, helping Edwards establish international connections and enrich his channels with films from multiple locations (Edwards, interview 2020).

The Great War is a history channel that covers the First World War and its aftermath from 1914 to 1923 in real time, one week at a time, 100 years later. Produced by Florian Wittig and hosted and written by Jesse Alexander, the idea was to mimic the newsreels displayed in cinema halls. *The Great War* is on YouTube because of the 'potential even for a niche product to reach a global audience' (Wittig and Alexander, interview 2020). This reach entails several benefits. First, the team gets comments and feedback from an international community of contributors located in various countries, considerably enriching the team's understanding of the chain of events that occurred a century ago. Second, the Berlin-based team can reach, via YouTube, the English-speaking markets (USA, United Kingdom, Australia, and Canada, by order of importance), where more than 80 per cent of its viewers and subscribers are located. Without access to these markets, the venture would simply be financially unviable (Wittig and Alexander, interview 2020).

On average, more than 60 per cent of YouTubers' traffic comes from outside their country (Kyncl and Peyvan, 2017: 72). For millions of YouTubers like Edwards, Wittig, and Alexander, access to multiple markets is not only essential to their business plan but informs their outlook. International access is what makes niche channels viable, and in turn attract viewers to the platform who find creators that match their tastes and interests. More than this, a reactive international audience creates a feedback loop that enriches creators' output with experiences and perspectives from beyond their national horizon.

YouTube's global reach is also attracting leading content rights holders. The growing presence of sports leagues and franchises on the platform provides a case in point. Their presence here is not purely driven by monetisation. Online advertising revenues are negligible compared to sports organisations' three proven sources of income: commercial, broadcasting and streaming rights, and match day. In addition, preparing professional-grade content involves costs. The reason lies elsewhere: fan engagement. YouTube enables them to grow their brands by widening access to their sport/team, maintain contact with fans during the off season, give them additional content to enjoy, and reach them wherever they are. The world's ten wealthiest football clubs have a strong presence on YouTube. On average, 69 per cent of their audience lies outside their domestic market, and the proportion never falls below 50 per cent (Table 10.2). In addition, the platform also hosts multiple local and international fan channels.

American sports leagues and organisations are also investing significant resources into social media and have incorporated YouTube into their all-out effort for attention. Their presence on the platform is complementary to the rights they sell to broadcasters and streamers, and none of the videos they post weaken their value. These organisations run multiple channels and post content tailored and edited for the platform, such as interviews, previews, game highlights, (delayed) full games, documentaries, tributes, career high-lights, and public messages, alongside thousands of edited reels (best moments, best plays, best shots, etc.). Three leagues, in particular, are making a sustained effort: World Wrestling Entertainment (WWE), which runs one of YouTube's most popular channels; the National Basketball League (NBA); and the National Football League (NFL). The Major League Baseball (MLB), the National Hockey League (NHL), and the Major League Soccer

Table 10.2 *Ten wealthiest football clubs' YouTube presence (key metrics),*
October 2021

Football club (2019/20 revenue, € million)	YouTube subscribers (millions)	Total views (millions)	Total number of videos	% of audience outside domestic market
FC Barcelona (715.1)	12.5	1,880	9,360	89
Read Madrid (691.8)	6.8	802	5,270	86
Bayern Munich (634.1)	2.3	625	4,830	51
Manchester United (580.4)	5.1	902	2,430	61
Liverpool (558.6)	6.1	1,210	1,790	56
Manchester City (549.2)	3.6	884	5,760	65
Paris Saint-Germain (540.6)	5.8	625	4,150	54
Chelsea (469.7)	3.2	680	3,800	91
Tottenham Hotspur (445.7)	1.9	489	2,590	64
Juventus (397.9)	3.5	604	2,990	73

Sources: Deloitte Sports Business Group, 2021: 11; noxinfluencer.com; youtube.com. 2019/
20 revenues are significantly lower than in 2019/19 due to the impact of the COVID-
19 pandemic.

(MLS) have more modest outputs. While these leagues' audience remains predominantly domestic, 36 per cent of their viewers reside overseas on average. For WWE and the NBA, their international fan base represents billions of views (Table 10.3).

Not all YouTube creators want to be seen everywhere. Geo-blocking is a platform feature that allows them to block access to their channel in certain locations (Lobato and Meese, 2016). This tool can be used to narrowcast a channel to a selection of countries. *Free Documentary* is a YouTube channel owned by Quintus Media, a German distribution company. Like any distributor, Quintus is seeking to get as much revenue as possible from the intellectual property it represents. They first propose content to broadcasters, and then turn their attention to selling AVoD and SVoD rights. In some countries, they sell both types of rights (linear and VoD), and in others, they sell none. When there is no expression of interest for the AVoD licence, Quintus puts the content on its

Table 10.3 *US sports leagues' YouTube presence (key metrics, main channel),*
October 2021

Sports league	YouTube subscribers (millions)	Total views (billions)	Total videos	% of audience outside domestic market
WWE	82.2	63	57,120	35
NBA	17	9.1	37,140	36
NFL	8.2	5.9	22,810	33
MLB	3.4	2.8	283,070	35
NHL	1.6	1.1	23,820	37
MLS	0.7	0.4	15,870	40

Sources: data from noxinfluencer.com; youtube.com.

YouTube channel, focusing on the three most lucrative markets: USA, the United Kingdom, and Australia. Thus, Quintus uses YouTube to complete its global puzzle of licenses, geo-blocking its documentaries according to which deals the company has signed. Either licences are sold to broadcasters or VoD operators, or the distributor retains them and puts content on YouTube. For Quintus, what YouTube offers is à la carte globalisation (Kemming, interview 2020).

YouTube: Worldwide Adoption – Local Adaptation

YouTube has been globally adopted and provides borderless access through a dashboard that is fully adapted to local languages. In the history of TV culture this constitutes a shift in status of the transnational by turning a professional practice into a popular one performed by millions. Users can choose content irrespective of where it comes from and take part in cross-border conversations through memetic videos and comments. For content creators, international access lowers the threshold of economic viability, and for larger organisations, the platform provides a complementary way to reach fans worldwide. Overall, YouTube is propelling the transnational to the forefront of TV culture.

Organisational Configuration: Towards the Transnational Solution

Running a firm in the TV GVC requires organisational capabilities that meet the challenges of operating in a globally integrated industry. Businesses' organisational response depends on their heritage, culture, geographical footprint, and position in the TV chain. In their classic study, Bartlett and Ghoshal have identified four ideal types of arrangement for international organisations (Bartlett and Ghoshal, 1998).

Multinational companies adopt a decentralised organisational structure that devolves assets and responsibilities to local subsidiaries. The multinational organisation runs 'the company's worldwide operations as a portfolio of national businesses', and it is a model that is often adopted in industrial sectors that require strong knowledge of, and adaption to, local markets (Bartlett and Ghoshal, 1998: 56).

In an *international organisation*, firms decentralise some assets and functions and give subsidiaries the necessary autonomy to adapt to the local environment. However, the overall organisation remains controlled by the parent company; knowledge, expertise, and strategic decisions flow from the core to the periphery.

The *global organisation* places the emphasis on economies of scale and efficiency. It is run from the headquarters, which keeps hold of assets, resources, and responsibilities. Subsidiaries are tightly controlled, and their role is limited to local operations such as the sale and distribution of standard products. This model suits companies operating in tech and consumer electronics (Bartlett and Ghoshal, 1998: 57–9).

Some firms have begun integrating the organisational characteristics of the fourth ideal type, the *transnational organisation model*. This architecture is labelled 'transnational' because it enables companies to achieve simultaneously global efficiency, local responsiveness, and worldwide knowledge transfer (Bartlett and Ghoshal, 1998: 65). It incites the corporation to move beyond a 'hub and spokes' organisational structure and adopt an *integrated network configuration* (Jones, 2005: 167). Local subsidiaries break the pattern of dependence/independence towards the headquarters to become units in a web of 'relationships based on mutual interdependence' (Bartlett and Ghoshal, 1998: 148).

The key organisational characteristics of the transnational company are network integration and flexibility. Some assets and decisions are centralised, and others are localised. Some subsidiaries are closely controlled from headquarters, others are given full autonomy. The headquarters is not the custodian of all centralised resources and responsibilities, which are dispersed throughout the network. The role of subsidiaries is differentiated, and some are relied on to make a distinct contribution to the company's worldwide and integrated operations. Local units continuously collaborate and share knowledge, sometimes with one another, sometimes in a small group, and sometimes at network level (Bartlett and Ghoshal, 1998: 75; Dicken, 2015: 136–41). In the global

Table 10.4 *Typical organisational configurations of firms in the TV GVC*

Segments	TV content production	Aggregation	Media delivery (publication)	Media delivery (transmission)
Type of company	Global TV studio	Lead firm	Industry-specific media delivery suppliers	Multi-sectoral suppliers
Most frequent organisational configuration	Transnational	International	Global	Global
Typical example	Banijay	Comcast; Disney	Red Bee Media	AWS

Source: author

TV industry, the nature of a firm's activities and position in the value chain play a determining role in the type of organisational structure it is most likely to adopt (Table 10.4).

Media Delivery Segments

Starting with the end of the chain, the organisational model of multi-sectoral tech suppliers such as AWS and Google Cloud (Chapter 8) is global. Economies of scale and efficiencies are paramount and dictate that research and development, technology, and infrastructure, are all centralised. While research usually occurs in multiple locations, these centres are interconnected and in effect operate as an integrated unit. Multi-sectoral suppliers have regional teams that are organised on a vertical basis according to the sector they serve (e.g. finance, health, public sector, media, and entertainment). At AWS, past a certain level of maturity, all these verticals are run on a global basis:

> We have a maturity model, which takes [the vertical] from incubation right through to a kind of individual business unit. And we have one of those, which is finance. So finance is organised globally. So everything reports into a centralised vertical solution. Then all the other industries are on the path to that. And I would say media and entertainment's probably next. And so we cross-fertilise in terms of knowledge, technique, training – a lot of the platforms we use, for example, are standardised across all the verticals.

> (Kilpatrick, interview 2019)

The industry–specific media delivery suppliers that populate the publication segment do not have the scale of big tech firms. Supplying services in playout and media management, they also have close working relationships with lead firms (Chapter 8). However, because of the borderless nature of IP delivery and cloud technology, their organisational structure is akin to a global configuration. Resources are centralised first and deployed locally second, even if the specific nature of the solutions may vary from one customer to another. In media assets management, for instance, Ericsson's Red Bee Media uses a unique cloud-based logistics platform. In distribution, Red Bee Media's six operating hubs are globally networked, and the company has developed the capability to produce and transmit TV channels and live events in full remote mode (IBC Showcase, 2020; Plunkett, interviews 2017).

Lead Firms

Lead firms in the aggregation segment vary greatly. The segment stretches from Netflix, which has no subsidiaries and a single revenue stream, to vertically integrated conglomerates with multiple activities. Overall, lead firms in the TV GVC are likely to adopt the international model of organisational configuration. Both Comcast and Disney fit neatly into this model. The core of Disney's competencies and assets are centralised, but the company attaches great importance to localisation and entrusts its local subsidiaries to adapt global franchises according to their knowledge and understanding of the markets in which they operate. Comcast has acted quickly to integrate Sky, its European subsidiary, to its core operations. For instance, Peacock, the conglomerate's AVoD platform, is powered by technology developed by Sky for Now TV. While, in this case, knowledge travelled from a subsidiary to the centre, Comcast intends to coordinate all development efforts to leverage technology and expertise across the entire group (Comcast, 2020).

There are at least two instances of transnational organisation among aggregators: MTV and YouTube. MTV Networks Europe was designed to encourage sharing and was organised into four regional groups: the United Kingdom and Nordic; Benelux; Germany and Central Europe; and Southern Europe, which held Italy, Spain, Portugal, and France. There was one large channel in every group (the United Kingdom, Germany, the Netherlands, and Italy) in order that the smaller stations learn from them. Teams had a strong incentive to share material, and instead of spending money on a new on-air look, a team just took it from any other channel.

Local teams were given autonomy to adapt and translate the MTV brand to the local market and collaborated with one another regularly. Certain channels developed expertise and capabilities in specific areas and the other teams went directly to them for advice and guidance. London was not interested in knowing who is borrowing what from whom. The Dutch were skilled at interactive applications, the Italians were good at on-air packaging, and the British knew how to position channels when competing with hundreds of other stations in a crowded market.

Local teams met constantly, covering advertising, marketing, and production issues. On-air departments, for instance, met regularly in order to share and repurpose material. A piece that was produced by a local team could be revoiced, rescripted, and aired by someone else. For instance, MTV Central ran a campaign for ringtones that was based on a cockroach. The idea originated in Argentina, was produced in Canada, and adapted to the German market.

Editorial teams had weekly video conference calls, and so did music people. Management met every year, senior executives every three months, and heads of channel every six weeks. Europe also participated in MTV's global creative gatherings. A fortnightly conference call brought together heads of region, who also took part in the larger annual global creative conference. These global get-togethers gave Europeans the opportunity to meet staff from MTV USA, the network's largest channel. Everything travelled across the network, short promos, marketing campaigns, interviews with musicians, and full-length pieces such as specials on artists (Flintoff, interview 2006; Godfrey, interview 2004; Guild, interview 2004).

Today, as music has transitioned to audio (Spotify) and video (YouTube Music) streaming services, the MTV network has become the home of youth-skewed reality TV formats. *Teen Mom, Geordie Shore, Ex on the Beach, Catfish,* and *Just Tattoo of Us* are among the staple shows. Depending on ratings, channels can either air the existing version of a format – not necessarily the American one – or produce their own adaptation. They can also come up with an extension or derivative version of an existing brand. The result is a multilayered network; any local team is part of an intricate web of relationships that juggle different layers of programming, ranging from the local to the global (e.g. MTV Awards), and anything in between. In addition to borrowing from one another, MTV channels share ratings analysis and knowledge about format production.

YouTube's structure differs but is based on a similar interplay between the local and the global. First, the company is aware that it needs to straddle the global dimension of tech and the local nature of content, and is filling in the layers. Regionally, the platform operates ten YouTube studios that provide equipment, post-production facilities, and training for creators. These studios are strategically located in London, Los Angeles, Tokyo, New York, São Paulo, Rio de Janeiro, Berlin, Paris, Mumbai, and Dubai (by opening date). In addition, all the content-facing and market-facing teams operate locally. These cover advertising sales, press, marketing, and creator and partner relationships. While tech is mostly run from the USA, local teams are in place to ensure that creators and advertisers understand its benefits and to address any specific local need (Frot-Coutaz, interview 2020). The overall principle remains the same, which consists of finding global synergies by centralising divisions whose work has worldwide ramifications, while adapting to local cultures by devolving certain tasks and decisions to country teams.

TV Production

TV content production is where transnational organisational patterns make most sense and are the most frequent. For multiple reasons, creativity is not an activity that can be centralised. Most creative talent likes to retain a certain amount of liberty, and production labels usually keep a degree of autonomy when integrating a major. Labels are left to get on with their tasks and the group acts as an administrative and financial support structure. Any top-down approach is coun-terproductive and can result in creative staff leaving the group (van Keulen et al., 2020). In addition, the local remains paramount in TV production. Labels' primary mission is to stay in business and develop the local market. Their role is to create shows that capture the interest of local audiences and work for them. For instance, international TV studios understand that global (unscripted) formats always begin life as local shows. While programmes that travel are sought after, studio executives know that it is impossible to predict where the next global hit will come from. Shine (now part of Banijay), refrained from setting up a global creative team in order to retain a diverse creative pallet and keep surprises coming (Hall, interview 2014). Senior managers at Endemol (also part of Banijay today) concurred that a creative organisation cannot be run centrally because 'ideas are incredibly local, even individual' (Hincks, interview 2010). The local remains important when labels adapt someone else's idea. They know which formats to choose from the catalogue and how to make it work for the local audience.

Large TV studios have jettisoned the position of chief creative officer, and the role of current heads of content is to identify trends, address gaps, avoid duplica-tions, and spread the fruits of creativity across the group. Among their challenges is to identify the best local ideas for travel, and on reaching the destination to ensure that production standards are met. TV production majors structure the creative flow of ideas according to these imperatives. Pan-network teams identify the best ideas and allocate funds once they have decided to champion them. If a local label is stuck on a project, these teams will send colleagues to help. They also encourage conversations among local teams to share ideas and learn from one another. International studios run schemes to ensure that an ongoing dialogue is taking place among creatives scattered across the network. They also organise international get-togethers with a similar purpose in mind. Sony, for instance, arranges a once-a-year Creative Leadership Conference whose aim is to highlight some of the projects that the production teams are working on, drive creative collaboration on ideas that deserve to get off the ground, and inspire teams with illustrious guest speakers (Carter, interview 2014; Flynn, interview 2014; Green, 2019; Hall, interview 2014; Wong, interview 2014).

In sum, global TV studios are coordinated federations of labels and subsidiaries, within which knowledge and information flow in multiple directions. Their transnational organisational structure and culture is dictated by the need to transit and adapt intellectual property from territory to territory. Labels talk to the group's coordinating team, as well as among each other.

The Local/Global Matrix

The transnational organisation structure does not fit businesses in all segments. Many lead firms prefer the international model, and tech giants are more interested in leveraging their infrastructure on a global scale. However, many companies have integrated some elements of this configuration without embracing the whole concept. This structure is particularly useful for those firms that need to break down the opposition between the local and the global, and to make each term an extension of the other. It gives them the ability to generate knowledge about both dimensions, combine global efficiency with responsiveness to local and regional markets, and move anywhere within the *local/global matrix*. Some actions and decisions are purely local, some are purely global, while others mix both dimensions (Figure 10.1). The transnational generation of knowledge and interaction between the two terms often becomes a driver for growth and innovation.

Conclusion

Transnationalisation is a key aspect of the global shift. Frontiers remain relevant and yet are blurred by the growth of cross-border flows. While streamers take linguistic borders into consideration, it remains that SVoD platform catalogues are more cosmopolitan than broadcasters' schedules, and video-sharing platforms make content posted by anyone available to everyone across the world. It is no longer place but technology that determines the fate of stories and ideas, and

Figure 10.1 The local/global organisational matrix of the transnational media firm

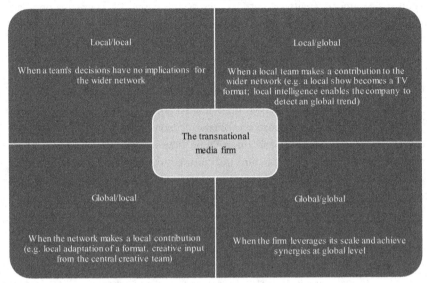

Source: author

internet delivery has loosened the ties between TV culture and national culture more than ever. By rendering TV cultures more cosmopolitan, global streamers are helping to bring about a new transcultural order.

Firms that straddle territories have a choice of organisational model. In the global TV industry, the structures they adopt vary and partly depend on the segment they occupy in the value chain (Table 10.4). While the transnational configuration makes most sense for global TV studios, many other companies have integrated some of its elements, without fully embracing it. This structure is particularly useful for those firms that need to break down the opposition between the local and the global, and benefit from the interplay between both dimensions.

11

Formulating GVC-Oriented Policies

This chapter examines the policy issues that influence the shape and contours of the TV GVC. As with any trading system, the global TV industry is based on a set of social and political values that are predominantly those of open societies and market economies. These values are not universal and the nature and amount of participation of a country into the TV GVC depends on its elites' degree of adherence to such values. Thus, the first section devotes special attention to China, which has largely shut its doors to the global TV industry. The second section examines the policy alternatives that exist for those countries that wish to embark on the path of GVC participation and economic upgrading. While no country has formulated an explicitly GVC-oriented media policy, internationally thriving TV production sectors are supported by a set of policies that integrate some of its elements. The chapter argues that such a policy has three key prongs: it must take into account the globalised nature of the TV industry and support firms that are best positioned to perform in the global marketplace, harness the benefits of trade, and incentivise creativity through regulation.

The Social and Political Values of the Global TV Industry

The global TV industry rests on a set of historically specific political values and economic conditions: those that prevail in open societies and market economies. Open societies are characterised by flexible social structures, political regimes that enable change without revolution, and ideals such as individual freedom. Among its core principles is freedom of opinion and expression. It is a fundamental right that is enshrined in the constitutions of all democratic regimes (and some non-democratic ones too), including the USA (First Amendment of the Constitution) and the EU (Article 10, European Convention on Human Rights). This right entails freedom of information and communication: opinions, to hold any value, need to be reasoned, thus citizens must have access to information. Freedom of communication stipulates that citizens have the right to both hold and voice opinions, and 'receive and impart information and ideas without interference by public authority and regardless of frontiers' (Article 10, European Convention on Human Rights).

While the nature of the relationship between open society and market economy remains subject to debate, historically it is the former that led to the latter (van Bavel, 2020). These economies are based upon a system of exchange and allocation driven by the market, leading to the commodification of 'land, labor and capital' (van Bavel, 2020: 795). Like other firms, media businesses abide by capitalist laws of free enterprise, competition, profit, and accumulation. In the twentieth century, this has driven the commodification of culture, in the same way that social media networks are commodifying social relations in the twenty-first century.

While the development of market economies can ultimately endanger the social and political foundations of open societies (van Bavel, 2020),[1] the TV industry and its globalisation rests, to a large extent, on the values of open societies and those same economic conditions set by market economies. The core of the global TV industry is made of firms that thrive under such political and economic contexts. Media multinationals primarily invest into – and collect revenue from – countries that share, at least to a certain extent, these values and market conditions. Their historical specificity and geographical limits first came to light during the New World Information and Communication Order (NWICO) debate in the 1980s (Chapter 1).

The governments calling for an alternative communication order in the UN arena were mostly concerned about Western hegemony. Indeed, the rationale for a NWICO was based on a critique of the free flow of communication and its capitalist foundations. These governments and representatives maintained that Western-based media corporations yield too much power and commodify both news and culture. They further contended that unfettered cross-border flows breached their cultural sovereignty and threatened national identity (Hamelink, 1997; Roach, 1997).

The NWICO argument rests on a set of political values that diverge from those of the West. Certain recommendations made by the MacBride report reflected the desire of some governments to control the flow of international communication the same way they controlled their domestic news media. Recommendation 48 called for an 'international right of reply and correction' enforceable by the UN in order 'to offset the negative effects of inaccurate or malicious reporting of international news' in the Western media (MacBride, 1980: 263). Should a newspaper criticise a dictatorial regime its government would have been able to publish its own version of events. Recommendation 58 was equally forthright and recommended 'effective legal measures ... to circumscribe the action of transnationals by requiring them to comply with specific criteria and conditions defined by national legislation and development policies' (MacBride, 1980: 266).

Western observers noted that UNESCO's report contained ambiguous attitudes towards freedom of expression. International associations of journalists, broadcasters, and newspapers were alarmed by its recommendations and the degree to which they imposed state control of news media (World Press Freedom Committee, 1981). For its part, the USA interpreted the NWICO call as a direct attack against its values and interests. In December 1983, US Secretary of State George P. Shultz informed UNESCO that his country was leaving the organisation (Shultz, 1984). The American government was followed by several other Western nations including the United Kingdom. Later, Jeane Kirkpatrick, then US ambassador at the UN, wrote: 'the language and the positions of the NAM [the Non-Aligned Movement that drove the NWICO movement] were simultaneously nationalist, socialist, and hostile to democratic values, alliances, and interests' (Kirpatrick, 2004: 238).

Forty years later, the conflict has resurfaced anew and the division lines remain similar, even though a few countries have switched sides. At stake is control of the Internet, with several nations attempting to increase their oversight of the network via the ITU. The battle came to the fore during the World Conference on International Telecommunications (WCIT) in Dubai, in 2012. In the course of negotiations aimed at revising the International Telecommunication Regulation (ITRs), provisions were put forward to expand the scope of the ITU recommendations on internet governance, and facilitate and legitimate governmental control over the network. Seven regimes with some of the poorest human rights records (Russia, the United Arab Emirates, China, Saudi Arabia, Algeria, Sudan, and Egypt) issued a joint proposal to sanction full national control over internet traffic (Wcitleaks.org, 2012). Western nations pushed back during weeks of intense negotiations; the final document remained unpalatable. Eighty-nine countries signed the WCIT 2012 Final Acts, and fifty-five abstained, meaning that the ITRs were left unchanged. Those who abstained are all democracies and include the Baltic countries, Norway, Switzerland, all the EU member states, Canada, USA, Australia, New Zealand, Japan, India, and Israel (Griffiths, 2019: 227–38; ITU, 2012).

As an observer noted, 'the split in the number of countries who signed the agreement and those who didn't clearly shows widely different views about the future of the Internet and the provision of telecommunication services' (EDRi, 2012). Since NWICO, the axis has shifted from North–South to West–East, and some countries such as India have crossed the line. But the two camps – liberal democracies on one side and authoritarian regimes on the other – remain divided.

Governments that wish to restrict freedom of communication do not need the blessing of the ITU to do so. They can erect a wide range of barriers and controls that generally expand in parallel with their financial means and technological capabilities. At their most basic, some of these measures are relatively benign and only affect the global TV industry momentarily. In 2019, there were 213 cases of internet shutdowns across thirty-three countries, located mostly in Asia, Africa, and the Middle East (Access Now 2020: 1). These internet blackouts last from a few hours to many months, usually targeted at 'members of oppressed or marginalized minority groups' within a country (Access Now 2020: 5). These blackouts aim to stifle voices at times of social dissent and political upheaval, and while social media platforms (YouTube included) are the main target, they equally affect streaming services.

Some countries go a step further. Russia, for instance, began to restrict foreign ownership of local media companies in the mid-2010s, forcing multinationals to disinvest from the country (Middleton, 2015). The Russian government is strengthening its grip over the Internet to limit its citizens' ability to access information from overseas (Matsnev, 2019).

However, none has gone further than China to insulate themselves from global media flows. Since the country's accession to WTO in 2001, content has crossed borders between the nation and the rest of the world. Chinese viewers have access to TV series, TV formats, and movies from Asia and the West. Conversely, China aims to become a 'strong cultural power (*wenhua qiangguo*)' and is ploughing resources into boosting the country's cultural exports (Keane and Zhang, 2017: 66). These flows are placed under surveillance and are limited in scope due to such restrictions. The Chinese government monitors and caps the amount of foreign content on TV channels and platforms. Import of both TV formats and TV series is constrained by quotas, and TV networks and platforms are limited by how many they can buy and when they can show them. No more than thirty-four foreign films, handpicked by the authorities, 'may be distributed annually on a revenue share basis' (ViacomCBS, 2020: 23). Any country whose foreign policy China disapproves of is threatened with a blanket ban (Keane and Zhang, 2017: 67).

Foreign media firms have long been attracted to the unique potential of the Chinese market. Sumner Redstone (Viacom), Rupert Murdoch (News Corp), and Larry Page and Sergey Brin (Google) have all invested fortunes to gain a foothold in the market. Apart from Viacom (which still has a small presence in the country but is trying to sell its local assets as it is unable to scale up operations), they were eventually forced to abandon the market and lost US$ billions in the process (Dover, 2009; Griffiths, 2019). None of the Western streamers operate in the country, and the top ten streaming services are all domestic (Lee, 2018: 166). Among the global TV studios, Fremantle alone has facilities in China.[2] Endemol

Shine (now part of Banijay) left China in 2019, stating that tight regulations make the market 'unsustainable' (in Middleton, 2019b).

With the Internet, China has realised the dream of all autocratic regimes: it has gained full control of its domestic online space and completely insulated itself from outside influence. All internet firms, from ISPs to content providers, operate in what is akin to a licensing system: platforms that allow user-generated content to employ hundreds of censors to ensure no red line is crossed, knowing they face closure should it occur too often. This is supplemented by the security services' own censorship apparatus, which combines automated and human control mechanisms. Repeat offenders, and their families, pay a heavy price (Griffiths, 2019: 71–5). The nation built a centralised network and censors can turn off the Internet in entire regions at the flick of a switch. Following Uyghur demonstrations, the Internet was shut down for more than a year in the entire Xinjiang province, with dramatic consequences for the cultural and business life of the region (Griffiths, 2019: 143–8). In between China's national network and the World Wide Web lies 'the great firewall'. It is a complex and multifaceted censorship system built to ensure that no undue foreign influence and nefarious voice contests nor questions the Communist Party's ideological construction and legitimacy to power (Griffiths, 2019).

No other country reflects more the determining influence of political values and participation in the global TV system. Regimes that do not share the values of open societies and market economies generally opt to limit or restrict the expansion and influence of the TV GVC on their territories.

Formulating GVC-Oriented Media Policies

Governments' range of policies towards the global media system fall into categories: *hostile, passive,* and *pro-active*. Non-democratic and autocratic regimes seek to insulate themselves from global news and entertainment. While success depends on the means at their disposal, the intent is to restrict incoming flows of communication as much as possible and promote regime-friendly narratives about history, politics, and culture.

Most governments do not seek to restrict international communication flows but show little interest in participating fully in the TV GVC, not deeming the creative industries a priority. Pro-active countries are a much smaller group including those which develop policies to upgrade in the global cultural and creative value chains (Lee and Lee, 2019).

Participation in any GVC is beneficial for nations and their citizens, particularly those from the Global South. The United Nations Conference on Trade and

Development (UNCTAD) reports that 'experience over the past 20 years shows that, as countries increase their participation in GVCs, their growth rates tend to increase as well' (UNCTAD, 2013: 151). Additional benefits include 'value added creation, employment generation and potential for learning and productivity growth' (UNCTAD, 2013: 148) (Table 11.1).

Local firms' participation in the TV GVC brings multiple benefits. It adds value to a domestic economy and leads to the creation of skilled and creative jobs. A thriving TV sector improves the trade balance before even a single show is exported by producing more local programmes and reducing broadcasters' reliance on foreign tapes. The content sustains local culture and, when exported, can lead to a surge in tourism revenues and have a positive impact on a nation's soft power.

Participation in a GVC requires the adoption of *GVC-oriented industrial policies* that seek to improve the position of local firms in existing international production networks, 'explicitly utiliz[ing] extra-territorial linkages that affect a country's positioning in global or regional value chains' (Gereffi and Sturgeon, 2013: 342). This type of industrial policy corresponds with strategies of economic upgrading (Chapter 1), which require producers 'to make better products, to make products more efficiently, or to move into more skilled activities' (Pietrobelli and Rabellotti, 2006: 1). What does a set of policies seeking to enhance a country's participation in the TV GVC look like? Each country faces different issues influenced by the capabilities of local firms, and the size and shape of the domestic media market. However, any GVC-oriented policy in the sector should be grounded on three building blocks.

Meeting the Challenges of a Globalised Industry

A GVC-oriented policy must take into account the globalised nature of the TV industry and support firms that are best positioned to perform internationally. Most often, governments' policy decisions tend to favour GVC's lead firms, such as national broadcasters. The temptation is easily explained: these organisations are often national champions employing staff in their thousands, are in the public eye, and are well versed in the dark arts of lobbying. In some instances, broadcasters are close to the field of political power, preventing governments from legislating against their commercial interests. But in an era of GVC-driven industrialisation, a lead-firm bias can impair economic development and cause a fatal blow to the prospects of economic upgrading for local firms. Furthermore, because the aggregation sector is dominated by global giants, it is impossible for national broadcasters to carve themselves a niche in this segment at the

Table 11.1 *Development impact of GVCs: selected highlights*

Impact areas	Selected highlights of findings
Local value capture	• GVC participation can generate value added in domestic economies and can contribute to faster GDP growth.
Job creation, income generation and employment quality	• GVC participation tends to lead to job creation in developing countries and to higher employment growth, even if GVC participation depends on imported contents in exports. GVC participation tends to have, with variations by country and industry, a positive effect on the employment of women. • GVC participation can lead to increases in both skilled and unskilled employment.
Technology dissemination and skills building	• Knowledge transfer from TNCs to local firms operating in GVCs depends on knowledge complexity and codifiability, on the nature of inter-firm relationships and value chain governance, and on absorptive capacities.
Social and environmental impacts	• GVCs can serve as a mechanism for transferring international best practices in social and environmental efforts, for example, through the use of CSR standards. Implementation of standards below the first tier of the supply chain remains a challenge.
Upgrading and building long-term productive capabilities	• GVCs can offer longer-term development opportunities if local firms manage to increase productivity and upgrade to activities with higher value added in GVCs. • At country level, successful GVC upgrading paths involve not only growing participation in GVCs but also the creation of higher domestic value added and the gradual expansion of participation in GVCs of increasing technological sophistication.

Source: adapted from UNCTAD, 2013: 149.

international level. For most nations, the best chance of participating in the TV GVC lies in the other segments of the chain.

The United Kingdom is among the best performing countries in the global TV industry, having become one of the largest exporters of TV programmes

(Chapter 3). The origin of its success lies in a multi-decade policy drive supporting the TV production sector. While no nation has explicitly formulated a GVC-oriented policy in television, British regulations contain its core elements.

In the early 1980s, the British government launched Channel 4, which was required to commission all its programming from independent producers. This decision created a cottage industry of micro-firms specialising in documentaries (Chapter 7). The fledgling sector was provided further support with the Broadcasting Act 1990, which introduced 'the statutory independent quota' to other terrestrial broadcasters. The Act stipulated that they must commission at least 25 per cent of their programming from independent producers; the Broadcasting Act 1996 expanded the principle to digital terrestrial television channels (Ofcom 2006: 34).

This policy strand culminated in 2003. The sector was growing but remained fragile and producers were at the mercy of a handful of powerful broadcasters who could dictate terms and conditions to their content suppliers. Broadcasters were able to bundle all the intellectual property (IP) rights attached to TV shows and keep them forever. The Communications Act 2003 forced the industry to introduce terms of trade between broadcasters and producers, considerably reinforcing the rights position of the latter. These terms disaggregated rights and allowed producers to keep all the rights not purchased by broadcasters, creating in the process a new IP regime that transformed the fortunes of the local independent production sector. The IP that used to end up in broadcasters' hands was now a bankable asset, leading to a wave of investment and consolidation in the sector (Chapter 7). In addition, the market for TV rights that the Act helped to develop created a 'natural' incentive for rights owners to exploit their IP, internationally or otherwise

This long-term policy effort facilitated the considerable growth of the UK–based TV production sector: its annual turnover has passed from £700 million in the mid-1990s to £3.3 billion in 2019 (Jones, 1995a: 5; Oliver and Ohlbaum, 2021: 9). The UK TV production sector's international revenues have increased by 120 per cent since 2013: standing at 1.25 billion in 2019, they represent 37.6 per cent of its total income (Oliver and Ohlbaum, 2021: 9).

The lesson to be learned is that the vested interests of lead firms must be challenged, and the power asymmetries between aggregators and producers must be addressed (Chapter 9). When the British Government created the nation's fourth channel, it did so in the face of formidable pressure from advertisers and ITV companies that had lobbied relentlessly for years for a second service. So certain were they to land their channel that TV sets on sale in the late 1970s already had an 'ITV-2' position on the dial (Darlow 2004: 103). The

Communications Act 2003 also challenged broadcasters' commercial interests, so much so that the terms of trade have gone through five full reviews since their implementation in 2004 (McVay, 2015).

By way of contrast, the power of lead firms is largely unchecked in most markets, making it difficult for local TV producers to develop their assets and export formats. The challenges they face are illustrated by Rapid Blue, one of Africa's leading production companies. Duncan Irvine, its CEO, explains:

> The beauty about the UK production environment is that you have terms of trade and thanks to the terms of trade, if you create a show, a really great show and you get it commissioned by the BBC for instance, you still get to retain the IP and you then can go off and sell the format. In South Africa that doesn't happen. If a broadcaster commissions you, they own everything, you no longer own the show; it's theirs. So down here I mean we'll develop shows for a broadcaster knowing that we basically are going to lose all the rights to it, so it makes it very, very hard to develop a format that you might be able to sell outside of the country.
>
> (Irvine, interview 2016)

Regulatory support for the sector, Irvine further argues, 'would unlock massive potential down here, because a lot of ideas we literally sit on, so we won't take them to a broadcaster because we're going to do everything else we can to try and find a way to make this without having to get it commissioned' (Irvine, interview 2016).

Middle Eastern TV producers face specific challenges. In addition to a catastrophic security situation, the drop in oil price, is having a significant impact on broadcasters' advertising revenue, and consequently on the regional content market. Broadcasters have sharply reduced the amount of programmes they commission, reducing sales opportunities for local producers.

However, Middle Eastern producers face exacerbated power asymmetries when dealing with local broadcasters, due to the latter's close association with governments and monarchies. In order to capture the relationship between the two parties, a Middle Eastern–based TV producer quotes La Fontaine's *The Wolf and the Lamb*, a fable that illustrates how those in power do not need to justify or explain the violence and coercion they exert on the less fortunate because 'the reason of the strongest is always the best' (TV producer, 2016). Broadcasters have no choice but to respect the IP owned by global studios when acquiring their content, 'but when it comes to small producers, most of the time the idea becomes their idea, the property of broadcasters, for not a lot of money' (TV producer 2016). While Middle Eastern TV producers have shown a strong potential for creativity (Khalil, 2017), they would perform much better in the global marketplace should local aggregators show a modicum of respect for their IP.

By way of contrast, Israel has emerged as a strong TV exporter, and has measures in place to protect the interests of TV producers: commercial broadcasters are required to commission 65 per cent of their original programming from independent producers, although they are still able to keep the rights of their original ideas if their show first airs in Israel (Armoza, interview 2016).

Regulators in continental Europe have yet to show strong support for the TV production sector and address the power asymmetries between aggregators and suppliers. There are some bright spots in TV production across the continent, including Spain and Scandinavia, while the Netherlands remains a leading TV format exporter. However, these countries' exports remain far behind those of the United Kingdom and the USA, and many large European territories should perform much better considering the size of their domestic market. As a whole, governments in Europe remain attached to the idea of nurturing vertically integrated national champions. European broadcasters also have the lobbying clout to block any threatening regulation: in some countries, an unspoken alliance exists between politicians who count on the support of broadcasters in times of need, who in turn rely on them not to threaten their dominant position in the content value chain. As a result, they enjoy a strong rights position that smothers local TV production and exports.

Harnessing the Benefits of Trade

When developing countries implemented an import substitution industrialisation (ISI) strategy, they restricted imports through levies and protectionist barriers. In the context of growing GVCs, this strategy is counterproductive, as nations need to import intermediate goods in order to export products (Gereffi and Sturgeon, 2013: 340–2). In the current era, 'the main emphasis is on how to use traded intermediates to capture more value in GVCs' (Milberg et al., 2014: 155). Research shows that in several value chains, original equipment manufacturers (OEMs) have learnt key skills from the firms they supplied. In East Asia for instance, several OEMs have used their skills to make the shift to original brand name manufacturing (OBM) (Gereffi, 1999; Gereffi et al., 2005). Open trade can support the same process in the TV GVC.

Evidence of the benefits of trade are strong, as illustrated in the format business: four of today's leading format exporters – the United Kingdom, Holland, Israel, and Japan – share one feature: all these countries were, and in certain respects remain, heavy importers of American television fare. Since the 1950s, the United Kingdom has been among the USA's top TV export market. From game shows to TV series, there has always been a British TV buyer willing to sign a licence contract for US content (Chapter 3). In the Netherlands, companies like Endemol cut their teeth on US game shows, some of which contained a reality element that became the firm's trademark. Israel is also a big importer of US content, and the savviness of the local audience raised on a diet of US programming is often cited as a factor for 'driving demand for edgy local content' (Waller, 2010). Even Japan (one of four countries with a positive trade balance in the format business) owes its prowess in the game show genre to a strong US cultural influence in the aftermath of World War Two (Ishita, 2000: 29–30). Proximity and familiarity with the birthplace of commercial TV creates producers, commissioners, and audiences who understand the discourse of commercial television.

The format trade plays an essential role in helping local producers to hone their skills. Local production communities learn from imported formats, enabling them to upskill more rapidly than if left to their own devices. As Armoza summarises: 'we started by bringing formats to Israel and producing them locally, and then we began developing our own. The next stage was to give our shows to others to distribute, but we know the formats so we can best do the work ourselves' (in Jenkinson, 2007). He himself learnt the trade from Sony and Action Time, a British company that specialised in game shows. Formats, he continues, allowed

the Israeli creative industry to engage in a creative dialogue with international companies ... the dialogue between international companies bringing their knowledge and their culture and their ambitions and the culture and ambitions of the Israelis kind of pushed the industry forward. So working with international format is certainly a way that can help any TV industry to develop and improve.

(Armoza, interview 2016)

Bibles and flying producers bring with them skills, knowledge, and techniques that can be transferred to other shows, as Duncan Irvine explains:

I think where it's had the biggest benefit is that every time we make one of those shows, all the crew and the people who work on it and so a production manager or a line producer, or anybody who's working on a show, they learn so much in terms of working on that show and I think that that's where we've seen a massive advantage in the sense that they then move on to other shows and they take a lot of that learning with them into other shows, so I think that's by far been the biggest advantage.

(Irvine, interview 2016)

In drama, co-productions play a similar role in the upgrading strategy of local producers. 'Korean producers', for instance, 'embraced international coproduction to learn from foreign firms and leverage their financial resources and distribution networks' (Lee and Lee, 2019: 148).

In sum, a GVC-oriented policy must not restrict international trade. Trade supports the cross-border flows of ideas and capital, and enables knowledge transfers to occur. Opening up borders also encourages competition that, ultimately, levels up production standards. Protectionist measures may offer temporary relief to local producers but not the incentives to export. In such circumstances, local firms are also less likely to reach international production standards. Most TV producers in developing countries would agree with Avi Armoza in arguing that building up the creativity of the local TV production sector necessitates engagement with the international market (Armoza, interview 2016).

In addition, restrictive trade policies expose countries to measures of retorsion, regardless of the origin of the conflict. The Chinese authorities have placed stringent restrictions on film, TV series, and format imports, and made it impossible for foreign platforms to operate in its territory. The reasons for the ban in India of fifty-nine Chinese apps, including social media networks such as TikTok, are diverse, complex, and lie outside the realm of media. The Trump administration's attempt to ban TikTok was blocked by US courts; had American platforms retained unfettered access to the Chinese market, a US administration would have thought twice about prohibiting the video platform (Chin, 2021; Paul, 2020).

Fostering Creativity through IP Laws

A GVC-oriented media policy must use IP laws to incentivise creativity, as the UK legislator did by ensuring that TV producers benefit from their work. This entails that IP rights are upheld and protected. In developing countries, however, the issue goes beyond the thorny relationship between broadcasters and producers, as there are question marks about the fairness and usefulness of the global IP regime itself.

The agreement on Trade-Related Aspects of Intellectual Property Rights (TRIPS), which came into effect in January 1995, binds WTO members into the most comprehensive multilateral agreement on IP (Taubman et al., 2012). To many observers, however, it instigated an IP regime that is iniquitous and favours developed countries, strengthening Western multinationals' ability to harvest royalties from their patents and copyrighted work worldwide (e.g. Olwan, 2013: 99–151). Sean Pager argues, however, that developing countries benefit from IP rights and their local protection is indispensable to the development of their creative industries. Developing nations should not merely be seen as IP consumers but producers who need the protection IP laws confer:

> Rather than rejecting IP rights as an alien appendage foisted upon them by external pressure, developing countries should consider their positive, yet unrealized, potential to function as engines of domestic innovation. Authors and inventors in developing countries deserve the same opportunity, enshrined in human rights law, to benefit from their creativity as their developed-world counterparts. Moreover, there are compelling reasons for supporting homegrown innovation as a pathway to sustainable development; increased technology transfer from developed countries is no substitute.
>
> (Pager, 2012: 235)

Without the protection and incentives an efficient IP regime offers, TV producers in developing countries are locked in a vicious cycle of low investment and poor creativity. Our interviewees, leading TV producers in the Middle East and Africa, agree that a stronger IP regime would enable them to unleash local creativity. They know, and potential investors know too, that they stand little chance of monetising their content. Nollywood, the Nigerian film industry that has become the country's largest private employee, loses 1 US$ billion every year to local and regional piracy (Pager, 2012: 263).

A key recommendation from the International Confederation of Authors and Composers Societies is to 'recognize the importance of IP and protection of copyright to the creative process' (CISAC, 2014: 13). The organisation cites several studies that report a positive correlation between the strength of IP rights and economic development. Among them, an OECD review 'found that for every 1% increase in copyright protection, there was an accompanying 6.8% increase in FDI' (CISAC, 2014: 56). An UNCTAD report concurs that 'intellectual property provides incentives to creators and entrepreneurs in the form of a tradable economic asset – a copyright – that is instrumental for investing in the development, production and distribution of goods and services, in a market economy' (in CISAC, 2014: 56–7).

Offering a viable IP regime for local producers must be part of any upgrading strategy in the TV GVC. It is the launch pad they need to perform in the global marketplace.

Conclusion

The TV GVC rests on the social and political values of open societies and market economies. The nations that do not share these values generally choose to opt out.

China is a case in point, having disentangled the nation from the Internet and set up its own sovereign network. The attitude of the Communist regime is typical of closed societies, and is consistent throughout the international regimes and agreements that underpin the TV GVC (e.g. Winseck, 2002). According to the Office of the United States Trade Representative, China is among the world's worst violators of foreign IP:

> In 2019, China again failed to reform measures that bar or limit the ability of foreign entities to engage in online publishing, broadcasting, and distribution of creative content, such as prohibitions in the Foreign Investment Catalogue and requirements that state-owned enterprises (SOEs) hold an ownership stake in online platforms for film and television content. Right holders report that growing advance approval requirements and other barriers have severely limited the availability of foreign TV content and prevented the simultaneous release of foreign content in China and other markets. Collectively, these measures create conditions that result in greater piracy and a market that is less open than others to foreign content and foreign entity participation.
>
> (Office of the United States Trade Representative, 2020: 45)

For those governments who wish to support the engagement of local firms with the global TV industry, they can find inspiration in nations that have successfully done so. No government has developed a media policy that is explicitly GVC-driven. However, most thriving TV production sectors are supported by local regulation that integrates, to varying degrees, elements of GVC-oriented policies.

GVC-oriented policies avoid the common mistake of supporting lead firms (aggregators). In the context of GVC-driven industrialisation, vertically integrated companies that may perform strongly in their national market can be an obstacle to economic development as, 'with GVCs, competitive improvements come not with the development of the fully integrated scope of activities in an industry, but by moving into higher-valued tasks associated with the industry' (Milberg et al., 2014: 170).

In the era of vertically specialised industrialisation, governments need to support those firms that perform best in an internationally fragmented system of production and adapt to vertical patterns of trade in intermediate goods between companies or subsidiaries of multinationals that specialise in a segment of the value chain (Milberg et al., 2014: 153; Miroudot and Ragoussis, 2009). It is what the United Kingdom, Israel, and South Korea have done by focusing their efforts on the TV content production sector.

GVC-oriented policies do not shield local producers from foreign competition but leverage trade in order to improve standards and engagement with the TV global industry. They incentivise creativity by enforcing the existing IP international regime, and fostering a legal framework that upholds and protects local IP rights.

Conclusion

Television has become a digital value chain that with the advent of streaming has entered the digital economy. Scale is a necessity in this economy in which oligopolistic markets prevail. The technology and infrastructure are designed and deployed at scale, and a similar logic drives M&A activities among lead firms and suppliers alike (Chapters 3–9). Platforms too work best at scale, not least because of network effects that can be exploited to full tilt in a digital environment (Chapters 4 and 10).

The global shift is not merely a matter of scale but structure. Based on a specific set of values, neither is the TV GVC universal. With varying degrees of intent and success, autocratic regimes restrain foreign media's ability to conduct business on their territories and limit their population's access to international media content (Chapter 11). Yet the TV GVC remains a globally integrated system of production and consumption because it consists of transnational networks of production and internationalised value–adding segments, and governs the strategies of firms scattered in different segments and territories (Chapter 9). The TV GVC offers lead firms and suppliers a distinct set of constraints and opportunities. In turn, their behaviour modifies the structure of the chain. The chain is altogether a *structural reality* – it is a coordinated sequence of international value–adding segments; and a *structuring reality* – it works as a global coordination mechanism.

Only a holistic perspective that takes into account all participating businesses can provide a full analysis of the globalising processes that are transforming the TV industry. Focusing on lead firms is not enough, suppliers too are adapting to the chain's coordinating influences and play an active role in the industry's integration. Global TV studios facilitate worldwide circulation of content, either through the distribution of finished tapes or the international production of TV formats. In media tech, many suppliers have a footprint equal in scope to those of the largest aggregators. Media delivery has become a multinational-to-multinational production network, and a global-scale production system with the capability to deliver content to and from any location in the world on a 24/7 basis.

In terms of country participation, how equal and diverse is the TV GVC? How much progress, if any, has been made since the NWICO debate? The USA remains the most widespread source of entertainment. US-based conglomerates still sell large amounts of programming to thousands of broadcasters and platforms overseas. American franchises, from *Star Wars* to the NBA, have fans across the planet. But diversity is on the rise. Regional trade routes and power players have emerged, and the South–South trade is growing faster than any other (Chapter 3). SVoD services commission programming from a wide array of territories, if only to drive local subscriptions (Chapters 4 and 10). Viewers in Western markets are becoming accustomed to foreign-language drama. YouTube's traffic and library epitomises a contemporary TV culture that is cosmopolitan in tone (Chapter 10).

However, our GVC analysis shows that the USA is more dominant than ever in the global TV system. While content production is diversifying and expanding to a wider range of countries, content aggregation is concentrated in American hands (Chapters 6–9). The online services of US-based media conglomerates and tech firms largely dominate the global streaming market. They hold the twin advantage of scale and capital. Aggregation is the most demanding segment in terms of investment and the barriers to entry are particularly high (Chapter 4). However, once a brand establishes itself as an entertainment destination, the return on investment is great. Content aggregation is also home to the industry's most powerful firms. Lead firms dictate terms and conditions to their suppliers, particularly when they are 'industry captive', such as TV producers (Chapters 7 and 9). As television transitions to a fully fledged digital GVC and an oligopolistic industry structure, the USA has emerged as the market's clear winner.

This research enriches the GVC literature in multiple ways. It illustrates a sociological approach to GVCs, emphasising the historical nature of value chains. It outlines a new value chain, whose evolution can be compared against others, as the forces that reshape it are active throughout the economy. Television is changing because it is at the heart of three key shifts of contemporary capitalism: digitisation, globalisation, and wealth generation through IP-based industries. This research provides a case study of the transformative power of these forces. Once they change industrial processes, as illustrated by the transition from broadcasting to streaming, these in turn have an impact on industry structure. Similar effects have been observed in other sectors (e.g. Sturgeon, 1999). This study is relevant to scholars examining industries with which television shares a global supply base.

This research analysed the formation of a global-scale production network focusing on each value-adding segment and firms within. It can be expanded into several areas. The relationship between globalisation and regionalisation, such as the connection between regional and global TV production networks, warrants further research. An example is the Asian TV trade and its connections to the rest of the world. Bringing together insights from the GPN and the GVC frameworks, more work is needed on intermediaries, particularly standards organisations (Chapter 5) and banking institutions. GVC scholars should make a distinct contribution to the debate on labour in the global creative industries. Finally, future research needs to take a closer look at the complex relationship between GVCs and platform ecosystems. The TV GVC involves several firms, such as tech giants and cloud providers, that govern vast ecosystems. What are their key features, and how do they differ from GVCs? How do they contribute and integrate into value chains, and what is their significance for GVC theory?

Personal Communications and Interviews by the Author

(Company names and job titles at time of interview)

Armoza, A. (2016) founder and chief executive officer, Armoza Formats, telephone interview by author, 13 April.

Carter, G. (2008) chief operating officer, FremantleMedia, interview by author, 20 November. London: digital recording.

———(2014) chairman, Northern Europe, and chairman, Shine 360°, Shine Group, interview by author, 10 October. London: digital recording.

Darnell, W. (2019) cloud solutions architect, Microsoft, interview by author, 11 April. London: digital recording.

Edwards, J. MBE (2020) founder, SBTV: Music, interview by author, 14 January. London: digital recording.

Flintoff, T. (2006) head of programming and production, MTV European, interview by author, 15 March. London: digital recording.

Flynn, D. (2014) chief creative officer, Endemol, UK, interview by author, 10 November. London: digital recording.

Porte, M. (2019) founder, Youngest Media, interview by author, 29 November. London: digital recording.

Frot-Coutaz, C. (2020) head of EMEA, YouTube, 13 January, interview by author: digital recording.

Godfrey, R. (2004) senior vice president, MTV Productions Europe, 26 February, interview by author: digital recording.

Google executive (2019) Google Cloud Media, interview by author, 21 March. London: digital recording.

Green, L. (2019) head of content, Banijay Group, interview by author, 14 August. London: digital recording.

Greenaway, S. (2019) chief technology and operations officer, UKTV, interview by author, 27 November. London: digital recording.

Guild, S. (2004) chief operating officer, MTV Networks Europe, interview by author, 20 July. London: digital recording.

Hall, B. (2014) managing director, Shine Network, interview by author, 12 October. London: digital recording.

Irvine. D. (2016) chief executive officer, Rapid Blue, telephone interview by author, 22 April. London: digital recording.

Kemming, G. (2020) director, Quintus Media, interview by author, 17 January. London: digital recording.

Kilpatrick G. (2019) industry lead, EMEA media and entertainment, Amazon Web Services, interview by author, 14 March. London: digital recording.

Lambert, S. (2012) chief executive, Studio Lambert, interview by author, 27 June. London: digital recording.

Mahon, A. (2014) group president, Shine Group, interview by author, 12 October. London: digital recording.

McVay, John (2009) chief executive, Pact, interview by author, 25 February. London: digital recording.

Nohr, N. (2020) international media consultant, interview by author, 2 March. London: digital recording.

Payne, C. (2019) chief executive, Endemol Shine International, interview by author, 13 November. London: digital recording.

Porte, M. (2009) head of format sales, Zodiak Entertainment Distribution, interview by author, circa November 2009. London: digital recording.

Plunkett, S. (2017) chief technology officer, Broadcast & Media Services, Ericsson, interviews by author, 28 June (2016), 27 January and 5 May. London: digital recording.

———(2009) head of format sales, Zodiak Entertainment Distribution, interview by author, circa November. London: digital recording.

Roth, J. (2008) head of distribution, Zodiak International, interview by author, circa December. London: digital recording.

Sargent, N. (2010) co-founder and CEO, The Farm Group, interview by author, 13 July. London: digital recording.

Stevens, H. (2017) director of broadcast operations, ITV, interview by author, 1 March. London: digital recording.

Tucker, S. (2017) broadcast engineering manager, technology strategy and operations, Channel Four Television, interview by author, 29 March. London: tape recording.

TV Producer (2016), Lebanon, Beirut, telephone interview with author, 4 March. London: digital recording.

Wittig, F. and J. Alexander (2020) producer and host, 'The Great War', interview by author, 5 February. London: digital recording.

Wong, A. (2014) vice president of alternative programming, 1998–2007, ABC; currently president of international production, Sony Pictures Television, president of international, Sony Pictures Entertainment, interview by author, 12 November. London: digital recording.

Notes

Introduction

1 The European Broadcasting Union (EBU) created a YouTube Eurovision Song Contest channel to complement its members' linear coverage of the event. RTVE in Spain, and ITV in the United Kingdom, are other examples of broadcasters that are leveraging the platform in order to expand the reach of their reality TV shows (Frot-Coutaz, 2019).

2 Sharing this aim, I have twice assembled essays written by scholars from a variety of world regions, including the Middle East, Africa, South and Southeast Asia, and Latin America (Chalaby, 2005b; Chalaby and Esser, 2017).

3 This book contains segments and develops themes and ideas that initially appeared in a series of articles published, in chronological order: the *Journal of Communication* (66/1) (Chapter 7), *International Journal of Digital Television* (8/1) (Chapter 11), *Communication Theory* (29/2) (Chapter 2), and the *Journal of Digital Media & Policy* (2021) (Chapter 10). Chapter 8 is a shortened version of an article co-authored with Steve Plunkett and published in *New Media & Society* (23/11).

Chapter 1

1 The concept is distinct from 'world-economy', a term that designates the global economy as a whole.

2 It was written in a German prisoner-of-war camp during the Second World War.

3 I am grateful to John Humphrey, who played a prominent role in this process, for clarification on its nature.

4 The World Trade Organization (WTO) has released a specific data set that provides insights on national economies' participation in GVCs, the volume of their trade in merchandise and commercial services intermediates, and their interconnection through GVCs (WTO, 2016).

Chapter 2

1 Offshoring necessarily entails the relocation of activities but, unlike outsourcing, the tasks can be carried out by the foreign subsidiary of a multinational (Contractor et al., 2011a: 7).

Chapter 3

1 A common complaint from foreign TV buyers is that they found British TV series too gritty for their markets (Jones, 1996).
2 Exchange rates GBP–USD at average closing price for corresponding year (www .macrotrends.net).
3 Viki is an amalgam of 'video' and 'wiki', reflecting the fact that subtitles are crowdsourced and written by fans.
4 The BBC used the 2020 annual meeting (on Zoom) for producers of *Dancing with the Stars* to share production tips on how to produce the dancing show safely during the COVID-19 pandemic (Phillips, 2020).

Chapter 4

1 Estimates given online vary widely, but a streamer reported that YouTube CPM was at US$4.08 in the USA compared to US$1.16 in India (Church, 2020).
2 This typology is based on a classification constructed by Matthew Ball for the US market (see Ball, 2019b).
3 Such as *All or Nothing*, the ground-breaking docuseries that offers behind-the-scenes access to a sports team for a season.

Chapter 5

1 RealNetworks filed a lawsuit against Microsoft in December 2003, alleging that 'Microsoft used its Windows OS [operating system] dominance to restrict RealNetworks' position in the market for digital media software for the PC' (Montalbano, 2005). The lawsuit was settled two years later at a cost of US$761 million for Microsoft, the two companies agreeing to cooperate in the delivery of digital media (Montalbano, 2005). Despite the cost, the agreement was seen as advantageous for Microsoft, who henceforth could use its own streaming technology in its operating system and the forthcoming Xbox 360. However, it was a pyrrhic victory, as neither RealNetworks nor Microsoft would be able to find a viable position in the future streaming industry.

Chapter 6

1 Submarine cable maps are available at https://submarine-cable-map-2019.telegeography .com and www.submarinecablemap.com.
2 In terms of resilience, the typical hyperscaler has several alternative power sources to mitigate a power interruption from the grid, such as rooms full of lithium-ion batteries and large diesel tanks.

3 Marshall McLuhan's notion of a global village constitutes an early conceptualisation of this transformation. The electric and digital media, he argued, have transformed the planet into a 'constricted space' within which 'each of us [is] present and accessible to every other person in the world' (McLuhan, 1962: 31, 1964: 248).

Chapter 7

1 Alex Graham is the founder of Wall to Wall Media, now part of Warner Bros. Television Productions UK.
2 The COVID-19 pandemic and the resulting delays in content production has made streamers more flexible about their rights position, creating a less rigid rights ecosystem and providing renewed opportunities for distributors, broadcasters, and AVoD platforms (Middleton, 2021).
3 The first independent distributors were established in the 1950s. Fremantle Corporation, which pioneered domestic franchising in the USA and the international sale of US TV series, was established by Paul Talbot in 1952. All American Television and King World, two syndication companies, provide other examples (Guider, 2005).
4 BBC Studios operates jointly with BBC's commercial distributor, BBC Worldwide.

Chapter 8

1 Also referred to as transnational first-tier suppliers in the literature (Raj-Reichert, 2019).
2 As illustrated by John Reith, the founder of the BBC, who famously stated: 'There is a grumble and a cause of complaining if the crofter in the North of Scotland or the agricultural labourer in the West of England has been unable to hear the King speak on some great national occasion' (Reith, 1924: 15).
3 Global suppliers were first detected in the electronics industry. The concept predates GVC theory and first appears in Sturgeon (1999: 71, 154–5).
4 The points of interconnection between Netflix's appliances and ISPs are known as peering locations, and these exchange points can be either public or private (https://openconnect.netflix.com).
5 Visit https://azure.microsoft.com/en-us/global-infrastructure/geographies for full map.
6 Smaller CDN providers can form federations to help them to improve reach, latency, and throughput (Mukerjee et al., 2016).

Chapter 9

1 Quibi was a short-form service for mobile consumption that shut down in October 2020. It ordered content from filmmakers such as Guillermo del Torro, Steven Soderbergh, and Steven Spielberg (Dams, 2019b).
2 Streamers are, however, subject to local regulations pertaining to content.

Chapter 10

1 ViacomCBS still managed to earn US$5.1 billion in advertising sales from its cable networks worldwide, including MTV, in 2019 (ViacomCBS, 2020: 73).

Chapter 11

1 Bas van Bavel argues that 'the rise of top wealth in all market economies subsequently allowed for the translation of economic wealth into political leverage and thus the erosion of the more equitable, open society that formed the foundation of the same market economy' (van Bavel, 2020: 810). He cites Rupert Murdoch and his collection of conservative news outlets as an example of 'the translation of wealth into political leverage' (van Bavel, 2020: 811). In a similar vein, Jürgen Habermas argues that capitalism is undermining the foundations of the public sphere, where reason and critical discourse should thrive unfettered by economic constraints and calculations (Habermas, 1989). Political economists contend that consolidation and conglomeration, which are inherent to unfettered market mechanisms, weaken media pluralism and are a threat to democratic political systems (e.g. Bagdikian, 2004).

2 Fremantle China is headed by Vivian Yin, a former student of mine.

References

3Vision (2019) *UK TV Exports Report, 2018–19*, London: 3Vision & Pact.

Access Now (2020) *Targeted, Cut Off, and Left in the Dark: The #KeepItOn Report on Internet Shutdown in 2019*, New York, NY: Access Now.

Achilles (2021) *Reform of Public Procurement Law after Brexit*, Abingdon: Achilles.

Afilipoaie, A., Iordache, C., and Raats, T. (2021) 'The "Netflix Original" and what it means for the production of European television content', *Critical Studies in Television*, 16(3): 304–25.

Aguete, M. (2021) 'Streaming ahead', *TBI Talks*, 28 January. Available at: https://tinyurl.com/ycksbp7r.

Aksoy, A. and Robins, K. (2000) 'Thinking across spaces: Transnational television from Turkey', *European Journal of Cultural Studies*, 3(3): 343–65.

Alexander, J. (2019) 'The Office will leave Netflix in 2021', *theverge.com*, 25 June. Available at: www.theverge.com/2019/6/25/18758714/the-office-netflix-2021-nbc-universal-streaming-wars.

Alloca, K. (2018) *Videocracy: How YouTube Is Changing the World . . . with Double Rainbows, Singing Foxes, and Other Trends We Can't Stop Watching*, London: Bloomsbury.

Alonzi, T. (1998) 'Growing up is hard to do', in C. Crowe (ed.), *Media and Marketing Europe Guide to Pan-European Television*, London: Emap media, pp. 18–19.

Alphabet (2020) *Annual Report 2019*, Mountain View, CA: Alphabet.

———(2021) *Year in Review 2020*, Mountain View, CA: Alphabet.

Alvino, C. and Basilico, J. (2015) 'Learning a personalized homepage', *netflixtechblog.com*, 9 April. Available at: https://netflixtechblog.com/learning-a-personalized-homepage-aa8ec670359a.

Amatriain, X. and Basilico, J. (2012) 'Netlix recommendations: Beyond the 5 stars' (Part 1), *netflixtechblog.com*, 6 April. Available at: https://netflixtechblog.com/netflix-recommendations-beyond-the-5-stars-part-1-55838468f429.

Ang, I. (1985) *Watching Dallas: Soap Opera and the Melodramatic Imagination*, London: Methuen.

Appadurai, A. (1990) 'Disjuncture and difference in the global cultural economy', in M. Featherstone (ed.), *Global Culture: Nationalism, Globalization and Modernity*, London: Sage, pp. 295–310.

Apple (2007) 'Award-winning MGM films now on the iTunes store, *apple.com*, 11 April. Available at: https://web.archive.org/web/20070416003909/www.apple.com/pr/library/2007/04/11itunes.html.

Aris, A. and Bughin, J. (2009) *Managing Media Companies: Harnessing Creative Value*, 2nd ed., Chichester: Wiley.

Arsenault, A. (2012) 'The structure and dynamics of communications business networks in an era of convergence: Mapping the global networks of the information business', in D. Winseck and D. Y. Jin (eds.), *The Political Economies of Media: The Transformation of the Global Media Industries*, London: Bloomsbury, pp. 101–20.

Ash, S. (2014) 'The development of submarine cables', in D. R. Burnett, R. C. Beckman, and T. M. Davenport (eds.), *Submarine Cables: The Handbook of Law and Policy*, Leiden: Martinus Nijhoff, pp. 19–60.

AT&T (2021) *2020 Annual Report*, Dallas, TX: AT&T.

Atkinson, L. (2017) 'Making OTT services better than broadcast', *AWS Media & Entertainment Symposium*, 4 December. Available at: www.slideshare.net/AmazonWebServices/making-ott-services-better-than-broadcast.

Bagdikian, B. H. (2004) *The New Media Monopoly*, Boston, MA: Beacon Press.

Bair, J. (2005) 'Global capitalism and commodity chains: Looking back, going forward', *Competition and Change*, 9(2): 153–80.

———(2009) 'Global commodity chains: Genealogy and review', in J. Bair (ed.) *Frontiers of Commodity Chain Research*, Stanford, CA: Stanford University Press, pp. 1–34.

Bakker, G. (2008) *Entertainment Industrialised: The Emergence of the International Film Industry, 1890–1940*, Cambridge: Cambridge University Press.

———(2012) 'How motion pictures industrialized entertainment', *The Journal of Economic History*, 72(4): 1036–63.

Baldwin, C. Y. (2008) 'Where do transactions come from? Modularity, transactions, and the boundaries of firms', *Industrial and Corporate Change*, 17(1): 155–95.

Baldwin, C. Y. and Woodard, C. J. (2009) 'The architecture of platforms: A unified view', in A. Gawer (ed.) *Platforms, Markets and Innovation*, Cheltenham: Edward Elgar, pp. 19–44.

Baldwin, R. (2013) 'Global supply chains: Why they emerged, why they matter, and where they are going', in D. B. Elms and P. Low (eds.), *Global Value Chains in a Changing World*, Geneva: World Trade Organization, pp. 13–59.

Ball, M. (2019a) 'Nine reasons why Disney+ will succeed (and why four criticisms are overhyped', *redef.com*, 17 March. Available at: https://redef.com/original/nine-reasons-why-disney-will-succeed-and-why-four-criticisms-are-overhyped.

———(2019b) 'The streaming wars: Its models, surprises, and remaining opportunities', *redef.com*, 12 July. Available at: https://redef.com/original/the-streaming-wars-its-models-surprises-and-remaining-opportunities.

Banerjee, I. (2002) 'The locals strike back? Media globalization and localization in the new Asian television landscape', *Gazette*, 64(6): 517–35.

Banks, M., Conor, B., and Mayer, V. (eds.) (2016) *Production Studies, The Sequel! Cultural Studies of Global Media Industries*, London: Routledge.

Barker, P. (1993) 'Nouvelles cuisine', *Cable & Satellite Europe*, February: 32.

Bartlett, C. A. and Ghoshal S. (1998) *Managing across Borders: The Transnational Solution*, 2nd ed., Boston, MA: Harvard Business School Press.

BBC (1946) 'Television is here again (1946) part one'. Available at: www.youtube.com/watch?v=b8XL0IfipLI.

Beck, U. (2000) 'The cosmopolitan perspective: Sociology of the second age of modernity', *British Journal of Sociology*, 51(1): 79–105.

———(2002) 'The cosmopolitan society and its enemies', *Theory, Culture & Society*, 19 (1–2): 17–44.

Beck, U. and Grande, E. (2010) 'Varieties of second modernity: The cosmopolitan turn in social and political theory and research', *The British Journal of Sociology*, 61(3): 409–43.

Bentaleb, A., Taani, B., Begen, A. C., Timmerer, C., and Zimmermann R. (2019) 'A survey on bitrate adaptation schemes for streaming media over HTTP', *IEEE Communications Surveys & Tutorials*, 21(1): 562–85.

Bernfeld, W. (2018) 'Telco and content world crossovers', *Content convergence: Why telcos need content and content providers need telco, IBC365 webinar*, 15 November. Available at: www.ibc.org/delivery/webinar-why-telcos-need-content-and-content-providers-need-telcos/3426.article.

Bernstein, W. (2009) *A Splendid Exchange: How Trade Shape the World*, London: Atlantic.

Bickerton, J. (2019a) 'Bankruptcy plan for post-production company Deluxe wins court approval', *screendaily.com*, 25 October. Available at: www.screendaily.com/news/bankruptcy-plan-for-post-production-company-deluxe-wins-court-approval/5144141.article.

———(2019b) 'Challenges of the post boom', *Broadcast TECH*, September 2019: 16–21.

Bisson, G. (2017) *SVoD Content Strategies: The Drive for Originality (Thinking Local, Going Global)*, London: Ampere Analysis.

Boudreau, B. (2016) *Global Submarine Cable Market Trends: What WAN Managers Need to Know*, San Diego, CA: TeleGeography.

———(2020) 'Pricing update: The TG decade challenge', *Pacific Telecommunications Council Annual Conference*, 19–22 January, Honolulu, HI.

Boudreau, Y. (2017) 'Podcast with Yves Boudreau talking heterogeneity in the edge', *soundcloud.com*, December. Available at: https://soundcloud.com/user-410091210/podcast-with-yves-boudreau-talking-heterogeneity-in-the-edge.

Bourdon, J. (2012) 'From discrete adaptations to hard copies: The rise of formats in European television' in T. Oren and S. Shahaf (eds.), *Global Television Formats: Understanding Television across Borders*, London: Routledge, pp. 117–27.

Boyd-Barrett, O. and D. K. Thussu (1992) *Contra-Flow in Global News: International and Regional News Exchange Mechanisms*, London: John Libbey.

Braudel, F. (1958) 'Histoire et Sciences Sociales: La longue durée', *Annales – Économies, Sociétés, Civilisations*, 13(4): 725–53.

———(1992a) *Civilization and Capitalism, 15th–18th Century, Volume I, The Structures of Every Day Life: The Limits of the Possible*, Berkeley: University of California Press.

———(1992b) *Civilization and Capitalism, 15th–18th Century, Volume I, The Wheels of Commerce*, Berkeley: University of California Press.

———(1992c) *Civilization and Capitalism, 15th–18th Century, Volume III, The Perspective of the World*, Berkeley: University of California Press

————(1996) *The Mediterranean and the Mediterranean World in the Age of Philip II, Volume 1*, Berkeley: University of California Press.

Briel, R. (2019) 'Netflix beats all SVOD services Europe', *Broadbandtvnews.com*, 6 March. Available at: www.broadbandtvnews.com/2019/03/06/netflix-beats-all-s-vod-services-in-europe.

Briggs, A. (1995). *The History of Broadcasting in the United Kingdom, Volume IV: Sound and Vision*, Oxford: Oxford University Press.

Brown, C. (2021) 'An industry transformed', *streamonomics.purely.capital*, 22 June. Available at: https://streamonomics.purely.capital/an-industry-transformed.

Brzoznowski, K. (2019) 'Keeping an eye on Big Brother', *worldscreen.com*, 16 September. Available at: https://worldscreen.com/tvformats/keeping-an-eye-on-big-brother.

Burgess, J. and Green J. (2018) *YouTube: Online Video and Participatory Culture*, 2nd ed., Cambridge: Polity.

Burke, P. (2015) *The French Historical Revolution: The Annales School, 1929-2014*, 2nd ed., Stanford, CA: Stanford University Press.

Bylykbashi, K. (2019) 'Will 2019 mark the end of niche SVOD?', *TBI*, October/November: 12–14.

C21 Media (2019) 'Africa Arrives', *2019 Global Drama Trends Report*: 71–5, London: C21 Media.

————(2019) 'Premium Player', *2019 Global Drama Trends Report*: 43–7, London: C21 Media.

Cable & Satellite Europe. (1994), 'A thorn on cable's side', January: 44.

Čandrlić, G. (2012) 'The history of Content Delivery Networks (CDN)', *globaldots.com*, 21 December. Available at: www.globaldots.com/blog/the-history-of-content-delivery-networks-cdn.

Carlini, S. (c.2020) 'Hyperscale: The next generation of data center architecture', *cisco.cioreview.com*. Available at: https://cisco.cioreview.com/cxoinsight/hyperscale-the-next-generation-of-data-center-architecture-nid-18356-cid-61.html.

Carrillo, J., Britto, J. and Gomis R. (2015) 'Industrial downgrading? The television industry in Mexico: Technological change and cluster "deformation"', *SASE Conference*, 2–4 July, London School of Economics and Political Science, UK.

Carugati, A. (2020) 'Walter presents' Walter Iuzzolino', *worldscreen.com*, 13 October. Available at: https://worldscreen.com/tvdrama/walter-presents-walter-iuzzolino-mipcom2020.

Castells, M. (2008) 'The new public sphere: Global civil society, communication networks, and global governance', *The Annals of the American Academy of Political and Social Science*, 616(1): 78–93.

————(2009) *Communication Power*, Oxford: Oxford University Press.

Caves R. E. (2000) *Creative Industries: Contracts between Art and Commerce*, Cambridge, MA: Harvard University Press.

Cerf, V. (2019) 'SubOptic 2019 Day 4 Keynote', 11 April, *suboptic2019.com*. Available at: https://suboptic2019.com/suboptic-2019-day-4-keynote.

Chalaby, J. K. (2005a) 'Deconstructing the transnational: A typology of cross-border television channels in Europe', *New Media & Society*, 7(2): 155–75.

————(ed.) (2005b) *Transnational Television Worldwide: Towards a New Media Order*, London: I. B. Tauris.

————(2009) *Transnational Television in Europe: Reconfiguring Global Communications Networks*, London: I. B. Tauris.

————(2010) 'The rise of Britain's super-indies: Policy-making in the age of the global market', *International Communication Gazette*, 72(8): 675–93.

————(2011) 'The making of an entertainment revolution: How the TV format trade became a global industry', *European Journal of Communication*, 26(4): 293–309.

————(2016a) 'Drama without drama: The late rise of scripted TV formats', *Television & New Media*, 17(1): 3–20.

————(2016b) *The Format Age: Television's Entertainment Revolution*, Cambridge: Polity.

————(2016c) 'Television and globalization: The TV content global value chain', *Journal of Communication*, 66(1): 35–59.

————(2017) 'Can a GVC-oriented policy mitigate the inequalities of the world media system? Strategies for economic upgrading in the TV format global value chain', *International Journal of Digital Television*, 8(1): 9–28.

————(2018) 'Hedging against disaster: Risk and mitigation in the media and entertainment industries', *International Journal of Digital Television*, 9(2): 167–84.

————(2019) 'Outsourcing in the U.K. television industry: A global value chain analysis', *Communication Theory*, 29(2): 169–90.

————(2021) 'Global streamers: Placing the transnational at the heart of TV culture', *Journal of Digital Media & Policy*, FastTrack, https://doi.org/10.1386/jdmp_00083_1.

Chalaby, J. K. and Esser, A. (eds.) (2017) Special issue: The TV format trade and the world media system, *International Journal of Digital Television*, 8(1): 1–165.

Chan-Olmsted, S. M. (1998) 'Mergers, acquisitions, and convergence: The strategic alliances of broadcasting, cable television, and telephone services', *The Journal of Media Economics*, 11(3), 33–46.

Chan-Olmsted, S. M. and Wirth, M. O. (eds.) (2006) *Handbook of Media Management and Economics*, Mahwah, NJ: Lawrence Erlbaum.

Chandrashekar, A., Amat, F., Basilico, J., and Jebara, T. (2017) 'Artwork personalization at Netflix', *netflixtechblog.com*, 7 December. Available at: https://netflixtechblog.com/art work-personalization-c589f074ad76.

Chesnoy, J. (2016) 'Presentation of submarine fiber communication', in J. Chesnoy (ed.) Undersea Fiber Communication *Systems*, 2nd ed., London: Academic Press, pp. 3–19.

Chin, M. (2021) 'TikTok reduces India staff after long-standing countrywide ban', *theverge.com*, 3 February. Available at: www.theverge.com/2021/2/2/22262940/tiktok-leaves-india-ban-app-china-government-security-privacy.

China Telecom (2020) *Connecting Infinity Empowering Future – Annual Report 2019*, Beijing: China Telecom Corporation.

Chon, B. S., Choi J. H., Barnett G. A., Danowski J. A., and Joo, S.-H. (2003) 'A structural analysis of media convergence: Cross-industry mergers and acquisitions in the information industries', *Journal of Media Economics*, 16(3): 141–57.

Chrisafis, A (2020) 'France's digital minister says tax on big tech is just the start', *theguardian.com*, 12 January. Available at: www.theguardian.com/world/2020/jan/12/frances-digital-minister-tax-on-tech-giants-just-the-start-cedric-o-gafa.

Christopherson, S. (2012) 'Hard jobs in Hollywood: How concentration in Distribution affects the production side of the media entertainment industry', in D. Winseck and D. Y. Jin (eds.), *The Political Economies of Media: The Transformation of the Global Media Industries*, London: Bloomsbury, pp. 123–41.

Church, S. (2020) 'This is how much YouTube paid me for my 1,000,000 viewed video', *onezero.medium.com*, 3 April. Available at: https://onezero.medium.com/this-is-how-much-youtube-paid-me-for-my-1-000-000-viewed-video-1453cad73847.

Cisco (2018) *Cisco Visual Networking Index: Forecast and Trends, 2017–2022*, San Jose, CA: Cisco.

CISAC (2014) *The Creative Industries and the BRICS: A Review of the State of the Creative Economy in Brazil, Russia, India, China and South Africa*, Paris: CISAC.

Coates, J. C. Jr. (2018) 'Mergers, acquisitions, and restructuring: Types, regulation, and patterns of practice', in J. N. Gordon and W.-G. Ringe (eds.), *The Oxford Handbook of Corporate Law and Governance*, Oxford: Oxford University Press, pp. 570–602.

Codding, G. A., Jr. (1990) *The Future of Satellite Communications*, Boulder, CO: Westview.

Coe, N. M. and Yeung, H. W.-C. (2015) *Global Production Networks: Theorizing Economic Development in an Interconnected World*, Oxford: Oxford University Press.

———(2019) 'Global production networks: Mapping recent conceptual developments', *Journal of Economic Geography*, 19: 775–801.

Collins, R. (1992) *Satellite Television in Western Europe*, revised ed., London: John Libbey.

———(1998) *From Satellite to Single Market: New Communication Technology and European Public Service Television*, London: Routledge.

Comcast (2021) *2020 Annual Report*, Philadelphia, PA: Comcast.

———(2020) *Investor meeting*, 16 January. Available at: https://corporate.comcast.com/peacockinvestormeeting.

Considine, P. (1997) 'Difficult Brits play co-pro game', *Broadcast Supplement – MIPCOM Special*, 26 September: 16–17.

Contractor, F. J., Kumar, V., Kundu, S. K., and Pedersen, T. (2011a). *Global Outsourcing and Offshoring: An Integrated Approach to Theory and Corporate Strategy*, Cambridge: Cambridge University Press.

Contractor, F. J., Kumar, V., Kundu, S. K., and Pedersen T. (2011b), 'Global outsourcing and offshoring: In search of the optimal configuration for a company' in F. J. Contractor, V. Kumar, S. K. Kundu, and T. Pedersen (eds.), *Global Outsourcing and Offshoring: An Integrated Approach to Theory and Corporate Strategy*, Cambridge: Cambridge University Press, pp. 3–46.

Cooper, T. (2018) 'Google owns 63,605 miles and 8.5% of submarine cables worldwide', *broadbandnow.com*, 12 September. Available at: https://broadbandnow.com/report/google-content-providers-submarine-cable-ownership.

Cooper-Chen, A. (ed.) (2005) *Global Entertainment Media: Content, Audiences, Issues*, Mahwah, NJ: Lawrence Erlbaum.

Cox, P. (1985) 'Sky: Still leading the pack', *Cable & Satellite Europe*, April: 22.

Crawford, S. (2013). *Captive Audience: The Telecom Industry and Monopoly Power in the New Gilded Age*, New Haven, CT: Yale University Press.

Crawford, S. (2021) 'Where the hell are all the formats?', *tbivision.com*, 26 August. Available at: https://tbivision.com/2021/08/26/where-the-hell-are-all-the-formats.

Cunningham, S. and Craig, D. (2019) *Social Media Entertainment: The New Intersection of Hollywood and Silicon Valley*, New York: New York University Press.

Curran, J. and Park, M.-J. (eds.) (2000*)* De-Westernizing Media Studies, London: Routledge.

Curry, E. (2016) 'The big data value chain: Definitions, concepts, and theoretical approaches', in J. M. Cavanillas, E. Curry, and W. Wahlster (eds.), *New Horizons for a Data-Driven Economy: A Roadmap for Usage and Exploitation of Big Data in Europe*, Switzerland: Springer Open, pp. 29–37.

Curtin, M. and Sanson, K. (eds.) (2016) *Precarious Creativity: Global Media, Local Labor*, Oakland: University of California Press.

Curtis, C. (2014) 'Mahon lifts lid on Endemol deal', *Broadcast*, 12 September: 1.

Daily Sabah (2019) 'Popular Turkish TV series raise exports of goods, services', 10 November. Available at: www.dailysabah.com/business/2019/11/10/popular-turkish-tv-series-raise-exports-of-goods-services.

Dams, T. (2019a) 'Apple bits into the streaming market', *ibc.org*, 31 October. Available at: www.ibc.org/publish/apple-bites-into-the-streaming-market/5153.article.

———(2019b) 'Quibi: Assessing the appetite for snackable streaming', *ibc.org*, 9 December. Available at: www.ibc.org/industry-trends/quibi-assessing-the-appetite-for-snackable-streaming/5272.article.

Darlow, M. (2004) *Independent Struggle: The Programme Makers Who Took on the TV Establishment*, London: Quarter.

DCD London (2019) 'Plenary panel: How should the data center industry now respond to the global climate emergency?', *DCD Europe Conference*, 5–6 November, Old Bilingsgate, London, UK. Available at: www.datacenterdynamics.com/en/conferences/london/2019/plenary-panel-how-should-data-center-industry-now-respond-global-climate-emergency.

DCD Magazine (2021) 'Hyperscale operator building reaches $150 billion in a year', July: 6.

Del Rey J. (2020) '6 reasons smaller companies want to break up Big Tech', *vox.com*, 22 January. Available at: www.vox.com/recode/2020/1/22/21070898/big-tech-antitrust-amazon-apple-google-facebook-house-hearing-congress-break-up.

Deloitte Sports Business Group (2021) *Testing Times: Football Money League*, London: Deloitte.

DePamphilis, D. M. (2019) *Mergers, Acquisitions, and Other Restructuring Activities: An Integrated Approach to Process, Tools, Cases, and Solutions*, 10th ed., London: Academic Press.

Devoncroft (2017) *Observations and Analysis of the Media Technology Industry*, Coronado, CA: Devoncroft.

———(2018) *The Devoncroft Media and Entertainment Cloud Adoption Index*, Coronado, CA: Devoncroft.

Dicken, P. (2015) *Global Shift: Mapping the Changing Contours of the World Economy*, 7th ed., New York, NY: The Guilford Press.

Digital, Culture, Media and Sport Committee (2021) *The Future of Public Service Broadcasting – Sixth Report of Session 2019–21*, London: House of Commons.

Discovery (2019) *Annual Report 2018*, Silver Spring (MA): Discovery.

Doerr, J. (2018) *Measure What Matters: OKRs – The Simple Idea That Drives 10x Growth*, London: Penguin Business.

Dong, S.-H. (2020) '"Viewership is not everything": K-dramas find norm-breaking recipe for success', *The Korea Times*, 25 July. Available at: www.koreatimes.co.kr/www/art/2020/07/688_293337.html.

Dorfman, A. and Mattelart, A. (1975) *How to Read Donald Duck: Imperialist Ideology in the Disney Comic*, New York, NY: International General.

Dover, B. (2009) *Rupert's Adventures in China: How Murdoch Lost a Fortune and Found a Wife*, Edinburgh: Mainstream.

Doyle, G. (2013) *Understanding Media Economics*, 2nd ed., London: Sage.

———(2016) 'Digitization and changing windowing strategies in the television industry: Negotiating new windows on the world', *Television & New Media*, 17(7): 629–45.

EAO (2017) *Trends in the EU SVOD Market*, Strasbourg: EAO.

———(2018a) *Audiovisual Media in Europe: Localised, Targeting and Language Offers*. Strasbourg: EAO.

———(2018b) *Online Video Sharing: Offerings, Audiences, Economic Aspects*, Strasbourg: EAO.

———(2018c) *The Production and Circulation of TV Fiction in the EU28*, Strasbourg: EAO.

Economy, E. C. (2018) *The Third Revolution: Xi Jinping and the New Chinese State*, New York, NY: Oxford University Press.

EDRi (2012) 'WCIR: what happened and what it means for the Internet', *edri.org*, 19 December. Available at: https://edri.org/our-work/edrigramnumber10-24wcit-what-happend.

Eisenstein, E. L. (1980) *The Printing Press as an Agent of Change: Communications and Cultural Transformations in Early-Modern Europe*, Cambridge: Cambridge University Press.

Elasmar, M. G. (ed.) (2003) *The Impact of International Television: A Paradigm Shift.* Mahwah, NJ: Lawrence Erlbaum.

El-Nawawy, M. and A. Iskander (2002) *Al-Jazeera: How the Free Arab News Network Scooped the World and Changed the Middle East*, Cambridge, MA: Westview.

Esser, A. (2002) 'The transnationalization of European television', *Journal of European Area Studies*, 10(1): 13–29.

European Commission (2020) *Shaping Europe's Digital Future*, Luxembourg: Publications Office of the European Union.

Eutelsat (2020) *Universal Registration Document, 2019-20*, Paris: Eutelsat.

Evans, J. (2016) 'Mastering chaos: A Netflix guide to microservices', *QCon San Francisco*, 8 November. Available at: www.youtube.com/watch?v=CZ3wIuvmHeM.

Feenstra R. C. (1998) 'Integration of trade and disintegration of production in the global economy', *Journal of Economic Perspectives*, 12(4): 31–50.

Fejes, F. (1981) 'Media imperialism: An assessment', *Media, Culture & Society*, 3(3): 281–9.

Fernandez-Stark, K., Bamber, P. and Gereffi, G. (2014) 'Global value chains in Latin America: A development perspective for upgrading', in R. A. Hernández, J. M. Martínez-Piva, and N. Mulder (eds.), *Global Value Chains and World Trade: Prospects and Challenges for Latin America*, Santiago: Economic Commission for Latin America and the Caribbean, pp. 79–106.

Fernandez-Stark, K., Frederick, S., and Gereffi, G. (2011) *The Apparel Global Value Chain: Economic Upgrading and Workforce Development*, Durham, NC: Center on Globalization, Governance & Competitiveness, Duke University.

Fiorino, E. (2019) 'From SDI to IP: The evolution of distribution', *smpte.org*. Available at: www.smpte.org/sdi-ip-evolution-distribution.

FitzGerald, D., Flint, J., and Mullin, B. (2021) 'AT&T's Hollywood ending erased billions in value; Telecom giant is giving up its dreams of marrying content and distribution – one of the biggest about-faces in corporate deal history', *wsj.com*, 18 May. Available at: www.wsj.com/articles/att-hollywood-ending-erased-billions-value-hbo-discovery-warner-11621297279.

Flew, T. (2013) *Global Creative Industries*, Cambridge: Polity.

Flex (2018) *Annual Report: Intelligence of Things*, Singapore: Flex.

Florida, R. (2005) 'The world is spiky', *The Atlantic Monthly*, 296(3): 48–51.

Flournoy, D. and Stewart, R. (1997) *CNN: Making News in the Global Market*, Luton: University of Luton Press.

Fontanella-Khan, J. and Nicolaou, A. (2021) 'AT&T nears deal to create $150bn streaming giant with Discovery', *ft.com*, 16 May. Available at: https://tinyurl.com/2jp9727e.

Foster, N., Steher, R., and Timmer, M. (2013). *International Fragmentation of Production, Trade and Growth: Impacts and Prospects for EU Member States*. Economic Papers 484, Brussels: European Commission.

Forbes (1999) Microsoft vs. RealNetworks. *Forbes.com*, 5 March. Available at: www.forbes .com/1999/03/05/feat.html#617638066ce0.

Foster-McGregor, N., Kaulich, F., and Stehrer, R. (2015) *Global Value Chains in Africa*, Vienna: United Nations Industrial Development Organization.

Fouchard, G. (2016) 'Historical overview of submarine communication systems', in J. Chesnoy (ed.) *Undersea Fiber Communication Systems*, 2nd ed., London: Academic Press, pp. 21–52.

FRAPA (2009) *The FRAPA Report 2009: TV Formats to the World*, Cologne: FRAPA.

Freeman, C. (1987) 'The challenges of new technologies', in *Interdependence and Co-operation in Tomorrow's World*, Paris: OECD, pp. 123–56.

Friedman, T. (2006) *The World Is Flat: The Globalized World in the Twenty-First Century*, London: Penguin.

Frot-Coutaz, C. (2019) 'IBC 2019 conference keynote: Opening keynote', *IBC Show 2019*, 12–16 September, Amsterdam. Available at: www.youtube.com/watch?v=hAsF7gSJIj8.

Fry, A. (1997) 'Export strength', *Broadcast Supplement – MIP TV Special*, 11 April: 9.

Fry, A. and Hazleton, J. (1999) 'Hollywood under scrutiny', *Broadcast – Mipcom Supplement*, 1 October: 2–3.

———(2019) 'Central perks', *c21media.net*, 12 April. Available at: www.c21media.net/379583-2.

———(2020) 'Fresh opportunities on horizon', *Broadcast – Distributors Survey 2019*: 14–18.

Gallagher, K. (2018) 'Scripted shows made for streaming services have surpassed cable and broadcast', *businessinsider.com*, 14 December. Available at: www.businessinsider.com/netflix-hulu-scripted-shows-surpass-cable-2018-12?r=US&IR=T.

Galloway, J. F. (1972) *The Politics and Technology of Satellite Communications*, Lexington, MA: Lexington Books.

Gamerman, E. (2020) 'What Netflix's lists of top foreign movies and TV series say about American taste', *www.wsj.com*, 9 December. Available at: www.wsj.com/articles/what-netflixs-lists-of-top-foreign-movies-and-tv-series-say-about-american-taste-11607562001.

García Canclini, N. (1995) *Hybrid Cultures: Strategies for Entering and Leaving Modernity*, Minneapolis: University of Minnesota Press.

Gawer, A. (2009) 'Platform dynamics and strategies: from products to services', in A. Gawer (ed.) *Platforms, Markets and Innovation*, Cheltenham: Edward Elgar, pp. 45–76.

———(2014) 'Bridging differing perspectives on technological platforms: Toward an integrative framework', *Research Policy*, 43(7): 1239–49.

Georgiou, M. (2012) 'Media, diaspora, and the transnational context: Cosmopolitanizing cross-national comparative research?', in I. Volkmer (ed.) (2012) *The Handbook of Global Media Research*, Chichester: Wiley-Blackwell, pp. 365–80.

Gereffi, G. (1994) 'The organization of buyer-driven global commodity chains: How U.S. retailers shape overseas production networks', in G. Gereffi and M. Korzeniewicz (eds.), *Commodity Chains and Global Capitalism*, Westport, CT: Praeger, pp. 95–122.

———(1999) 'International trade and industrial upgrading in the apparel commodity chain', *Journal of International Economics*, 48(1): 37–70.

———(2014) 'Global value chains in a post-Washington Consensus world', *Review of International Political Economy*, 21(1): 9–37.

Gereffi, G. and Fernandez-Stark, K. (2016). *Global Value Chain Analysis: A Primer*, 2nd ed., Duke University, Durham, NC: Center on Globalization, Governance & Competitiveness.

Gereffi, G., Humphrey, J., Kaplinsky, R., and Sturgeon, T. J. (2001) 'Introduction: globalisation, value chains and development, *IDS Bulletin*, 32(3): 1–8.

Gereffi, G., Humphrey, J., and Sturgeon, T. J. (2005) 'The governance of global value chains', *Review of International Political Economy*, 12(1), 78–103.

Gereffi, G. and Korzeniewicz, M. (eds.) (1994) *Commodity Chains and Global Capitalism*, Westport, CT: Praeger.

Gereffi, G., Korzeniewicz, M., and Korzeniewicz, R. P. (1994) 'Introduction: Global commodity chains', in G. Gereffi and M. Korzeniewicz (eds.), *Commodity Chains and Global Capitalism*, Westport: Praeger, pp. 1–14.

Gereffi, G. and Sturgeon, T. J. (2013) 'Global value chains-oriented industry policy: the role of emerging economies', in D. K. Elms and P. Low (eds.), *Global Value Chains in a Changing World*, Geneva: WTO, pp. 329–60.

Gilboa, E. (2005) 'The CNN effect: The search for a communication theory of international relations', *Political Communication*, 22: 27–44.

Gittlen, S. (1998) 'Internet braces for Clinton's video testimony', *CNN.com*, 17 September. Available at http://edition.cnn.com/TECH/computing/9809/17/videobc.idg/index.html.

Glaser, R. (c 2015) founder & CEO, RealNetworks, interview with Brian McCover, *Internet History Podcast*. Available at: https://hwcdn.libsyn.com/p/7/4/8/748c13c58cb59a60/Ch._5_Int._4_-_Real_Networks_CEO_Rob_Glaser.mp3?c_id=7598746&cs_id=7598746&expiration=1586687868&hwt=dc4d4da45abd0472d8789c472f25b625.

Grand View Research (2020) 'Video streaming market size, share & trends analysis report', February. Available at: www.grandviewresearch.com/industry-analysis/video-streaming-market.

Graz, J.-C. (2019) *The Power of Standards: Hybrid Authority and the Globalisation of Services*, Cambridge: Cambridge University Press.

Grey, V. (1997) 'Stetting standards: A phenomenal success story', in *Friendship among Equals: Recollections from ISO's First Fifty Years*, ISO: Geneva, pp. 33–42.

Griffiths, J. (2019) *The Great Firewall of China: How to Build and Control and Alternative Version of the Internet*, London: Zed Books.

Griffiths, R. (2018) Vice President, Huawei Consultant Office, 'Media convergence in 2018', in *Content convergence: Why telcos need content and content providers need telco, IBC365 webinar*, 15 November. Available at: www.ibc.org/delivery/webinar-why-telcos-need-content-and-content-providers-need-telcos/3426.article.

Guider, E. (2005) 'Talbot created int'l formats', *Variety*, 18 July: 48.

Guider, E. and Hils, M. (1997) 'MGM, Kirch cinch digital output deal', *variety.com*, 29 April. Available at: https://variety.com/1997/scene/vpage/mgm-kirch-cinch-digital-output-deal-1117433620.

Gustafsson, V. and Schwarz, E. J. (2013). 'Business modelling and convergence', in S. Diehl and M. Karmasin (eds.), *Media and Convergence Management*, Heidelberg: Springer, pp. 9–23.

Habermas, J. (1989) *The Structural Transformation of the Public Sphere*, Cambridge: Polity Press.

Hacklin, F., Klang, D. and Baschera, P. (2013) 'Managing the convergence of industries: Archetypes for successful business models', in S. Diehl and M. Karmasin (eds.), *Media and Convergence Management*, Heidelberg: Springer, pp. 25–36.

Hahn, D. (2015) 'A day in the life of a Netflix engineer using 37% of the Internet', *AWS re: Invent*, Las Vegas, 6–9 October. Available at: www.youtube.com/watch?v=-mL3zT1iIKw.

Hale, J. (2019) 'More than 500 of content are now being uploaded to YouTube every minute', *tubefilter.com*, 7 May. Available at: www.tubefilter.com/2019/05/07/number-hours-video-uploaded-to-youtube-per-minute.

Hamburger, E. (2020) 'Transnational mediation, telenovela and series', in S. Shimpach (ed.), *The Routledge Companion to Global Television*, New York, NY: Routledge, pp. 175–89.

Hamelink, C. (1997) 'MacBride with hindsight', in P. Golding and P. Harris (eds.), *Beyond Cultural Imperialism*, London: Sage, pp. 69–93.

Han, J. K, Chung, S. W., and Sohn, Y. S. (2009) 'Technology convergence: When do consumers prefer converged products to dedicated products?' *Journal of Marketing* 73 (July): 97–108.

Hastings, R. and Meyer, E. (2020) *No Rules: Netflix and the Culture of Reinvention*, London: WH Allen.

Havens, T. (2006) *Global Television Marketplace*, London: British Film Institute.

Hecht, J. (2018) 'Submarine cable goes for record: 144,000 gibabits from Hong Kong to L.A. in 1 second', 5 January, *news.itu.int*. Available at: https://news.itu.int/submarine-cable-hk-la.

Herman, E. S. and McChesney, R. W. (1997) *The Global Media: The New Missionaries of Corporate Capitalism*, London: Cassell.

Hess, T. and Matt, C. (2013) 'The Internet and the value chains of the media industry', in S. Diehl and M. Karmasin (eds.), *Media and Convergence Management*, Heidelberg: Springer, pp. 37–55.

Hills, J. (2002) *The Struggle for Control of Global Communication: The Formative Century*, Urbana: University of Illinois.

HMSO (1861) *Report of the Joint Committee Appointed by the Lords of the Committee of Privy Council for Trade the Atlantic Telegraph Company to Inquire into the Construction of Submarine Telegraph Cables; together with the Minutes of Evidence and Appendix*, London: HMSO.

Holleran, T. (2020) 'SVoD subscriptions to overtake pay TV in more than 30 countries by end of 2020', *Ampere Analysis*, 20 January. Available at: www.ampereanalysis.com/insight/svod-subscriptions-to-overtake-pay-tv-in-more-than-30-countries-by-end-of-2020.

Holt, J. and Perren, A. (eds.) (2009) *Media Industries: History, Theory, and Method*, Chichester: Wiley-Blackwell.

Hopkins, T. K. and Wallerstein, I. (1977) 'Patterns of development of the modern world-system', *Review* 1(2): 111–45.

———(1986) 'Commodity chains in the world economy prior to 1800', *Review* 10(1): 157–70.

Horsman, M. (1997) *Sky High: The Amazing Story of BskyB – and the Egos, Deals and Ambitions that Revolutionised TV Broadcasting*, London: Orion Business.

IBC Showcase (2020) 'Transformation of content delivery and linear playout', panel conversation with J. Arnold, A. Dubiez, J. Stinehour, and J. Zaller, *ibc.org*, 9 September. Available at: www.ibc.org/exhibitor-programmes/business-transform ation-in-an-uncertain-world/6393.article.

IBC365 Webinar (2020) 'CDNs: Building a better video experience', *ibc.org*, 5 August. Available at: www.ibc.org/webinars-and-papers/cdns-building-a-better-video-experi ence/6366.article.

———(2021) 'CDNs: Delivering a seamless and engaging viewing experience', *ibc.org*, 17 February. Available at: www.ibc.org/webinars/cdns-delivering-a-seamless-and-engaging-viewing-experience/7166.article.

ILO (2016) *Decent Work in Global Supply Chains*, Geneva: International Labour Office.

Ingold, M. (2020) 'Tech expert: Inside OTT', *ibc.org*, 30 January. Available at: https://tinyurl.com/442mh86e.

Intelsat (2020) *Annual Report 2019*, Luxembourg: Intelsat.

———(2021) *Annual Report 2020*, Luxembourg: Intelsat.

International Bank for Reconstruction and Development/The World Bank (2017) *Global Value Chain Development Report 2017: Measuring and Analyzing the Impact of GVCs on Economic Development*, Washington, DC: The World Bank.

Ishita, S. (2000) 'Television genre and audience: Quiz shows in Japanese television', *Studies in the Humanities: Bulletin of the Faculty of Literature and Human Sciences*, 52(5): 25–38.

ITU (2012) 'WCIT2012: Signatures of the final acts: 89', *itu.int*. Available at: www.itu.int/osg/wcit-12/highlights/signatories.html.

———(2019a) 'Why do we need international standards in telecommunications?', *itu.int*. Available at: www.itu.int/net/ITU-T/info/answers.aspx?Fp=faqs.aspx&Qn=2&ewm= False.

———(2019b) 'ITU-T Recommendations', *itu.int*. Available at: www.itu.int/en/ITU-T/publications/Pages/recs.aspx.

ITV (2020) *Accelerating ITV's Digital Transformation – ITV plc Annual Reports and Accounts for the year ended 31 December 2019*, London: ITV.

Jacobides, M. G., Cennamo, C., and Gawer, A. (2018) 'Towards a theory of ecosystems', *Strategic Management Journal*, 39(8): 2255–76.

Jarnikov, D. and Özçelebi, T. (2011) 'Client intelligence for adaptive streaming solutions', *Signal Processing: Image Communication*, 26(7): 378–89.

Ji, S. W. and Waterman, D. (2015) 'Vertical ownership, technology and programming content', in R. G. Picard and S. S. Wildman (eds.), *Handbook on the Economics of the Media*, Cheltenham: Edward Elgar Publishing, pp. 36–52.

Jia, L. and Liang, F. (2021) 'The globalization of TikTok: Strategies, governance and geopolitics', *Journal of Digital Media & Policy*, 12(2): 273–92.

Jin, D. Y. (2013) *De-convergence of Global Media Industries*, New York, NY: Routledge.

———(2016) *New Korean Wave: Transnational Cultural Power in the Age of Social Media*, Urbana: University of Illinois Press.

Johnson, C. (2019) *Online TV*, London: Routledge.

Jones, G. (2005) *Multinationals and Global Capitalism: From the Nineteenth to the Twenty-First Century*, Oxford: Oxford University Press.

Jones, M. (1995a) 'Analysis', *Broadcast – The Indie Survey*, 21 July: 5.

———(1995b) 'Denied the big time', *Broadcast – Indie Special*, 5 May: 9.

———(1996) 'Who wants to rule the world?', *Broadcast – MIP TV Special*, 19 April: 22–3.

Jowitt, T. (2019) 'Google transatlantic cable transmits 250TB/s of data', *silicon.co.uk*, 10 April. Available at: www.silicon.co.uk/cloud/datacenter/google-transatlantic-cable-250tbs-243821.

Junni, P. and Teerikangas, S. (2019) 'Mergers and acquisitions', *Oxford Research Encylopedia of Business and Management*. Available at: https://oxfordre.com/business/view/10.1093/acrefore/9780190224851.001.0001/acrefore-9780190224851-e-15?rskey=o7QGo9&result=1.

K7 Media (2019) *Tracking the Giants: The Top 100 Travelling Unscripted Formats, 2018-19*, Manchester: K7 Media.

———(2021) *Tracking the Giants: The Top 100 Travelling Unscripted Formats, 2020-2021*, Manchester: K7 Media. Available at https://k7.media/tracking_the_giants.

Kava, J. (2020) Vice President Global Data Centres, Gloogle Cloud, 'Green zettabytes: How we power global computing in a low-carbon economy', *DCD New York Virtual Conference*, 31 March–2 April. Available at: https://tinyurl.com/yxnjnzks.

Keane, M. and Zhang, J. D. (2017) 'Formats, cultural security and China's going out policy', *International Journal of Digital Television*, 8(1): 65–80.

Kempton, M. (2020). 'Introduction', *tvstudiohistory.co.uk*. Available at: www.tvstudiohistory.co.uk/introduction.htm.

Kenney, M., Bearson, D., and Zysman, J. (2021) 'The platform economy matures: Measuring pervasiveness and exploring power', *Socio-Economic Review*. DOI: 10.1093/ser/mwab014.

Kenney, M. and Zysman, J. (2016) 'The rise of the platform economy', *Issues in Science and Technology*, 32(3): 61–9.

Khalil, J. F. (2017) 'From Big Brother to Al Maleka: The growing pains of TV format trade in the Arab region', *International Journal of Digital Television*, 8(1): 29–46.

Khalsa, B. (2013) 'C5 and cashflow worry for indies', *Broadcast*, 31 May: 1.

Kieve, J. (1973) *The Electric Telegraph: A Social and Economic History*, Newton Abbot: David & Charles.

Kim, Y. (ed.) (2013a) *The Korean Wave: Korean Media Go Global*, Abingdon: Routledge.

———(2013b) 'Introduction', in Y. Kim (ed.), *The Korean Wave: Korean Media Go Global*, Abingdon: Routledge, pp. 1–28

Kirkpatrick, J. (2004) 'Neoconservatism as a response to the counter-culture', in I. Stelzer (ed.) *Neoconservatism*, London: Atlantic Books, pp. 235–40.

Klinge, N. (2020) 'Watch parties and K-pop. How San Mateo streamer Rakuten Viki is growing in a pandemic', *latimes.com*, 22 July. Available at: www.latimes.com/entertainment-arts/business/story/2020-07-22/kpop-rakuten-viki-korean-dramas-streaming-watch-parties-parasite.

Krechmer, K. (2014) 'Standardization: A primer', *Proceedings of the 2014 ITU Kaleidoscope Academic Conference* (3–5 June, St. Petersburg, Russian Federation), Geneva: ITU.

Küng, L. (2017) *Strategic Management in the Media: Theory to Practice*, 2nd ed., London: Sage.

Kunz, W. M. (2007) *Culture Conglomerates: Consolidation in the Motion Picture and Television Industries*, Lanham: Rowman & Littlefield.

Kyncl, R. and Peyvan, M. (2017) *Streampunks: How YouTube and the New Creators Are Transforming Our Lives*, London: Virgin.

Labrador, V. S. and Galace, P. I. (2005) *Heavens Fill with Commerce: A Brief History of the Communications Satellite Industry*, Sonoma, CA: Satnews.

Langlois R. N. (2003) 'The vanishing hand: The changing dynamics of industrial capitalism', *Industrial and Corporate Change*, 12(2): 351–85.

Lavender, A. (1993) 'Edge of darkness (Troy Kennedy Martin)', in G. W. Brandt (ed.) *British Television Drama in the 1980s*, Cambridge: Cambridge University Press, pp. 103–18.

Lee, C. S. (2018) *Soft Power Made in China: The Dilemmas of Online and Offline Media and Transnational Audiences*, London: Palgrave Macmillan.

Lee, J. (2010) 'Global commodity chains and global value chains', in R. A. Denemark (ed.) *The International Studies Encyclopedia*, Oxford: Wiley-Blackwell, pp. 2987–3006.

Lee, J. and Lee, M. (2019) 'Governance and upgrading in global cultural and creative value chains', in S. Ponte, G. Gereffi, and G. Raj-Reichert (eds.) *Handbook on Global Value Chains*, Cheltenham: Edward Elgar, pp. 138–52.

Lee, J. and Lim, H.-C. (2018) *Mobile Asia: Capitalisms, Value Chains and Mobile Telecommunication in Asia*, Seoul: Seoul National University Press.

Lerner, D. (1958) *The Passing of Traditional Society: Modernizing the Middle East*, New York, NY: The Free Press.

Levinson, M. (2006) *The Box: How the Shipping Container Made the World Smaller and the World Economy Bigger*, Princeton, NJ: Princeton University Press.

Li & Fung (2019) 'Our reach', *lifung.com*. Available at: www.lifung.com/about-lf/our-reach.

Liebes, T. and Katz, E. (1993) *The Export of Meaning: Cross-Cultural Readings of Dallas*, Cambridge: Polity.

Lobato, R. (2019) *Netflix Nations: The Geography of Digital Distribution*, New York: New York University Press.

Lobato, R. and Meese, J. (eds.) (2016) *Geoblocking and Global Video Culture*, Amsterdam: Institute of Network Cultures.

Lotz, A. D. (2007) *The Television Will Be Revolutionized*, New York: New York University Press.

Macaulay, T. (2018) 'Ten years on: How Netflix completed a historic cloud migration with AWS', *Computerworld*, 10 September. Available at www.computerworld.com/article/3427839/ten-years-on-netflix-completed-a-historic-cloud-migration-with-aws.thml.

MacBride, S. (1980) *Many Voices One World*, London: Kogan Page; Paris: Unesco.

Madrigal, A. (2014) 'How Netflix reverse-engineered Hollywood', *theatlantic.com*, 2 January. Available at: www.theatlantic.com/technology/archive/2014/01/how-netflix-reverse-engineered-hollywood/282679.

Malim, G. (2018) 'How telcos are pushing into content', *ibc.org*, 23 July. Available at: www.ibc.org/publish/how-telcos-are-pushing-into-content/2981.article.

MarketsandMarkets (2020) 'Submarine cable system market by application (communication (component, offering (installation & commissioning, upgrades)), power (type, voltage, end user (offshore wind power generation, offshore oil & gas), and region – global forecast to 2025', *marketsandmarkets.com*, February. Available at: www.marketsandmarkets .com/Market-Reports/submarine-cable-system-market-184625.html.

MarketWatch (2019) 'Pay TV services market: Key vendors, trends, analysis, segmentation, forecast to 2019–2026', 25 September. Available at: www.marketwatch.com/press-release/pay-tv-services-market-key-vendors-trends-analysis-segmentation-forecast-to-2019-2026-2019-09-25.

Maroulis, T. (2018) 'Media-Telco convergence', in *Content convergence: Why telcos need content and content providers need telco, IBC365 webinar*, 15 November. Available at: www.ibc.org/delivery/webinar-why-telcos-need-content-and-content-providers-need-telcos/3426.article.

Matsnev, O. (2019) 'Kremlin moves toward control of Internet, raising censorship fears', *The New York Times*, 11 April. Available at: www.nytimes.com/2019/04/11/world/europe/russia-internet-censorship.html.

Mattelart, A. (1979) *Multinational Corporations and the Control of Culture. The Ideological Apparatuses of Imperialism*, Lewes: Harvester Press.

McCann, K. (2020) 'IBC tech expert: Inside codecs', *ibc.org*, 26 February. Available at: www.ibc.org/manage/tech-expert-inside-codecs/5500.article.

McChesney, R. W. and Schiller, D. (2003) *The Political Economy of International Communications: Foundations for the Emerging Global Debate about Media Ownership and Regulation*, Geneva: The United Nations Research Institute for Social Development.

McGrath, J. and Vachhrajani, I. (2020) 'Opening keynote: Cloud city: A&E network's cloud journey and lessons learned', *AWS Insights Online Conference*, 28 May. Available at: https://onlinexperiences.com/scripts/Server.nxp.

McLuhan, M. (1962) *The Gutenberg Galaxy: The Making of the Typographic Man*, Toronto: University of Toronto Press.

———(1964) *Understanding Media*, London: Routledge.

McVay, J. (2015) 'There is no reason to change ToT', *Broadcast*, 27 November: 8.

Medianova (2020) 'Webinar – the state of private CDN in 2020, and how you can use it for edge computing', *medianova.com*, 9 June. Available at: www.medianova.com/en-blog/2020/06/09/webinar-recap-the-state-of-private-cdn-in-2020.

Mercer, C. (2018) 'A history of UK broadband roll out: BT, Openreach and other major milestones', 23 July. Available at: www.computerworld.com/article/3412338/a-history-of-uk-broadband-roll-out–bt-openreach-and-other-major-milestones.html#slide3.

Microsoft (2020) 'What is the cloud?', *azure.microsoft.com*. Available at: https://azure .microsoft.com/en-gb/overview/what-is-the-cloud.

Middleton, R. (2015) 'MTG offloads Russian nets', 26 October. Available at: www .c21media.net.

———(2019a) 'The drama of distribution', *TBI Distributor Survey*, October/November: 22–5.

———(2019b) 'Endemol Shine closes China office, William Tan to depart', *tbivision.com*, 7 November. Available at: https://tbivision.com/2019/11/07/endemol-shine-closes-china-office-william-tan-to-step-down.

————(2019c) 'Screening thoughts', *C21 Media*, 20 February. Available at: www.c21media
.net/screening-thoughts.

————(2019d) 'Turkey retains flavour', *C21 Media*, 24 April. Available at: www.c21media
.net/turkey-retains-flavour.

————(2021) 'Life after Netflix', *TBI UK Screenings*, February/March: 6–8.

Middleton, R. and J. Easton (2021) 'HBO Max won't launch in UK, Germany or Italy until Sky deal ends in 2025', *tbivision.com*, 23 March. Available at: https://tbivision .com/2021/03/23/hbo-max-wont-launch-in-uk-germany-or-italy-until-sky-deal-ends-in-2025.

Mikos, L. (2020) 'Transnational television culture', in S. Shimpach (ed.) *The Routledge Companion to Global Television*, New York, NY: Routledge, pp. 74–83.

Milberg, W., Jiang, X., and Gereffi, G. (2014), 'Industrial policy in the era of vertically specialized industrialization', in J. M. Salazar-Xirinachs, I. Nübler, and R. Kozul-Wright (eds.), *Transforming Economies: Making Industrial Policy Work for Growth, Jobs and Development*, Geneva: International Labour Organization, pp. 151–78.

Milberg, W. and Winkler, D. (2013) *Outsourcing Economics: Global Value Chains in Capitalist Development*, Cambridge: Cambridge University Press.

Miller, R. (2019) *Hyperscale Data Centers – Date Center Frontier Special Report*, Data Center Frontier.

Miroudot, S. and Ragoussism A. (2009) 'Vertical trade, trade costs and FDI', *OECD Trade Policy Papers*, No. 89, Paris: OECD.

Mittel, J. (2009) *Television and American Culture*, New York, NY: Oxford University Press.

Ministry of Culture, Sports and Tourism and Kocca (2020) *2019 Broadcasting Industry White Paper*, Seoul: Ministry of Culture, Sports and Tourism and Kocca.

Mohney, D. (2020) 'AWS ground station connects the Amazon cloud to space satellites', *datacenterfrontier.com*, 2 June. Available at: https://datacenterfrontier.com/aws-ground-station-connects-the-amazon-cloud-to-space-satellites.

Montalbano, E. (2005) 'Microsoft, RealNetworks Settle for $761 million', *PCWorld.com*, 11 October. Available at: www.pcworld.com/article/122978/article.html.

Moran, A. (1998) *Copycat Television: Globalisation, Program Formats and Culture Identity*, Luton: University of Luton Press.

————(2013) 'Global television formats: genesis and growth', *Critical Studies in Television*, 8(2): 1–19.

Morley, D. and Robins, K. (1995) *Spaces of Identity: Global Media, Electronic Landscapes and Cultural Boundaries*, London: Routledge.

MPEG (2020) 'About MPEG', *Moving Picture Experts Group*. Available at: https://mpeg .chiariglione.org/about.

Mytton, G., Teer-Tomaselli, R., and Tudesq, A.-J. (2005) 'Transnational television in sub-Saharan Africa', in J. Chalaby (ed.) *Transnational Television Worldwide: Towards a New Media Order*. London: I. B. Tauris, pp. 96–127.

Ndlela, M. N. (2017) 'TV formats in anglophone Africa: The hegemonic role of South Africa in the TV format value chain', *International Journal of Digital Television*, 8(1): 47–64.

Nederveen Pieterse, J. (2001) 'Hybridity, so what? The anti-hybridity backlash and the riddles of recognition', *Theory, Culture & Society*, 18(2–3): 219–45.

Negrine, R. (ed.) (1988) *Satellite Broadcasting: The Politics and Implications of the New Media*, London: Routledge.

Netflix (2018) *2017 Annual Report*, Los Gatos, CA: Netflix.

———(2021) *2020 Annual Report*, Los Gatos, CA: Netflix.

———(2022) Global Top 10, *top10.netflix.com*, 18 November. Available at: https://top10 .netflix.com/tv-non-english.html.

Nicas, J., Weise, K., and M. Isaac (2019) 'How each big tech company may be targeted by regulators', *nytimes.com*, 8 September. Available at: www.nytimes.com/2019/09/08/ technology/antitrust-amazon-apple-facebook-google.html.

Nicolaou, A. and Rennison, J. (2019) 'Netflix changes the way TV production is paid for', *ft.com*, 16 April. Available at: www.ft.com/content/cf0f0bd6-4596-11e9-a965-23d669740bfb.

Nordenstreng, K. (1984) *The Mass Media Declaration of Unesco*, Norwood, NJ: Ablex Publishing.

Nordenstreng, K. and Schiller, H. I. (eds.) (1979) *National Sovereignty and International Communication*, Norwood, NJ: Ablex Publishing Corporation.

Noxinfluencer.com (2021a) 'Top 100 most subscribed Youtubers', 8 May. Available at: www.noxinfluencer.com/youtube-channel-rank/top-100-all-all-youtuber-sorted-by-subs-weekly.

———(2021b) 'Top 100 Most Subscribed Youtubers in India, 8 May. Available at: www.noxinfluencer.com/youtube-channel-rank/top-100-in-all-youtuber-sorted-by-subs-weekly.

OCWG (2019a) *SubOptic Open Cables Working Group Update*, 8 April. Available at: https://suboptic2019.com/suboptic-2019-papers-archive.

———(2019b) *Subsea Open Cables: A Practical Perspective on the Guidelines and Gotchas*, 8 April. Available at: https://suboptic2019.com/suboptic-2019-papers-archive.

Ofcom (2006), *Review of the Television Production Sector: Consultation Document*, London: Ofcom.

———(2019) *Media Nations: UK 2019*, London: Ofcom.

———(2021) *Media Nations: UK 2021*, London: Ofcom.

O'Halloran, J. (2019) 'India set for 'negligible' pay-TV revenue growth over next five years', 24 September, *Rapidtvnews.com*. Available at: www.rapidtvnews.com/ 2019092457396/india-set-for-negligible-pay-tv-revenue-growth-over-next-five-years .html#axzz6H8oPXSbu.

———(2020a) 'A+E Networks UK moves EMEA broadcast operations to the cloud', 14 July, *Rapidtvnews.com*. Available at: www.rapidtvnews.com/2020071458766/a-e-networks-uk-moves-emea-broadcast-operations-to-the-cloud.html#axzz6VYiUqRN9.

———(2020b) 'Major US pay-TV providers lose 5MN subscribers in 2019, 4 March, *Rapidtvnews.com*. Available at: www.rapidtvnews.com/2020030458158/major-us-pay-tv-providers-lose-5mn-subscribers-in-2019.html#axzz6H8oPXSbu.

———(2021) 'Discovery breaks records for Olympic digital engagement, sues Polish government', 13 August, *Rapidtvnews.com*. Available at: www.rapidtvnews.com/

2021081361030/discovery-breaks-records-for-olympic-digital-engagement-sues-polish-government.html#axzz741dKE1i6.

Oh, D. C. (2017) 'K-Pop fans react: Hybridity and the white celebrity-fan on YouTube', *International Journal of Communication*, 11: 2270–87.

Oliver, J. J. and Picard, R. G. (2020) 'Shaping the corporate perimeter in a changing media industry', *International Journal on Media Management*, 22(2): 67–82.

Oliver and Ohlbaum (2021) *UK Television Production Survey: Financial Census 2021*, London: Pact.

Olwan, R. M. (2013) *Intellectual Property and Development: Theory and Practice*, New York, NY: Springer.

Pact (2008) *Response to OFCOM PSB Review: Phase 1*, London: Pact.

———(2018) *UK TV Exports: A Global View in 2016/17*, London: Pact.

Page, D. and Crawley, W. (2005) 'The transnational and the national: Changing patterns of cultural influence in the South Asian TV market', in J. Chalaby (ed.) *Transnational Television Worldwide: Towards a New Media Order*, London: I. B. Tauris, pp. 128–55.

Pager, S. A. (2012), 'Accentuating the positive: Building capacity for creative Industries into the development agenda for global intellectual property law', *American University International Law Review*, 28(1): 223–94.

Panettieri, J. (2018) 'Cloud market share 2018 by region: Amazon AWS, Microsoft Azure, Google, IBM', *CHANNELe2e.com*, 2 August. Available at: www.channele2e.com/channel-partners/csps/cloud-market-share-2018-aws-microsoft-google.

Parker, G. G., Van Alstyne, M. W., and Choudary, S. P. (2016) *Platform Revolution: How Networked Markets Are Transforming the Economy and How to Make Them Work for You*, New York, NY: W. W. Norton.

Park, J. and Lee, A.-G. (eds.) (2019) *The Rise of K-Dramas: Essays on Korean Television and its Global Consumption*, Jefferson, NC: McFarland & Company.

Parks, L. and N. Starosielski (2015) *Signal Traffic: Critical Studies of Media Infrastructures*, Urbana: University of Illinois Press.

Parrot Analytics (2019) *The Global Television Demand Report: Global SVOD Platform Demand Share, Digital Original Series Popularity and Gender Demand Share Trends in 2018*, Los Angeles, CA: Parrot Analytics.

Paterson, C. and Sreberny, A. (eds.) (2004) *International News in the 21st Century*, Eastleigh: John Libbey.

Pathan, M, Buyya, R., and Vakali, A. (2008) 'Content delivery networks: State of the art, insights, and imperatives', in R. Buyya, M. Pathan, and A. Vakali (eds.), *Content Delivery Networks*, Berlin: Springer, pp. 3–32.

Paul, K. (2020) 'Trump bid to ban TikTok and WeChat: where are we now?', 29 September, *theguardian.com*. Available at: www.theguardian.com/technology/2020/sep/29/trump-tiktok-wechat-china-us-explainer.

Pawley, E. (1972) *BBC Engineering 1922–1972*, London: British Broadcasting Corporation.

Peil, C. and Sparviero, S. (2017) 'Media convergence meets deconvergence', in S. Sparviero, C. Peil, and G. Balbi (eds) *Media Convergence and Deconvergence: Global*

Transformations in Media and Communication Research, Cham: Palgrave Macmillan, pp. 3–30.

Pennington, A. (2011). Surviving then, thriving in 2010. *Broadcast – Business Book*: 14–15.

———(2014). Eventful year for OB firms. *Broadcast*, 12 December: 39–41.

———(2019) 'Netflix original: Inside Netflix's post-production operation', *ibc.org*, 8 April. Available at: www.ibc.org/trends/netflix-original-inside-netflixs-post-production-oper ation/3720.article?utm_source=Adestra&utm_medium

Philips, W. (1997) 'Bored with the USA?', *Broadcast*, 10 January: 30.

Phillips, K. (2020) Presentation in 'Exploring UK production, commissioning & international potential', *TBI Talks*, 30 July. Available at: https://tinyurl.com/2p9cd7h4.

Picard, R. G. (2002) *The Economics and Financing of Media Companies*, New York, NY: Fordham University Press.

Picard, R. G. and Wildman, S. S. (eds.) (2015) *Handbook on the Economics of the Media*, Cheltenham: Edward Elgar Publishing.

Pietrobelli, C., and Rabellotti, R. (2006) 'Clusters and value chains in Latin Americas: In search of an integrated approach', in C. Pietrobelli and R. Rabellotti (eds.), *Upgrading to Compete: Global Value Chains, Clusters and SMEs in Latin America*, New York, NY: Inter-American Development Bank, pp. 1–40.

Plummer, L. (2017) 'This is how Netflix's top-secret recommendation system works', *wired .co.uk*, 22 August. Available at: www.wired.co.uk/article/how-do-netflixs-algorithms-work-machine-learning-helps-to-predict-what-viewers-will-like.

Ponte, S. and Sturgeon, T. J. (2014) 'Explaining governance in global value chains: A modular theory-building effort', *Review of International Political Economy*, 21(1): 195–223.

Porter, J. (2021) 'Amazon buys MGM for $8.45 billion', *theverge.com*, 26 May. Available at: www.theverge.com/2021/5/26/22441644/amazon-mgm-acquisition-prime-video-subscription-service-james-bond.

Porter, M. E. (1985). *Competitive Advantage: Creating and Sustaining Superior Performance*, New York, NY: Free Press.

Potter, I. (2008) *The Rise and Rise of the Independents*, Isleworth: Guerilla.

Pratt, A. and Gornostaeva, G. (2009) 'The governance of innovation in the film and television industry: A case study of London, UK', in A. Pratt and P. Jeffcut (eds.), *Creativity, Innovation and the Cultural Economy*, London: Routledge, pp. 119–36.

Raikes, P., Jensen, M. F., and Ponte, S. (2000) 'Global commodity chain analysis and the French *filière* approach: comparison and critique', *Economy and Society*, 29(3): 390–417.

Raj-Reichert, G. (2019) 'The role of transnational first-tier suppliers in GVC governance', in S. Ponte, G. Gereffi, and G. Raj-Reichert (eds.) *Handbook on Global Value Chains*, Cheltenham: Edward Elgar, pp. 354–69.

Randolph, M. (2019) *That Will Never Work: The Birth of Netflix and the Amazing Life of an Idea*, London: Endeavour.

Rantanen, T. (2009) *When News Was New*, Chichester: Wiley-Blackwell.

Rapidtvnews (2021) 'Netflix, Disney+ Hotstar account for half of SVOD subscribers in India', *rapidtvnews.com*, 31 March. Available at: https://tinyurl.com/vex9k4b7.

Rayburn, D. (2016) 'The early history of the streaming media industry and the battle between Microsoft & Real', *streamingmediablog.com*, 9 March. Available at: hwww .streamingmediablog.com/2016/03/history-of-the-streaming-media-industry .html#disqus_thread.

Reith J. C. W. (1924) *Broadcast over Britain*, London: Hodder and Stoughton.

Richardson, I. E. (2010) *The H.264 Advanced Video Compression Standard*, 2nd ed., Chichester: Wiley.

Riffaterre, M. (1984) *Semiotics of Poetry*, Bloomington: Indiana University Press.

Roach, C. (1997) 'The Western world and the NWICO: United they stand?' in P. Golding and P. Harris (eds.), *Beyond Cultural Imperialism*, London: Sage, pp. 94–116.

Robins, K. and Aksoy, A. (2005) 'Whoever looks always finds: Transnational viewing and knowledge-experience', in J. Chalaby (ed.) *Transnational Television Worldwide: Towards a New Media Order*, London: I. B. Tauris, pp. 14–42.

Rochet, J.-C. and Tirole, J. (2003) 'Platform competition in two-sided markets', *Journal of the European Economic Association*, 1(4): 990–1029.

Roddick, N. (1998) 'Brits track the vital mix', *Broadcast – Mipcom pull-out*, 2 October: 20–1.

Rogers, R. (ed.) (2019) *Understanding Esports: An Introduction to the Global Phenomenon*, London: Lexington Books.

Russell, A. L. (2014) *Open Standards and the Digital Age*, Cambridge: Cambridge University Press.

Ryan, M. and Littleton, C. (2017) 'TV series budgets hit the breaking point as costs skyrocket in peak TV era', *variety.com*, 26 September. Available at: https://variety.com/ 2017/tv/news/tv-series-budgets-costs-rising-peak-tv-1202570158.

Rysman, M. (2009) 'The economics of two-sided markets', *Journal of Economic Perspectives*, 23(3): 125–43.

Sakr, N. (2005) 'Maverick or model? Al-Jazeera's impact on Arab satellite television', in J. Chalaby (ed.) *Transnational Television Worldwide: Towards a New Media Order*, London: I. B. Tauris, pp. 66–95.

Sandvine (2022) *The Global Internet Phenomena Report*. San Jose, CA: Sandvine.

Scannell, P. (1990) 'Public service broadcasting: The history of a concept', in A. Goodwin and G. Whannel (eds.) *Understanding Television*, London: Routledge, pp. 11–29.

Schiller, H. I. ([1969] 1992) *Mass Communications and American Empire*, 2nd ed., Boulder, CO: Westview.

Schmidt, E. and Rosenberg, J. (2017) *How Google Works*, London: John Murray.

Schneider, M. (2022) 'Peak TV tally: According to FX research, a record 559 original scripted series aired in 2021', *variety.com*, 14 January. Available at: https://variety.com/ 2022/tv/news/original-tv-series-tally-2021-1235154979.

Schramm, W. (1964) *Mass Media and National Development: The Role of Information in the Developing Countries*, Stanford, CA: Stanford University Press; Paris: Unesco.

Schudson, M. (1978) *Discovering the News*, New York, NY: Basic Books.

Schumpeter, J. A. (1947) *Capitalism, Socialism, and Democracy*, 2nd ed., New York, NY: Harper & Brothers.

Scott A. J. (2005) *On Hollywood: The Place, The Industry*, Princeton, NJ: Princeton University Press.

Seib, P. (2012) (ed.) Al Jazeera English: Global news in a changing world, New York, NY: Palgrave Macmillan.

Sendall, B. (1983) *Independent Television in Britain, Volume 2: Expansion and Change, 1958–68*, London: Macmillan.

Seufert, M., Eggger, S., Slanina, M., Zinner, T., Hossfeld, T., and Tran-Gia, P. (2015) 'A survey on quality of experience of HTTP adaptive streaming, *IEEE Communication Surveys & Tutorials*, 17(1): 469–92.

Shifman, L. (2011) 'An anotomy of a YouTube meme', *New Media & Society*, 14(2): 187–203.

Shimpach, S. (ed.) (2020) *The Routledge Companion to Global Television*, New York, NY: Routledge.

Shultz, G. P. (1984) 'Letter from U.S. Secretary of State George P. Shultz', *Journal of Communication*, 34(4): 82–4.

Sigismondi, P. (ed.) *World Entertainment Media: Global, Regional and Local Perspectives.* New York, NY: Routledge.

Sky Group (2021) 'Comcast and ViacomCBS announce "SkyShowtime", a new streaming service to launch in select European markets', 18 August, *skygroup.sky*. Available at: www.skygroup.sky/article/comcast-and-viacomcbs-announce-skyshowtime-a-new-streaming-service-to-launch-in-select-european-markets.

Sloman, J., Garratt, D., Guest, J., and Jones, E. (2016) *Economics for Business*, Harlow: Pearson.

Smalley, E. (1993) 'Fast forward to LAN-based video', *Network Week*, 10(30): 39–42.

Smith, A. with Paterson, R. (eds.) (1998) *Television: An International History*, Oxford: Oxford University Press.

SMPTE (2019) 'About standards', *smpte.org*. Available at: www.smpte.org/standards/about.

Société Européenne des Satellites (2021) *Annual Report 2020*, Luxembourg: SES.

Srnicek, N. (2017) *Platform Capitalism*, Cambridge: Polity.

Starks M. (2013) *The Digital Television Revolution: Origins to Outcomes*, Basingstoke: Palgrave Macmillan.

Starosielski, N. (2015) *The Undersea Network*, Durham, NC: Duke University Press.

Steinberg, M. (2019) *The Platform Economy: How Japan Transformed the Consumer Internet*, Minneapolis: University of Minnesota Press.

Stocker, V., Smaragdakis, G., Lehr, W., and S. Bauer (2017) 'The growing complexity of content deliver y networks: Challenges and implications for the internet ecosystem', *Telecommunications Policy* 41(10): 1003–16.

Straubhaar, J. (1991) 'Beyond media imperialism: Asymmetrical interdependence and cultural proximity', *Critical Studies in Media Communication*, 8(1): 29–59.

Stronge, T. (2020) 'How much growth is too much growth?', *Pacific Telecommunications Council Annual Conference*, 19–22 January, Honolulu, HI.

Sturgeon, T. J. (2002) 'Modular production networks: A new American model of industrial organization', *Industrial and Corporate Change*, 11(3): 451–96.

———(1999) *Turn-Key Production Networks: Industry Organization, Economic Development, and the Globalization of Electronics Contract Manufacturing*, PhD Dissertation, Berkeley: University of California at Berkeley.

———(2009) 'From commodity chains to value chains: Interdisciplinary theory building in an age of globalization', in J. Bair (ed.) *Frontiers of Commodity Chain Research*, Stanford, CA: Stanford University Press, pp. 110–35.

———(2019) 'Upgrading strategies for the digital economy', *Global Strategy Journal*, 11(1): 34–57.

Sturgeon T. J. and Florida, R. (2004) 'Globalization, deverticalization and employment in the motor vehicle industry', in M. Kenney and R. Florida (eds.), *Locating Global Advantage: Industry Dynamics in the International Economy*, Stanford CA: Stanford University Press, pp. 52–81.

Sturgeon, T. J., Humphrey, J., and Gereffi, G. (2011) 'Making the global supply base', in G. Hamilton, M. Petrovic, and B. Senauer (eds.), *The Market Makers: How Retailers Are Reshaping the Global Economy*, Oxford: Oxford University Press, pp. 231–54.

Sturgeon, T. J. and Kawakami, M. (2010) 'Global value chains in the electronics industry: Was the crisis a window of opportunity for developing countries?', *Policy Research Working Paper 5417*. Washington, DC: The World Bank.

Sturgeon T. J. and Lee, J.-R. (2005) 'Industry co-evolution: A comparison of Taiwan and North American electronics contract manufacturers', in S. Berger and R. K. Lesters (eds.), *Global Taiwan: Building Competitive Strengths in a New International Economy*, Armonk, NY: M. E. Sharpe, pp. 33–75.

Sturen, O. (1972) 'Towards international standardization', *Technical News Bulletin*, 56(1), January: 236–7, 250.

———(1997) 'The expansion of the ISO: Decade by decade', in *Friendship among Equals: Recollections from ISO's First Fifty Years*, ISO: Geneva, pp. 57–67.

Sullivan, D. and Jiang, Y. (2010) 'Media convergence and the impact of the Internet on the M&A activity of large media companies', *Journal of Media Business Studies*, 7(4), 21–40.

Susen, S. (2015) *The 'Postmodern Turn' in the Social Sciences*, Basingstoke: Palgrave Macmillan.

Swartz, J. (2020) 'Big Tech keeps getting bigger, as antitrust inquiries continue to multiply', *marketwatch.com*, 12 February. Available at: www.marketwatch.com/story/big-tech-keeps-getting-bigger-as-antitrust-inquiries-continue-to-multiply-2020-02-11.

Synergy (2020) *Hyperscale Market Primer Report*, March. London: Synergy.

Taubman, A., Hannu, W., and Watal, J. (eds.) (2012) *A Handbook on the WTO TRIPS Agreement*, Cambridge: Cambridge University Press.

TBI Formats (2014) 'Europe's most valuable formats', April/May: 22–5.

Thomas, A. O. (1998) 'Transnational satellite television and advertising in South East Asia', *Journal of Marketing Communications*, 4(4): 221–36.

Thussu, D. K. (2002) 'Privatizing intelsat: Implications for the global South', in M. Raboy (ed.) *Global Media Policy in the New Millennium*, Luton: University of Luton Press, pp. 39–53.

———(2005) 'The transnationalization of television: The Indian experience', in J. Chalaby (ed.) *Transnational Television Worldwide: Towards a New Media Order*, London: I. B. Tauris, pp. 156–72.

———(2019) *International Communication: Continuity and Change*, 3rd ed., London: Bloomsbury Academic.

Tobagi, F. A., Pang, J., and Baker, B. A. ([1993], 1996) 'Starworks – A video application server', pp. 84–100 in S. Reisman (ed.) *Multimedia Computing: Preparing for the 21st Century*, Harrisburg, PA: Idea Group Publishing.

Tomlinson, J. (1991) *Cultural Imperialism: A Critical Introduction*, London: Continuum.

———(1997) 'Cultural globalization and cultural imperialism', in A. Mohammadi (ed.) *International Communication and Globalization: A Critical Introduction*, London: Sage, pp. 170–90.

Torre, P. J. (2009) 'Block booking migrates to television: The rise and fall of the international output deal', *Television & New Media*, 10(6): 459–81.

Tracey, M. (1985) 'The poisoned chalice? International television and the idea of dominance', *Daedalus*, 114(4): 17–56.

Turton, J. and L. Opie (2019) 'Global gamechangers: Creative challenges and digital giants', *IBC Show 2019*, 12–16 September, Amsterdam. Available at: www.ibc.org/global-gamechangers-creative-challenges-and-digital-giants/4711.article.

Tydeman, J. and E. J. Kelm (1986) *New Media in Europe: Satellites, Cable, VCRs and Videotex*, London: McGraw-Hill.

Ulin, J. C. (2019) *The Business of Media Distribution: Monetizing Film, TV, and Video Content in an Online World*, 3rd ed., New York, NY: Routledge.

UNCTAD (2013) *World Investment Report 2013: Global Value Chains: Investment and Trade for Development*, Geneva: United Nations.

———(2017) *World Investment Report 2017: Investment and the Digital Economy*, Geneva: United Nations.

Uribe-Jongbloed, E. and Pis Diez, E. (2017) 'The TV format market in Latin America: Trends and opportunities', *International Journal of Digital Television*, 8(1): 99–115.

Vachhrajani, I. (2020) 'Opening keynote: Cloud city: A&E network's cloud journey and lessons learned', *AWS Insights Online Conference*, 28 May. Available at: https://onlineexperiences.com/scripts/Server.nxp.

Valderrama, F. (1995) *A History of UNESCO*, Paris: UNESCO.

van Bavel, B. J. P. (2020) 'Open societies before market economies: Historical analysis', *Socio-Economic Review*, 18(3): 795–815.

Van Keulen, J., Bauwens, J., and Krijnen, T. (2020) '"Everyone working a little more closely together": Transnationalization of creative production in TV production conglomerates', *Television & New Media*, 21(7): 749–67.

Verevis, C. and Perkins, C. (2015) 'Transnational television remakes', *Continuum*, 29(6): 677–83.

Vickers, G. (1994) 'Secrets of the hard sell', *Broadcast MIPCOM Supplement*, 7 October: 22–3.

Vogel, H. L. (2020) *Entertainment Industry Economics: A Guide for Financial Analysis*, 10th ed., Cambridge: Cambridge University Press.

Volkmer, I. (2014) *The Global Public Sphere: Public Communication in the Age of Reflective Interdependence*, Cambridge: Polity.

Von der Leyen, U. (2019) *A Union that Strives for More: My Agenda for Europe*, 9 October, Luxembourg: Publications Office of the European Union.

Waade, A. M., Redvall, E. N., and Jensen, P. (eds.) (2020) *Danish Television Drama: Global Lessons from a Small Nation*. London: Palgrave Macmillan.

Waisbord, S. (2004) 'McTV: Understanding the global popularity of television formats', *Television & New Media*, 5(4): 359–83.

Waller, E. (2010) 'Israeli format wave arrives', *c21media.net*, 20 April. Available at: www .c21media.net/israeli-format-wave-arrives.

Wallerstein, I. (1983) *Historical Capitalism*, London: Verso.

———(1974) *The Modern World-System I: Capitalist Agriculture and the Origins of the European World-Economy in the Sixteenth Century*, San Diego, CA: Academic Press.

———(1980) *The Modern World-System II: Mercantilism and the Consolidation of the European World-Economy, 1600-1750*, New York, NY: Academic Press.

———(1983) *Historical Capitalism*, London: Verso.

———(1984) 'World networks and the politics of the world economy', in *The Politics of the World-Economy: The States, the Movement and the Civilizations*. Cambridge and Paris: Cambridge University Press and Maison des Sciences de l'Homme, pp. 1–12.

———(1989) *The Modern World-System III: The Second Era of Great Expansion of the Capitalist World-Economy, 1730–1840s*, San Diego, CA: Academic Press.

Walt Disney (2019a) *Fiscal Year 2019 Annual Financial Report*, Burbank, CA: The Walt Disney Company.

———(2019b) *Investor Day*, 11 April. Burbank, CA: The Walt Disney Company.

Wcitleaks.org (2012) 'Russia, UAE, China, Saudi Arabia, Algeria, Sudan, and Egypt: Proposals for the work of the conference', 5 December. Available at: http://files .wcitleaks.org/public/Merged%20UAE%2081212.pdf.

Weissmann, E. (2012) *Transnational Television Drama: Special Relations and Mutual Influence between the US and the UK*, Basingstoke: Palgrave Macmillan.

Wescott, T. (2021) 'Landing a format hit', *TBI Talks*, 2 March. Available at: http://tinyurl .com/2fbac6a6.

White, P. (2020) 'BBC & ITV-backed U.S. streamer Britbox hits 1M subscribers', *deadline .com*, 4 March. Available at: https://deadline.com/2020/03/britbox-1m-subscribers-1202873964.

Widdicks, K., Hazas, M., Bates, O., and Friday, A. (2019) 'Streaming, multi-screens and YouTube: The new (unsustainable) ways of watching in the home', *CHI 2019 Conference*, 4–9 May, Glasgow.

Williamson, M. (1988) 'Broadcasting by satellite: Some technical considerations', in R. Negrine (ed.) *Satellite Broadcasting: The Politics and Implications of the New Media*, London: Routledge, pp. 23–48.

Winseck, D. (2002) 'The WTO, emerging policy regimes and the political economy of transnational communications', in M. Raboy (ed.) *Global Media Policy in the New Millennium*, Luton: University of Luton Press, pp. 19–37.

——(2012) 'Financialization and the "crisis of the media": The rise and fall of (some) media conglomerates in Canada', in D. Winseck and D. Y. Jin (eds.), *The Political Economies of Media: The Transformation of the Global Media Industries*, London: Bloomsbury, pp. 142–66.

Winseck, D. and Pike, R. M. (2007) *Communication and Empire: Media, Markets, and Globalization, 1860–1930*, Durham, NC: Duke University Press.

Winseck, D. and Jin, D. Y. (2012) *The Political Economies of Media: The Transformation of the Global Media Industries*, London: Bloomsbury.

Wirz, B. W. (2017) *Media Management*, Speyer: German University of Administrative Sciences Speyer.

Wood, D. (2010) 'Indie chief with ambition', *Broadcast*, 16 July, 18–21.

Woodman, C. (1999) '15 years of intelligence', *Cable & Satellite Europe*, May: 32.

Woody, T. (2003) 'The race to kill Kazaa', *Wired.com*, 1 February. Available at: www.wired.com/2003/02/kazaa.

World Press Freedom Committee (ed.) (1981) *The Media Crisis . . .: The Problems Faced in UNESCO; the MacBride Commission Report; the New Information Order; the Challenges of Belgrade*, Miami, FL: World Press Freedom Committee.

WTO (2013) *International Trade Statistics 2013*, Geneva: WTO.

——(2016) 'Trade in value-added and global value chains: statistical profiles'. Available at: www.wto.org/english/res_e/statis_e/miwi_e/countryprofiles_e.htm.

——(2017) *Annual Report 2017*, Geneva: WTO.

Yates, J. and Murphy, C. N. (2019) *Engineering Rules: Global Standard Setting since 1880*, Baltimore, MD: Johns Hopkins University Press.

Zambelli, A. (2013) 'A history of media streaming and the future of connected TV', *theguardian.com*, 1 March. Available at: www.theguardian.com/media-network/media-network-blog/2013/mar/01/history-streaming-future-connected-tv.

Zanni, L. (2019) 'AI: Content chain analysis', *ibc.org*, 6 February. Available at: www.ibc.org/ai-a-content-chain-analysis/3572.article.

Zayani, M. (ed.) (2005) *The Al Jazeera Phenomoneon: Critical Perspectives on New Arab Media*, London: Pluto.

Zodiak Television (2008) *Annual Report: 2007 Was a Good Year*, Stockholm.

Index

5G network, 27

A&E Networks, 52
  and the cloud, 88, 140–1
Acorn TV, 73, 161
Advanced Research Projects Agency
  (ARPA), 75
Adventure Line Production, 113
advertising video on demand (AVoD), 3,
  63, 66
  leading platforms, 70–1
Africa, 178
  Nollywood, 187
  Transnational TV networks, 51
  TV producers, 40, 183, 187
Aggregation, 6, 27, 61, 102, 115–18, 143,
  148, 169–70, 181, 190
  definition, 115
Agreement on Trade-Related Aspects of
  Intellectual Property Rights (TRIPS),
  186
Akamai Technologies, 86, 138
Aksoy, Asu, 13
Alibaba, 141
All3Media, 111
Allocca, Kevin, 162
Alphabet, 71, 155–6
Amazon, 155
  Amazon CloudFront, 86, 138
  Amazon Fire TV, 64
  Amazon Video, 83
  Amazon Web Services (AWS), 80, 137,
    139–42, 169
  content investment, 61
  and undersea cable networks, 95

Amazon Prime Video, 27, 43, 60–1, 67, 72,
  101, 155, 160
  and content delivery networks (CDNs),
    137
  and TV producers, 150
Antioco, John, 144
Appadurai, Arjun, 12
Apple, 32, 82, 155
  and content delivery networks (CDNs),
    137
  App Store, 100
  content investment, 61
  iCloud, 100
  iTunes, 83
Apple TV, 27, 64
Apple TV+, 27, 43, 61, 67, 69, 155, 160
Armoza, Avi, 185
Arqiva, 125, 127
Arsenault, Amelia, 21
artificial intelligence and machine learning
  (AI/ML), 25, 142
Asia, 178, 184
  communications satellites, 51–4
  Transnational TV networks, 51–4
  TV formats, 49
  web application traffic share, 101
Aspera, 131
Asset specificity, 118, 145, 157
AT&T, 27, 30, 63, 73, 111, 131, 149

Bair, Jennifer, 18
Bakker, Gerben, 58
Banerjee, Indrajit, 13
Banijay, 46, 106–8, 111, 113, 169, 172, 179
Bartlett, Christopher A., 167–9

BBC, 38, 40, 43–4, 54, 66, 122, 125, 140, 150
  BBC Studios, 46, 111, 119
  BBC Worldwide, 106
  broadcast engineering, 122
  and the cloud, 88
  and content delivery networks (CDNs), 137
  introduction to television, 58
  iPlayer, 59, 88, 126, 129, 140
  media delivery outsourcing, 127–9
  and TV rights, 41–2
Beck, Ulrich, 15
Berners-Lee, Tim, 91
Beuve-Mery, Hubert, 12
Big Brother, 46–7, 106
Blockbuster, 144–5
Bloem, Adriaan, 137
Bloomberg TV+, 73
Boudreau, Yves, 139
Braudel, Fernand, 16
Brin, Sergey, 28, 178
BritBox, 66, 73, 161
British Telecom (BT), 77–8
  BT Media & Broadcast, 127
  BT Sport, 127, 129
broadcaster video on demand (BVoD), 3, 59, 70
broadcasting, 36, 45, 55–6, 120
  and history of sreen entertainment, 58–9
  and streaming, 1, 3–4, 59, 72, 99, 161, 190
  media delivery, 121–2, 126
BT Sport. *See* British Telecom (BT)
Burgess, Jean, 2

Cable TV, 58, 60
Canal Plus, 38
capitalism, 10
  and creative destruction, 144
  and financialisation, 32
  and globalisation, 15
  and GVCs, 2, 32
  and open societies, 175–6

  and television, 190
  and the world-system, 16
Castells, Manuel, 65–6
Caves, Richard, 31
CBS, 122
Cerf, Vint, 93
Channel 4 (UK), 38, 40, 105, 129, 140, 182
  4oD, 59
  All 4, 88
  media delivery outsourcing, 127–8
Chaplin, Charlie, 58
China, 8
  and the global media system, 178–9
  and IP rights, 188
  and media import restrictions, 186
China Telecom, 26
cinema, 58
cloud, the, 1, 25, 74, 86–9, 121, 170
  definition, 88
  infrastructure, 93–9
  and media delivery, 130
  providers, 140–2
clusters, 103
CNN, 49, 54
codecs, 92, 124
  and MPEG-1 81
Coe, Neil M., 22–3
Cold War, 11–12, 75
Comcast, 27, 30, 51–2, 63, 131, 140, 149, 169
  organisational configuration, 170
communications satellites, 49, 60, 74
  Astra 1A, 78
  Astra fleet, 78
  direct broadcast satellites (DBS), 76–7
  direct to home (DTH) satellites, 76–7
  European Communications Satellite (ECS) programme, 76
  Hotbird fleet, 78
  Intelsat 1, 75
  Syncom 2, 75
  Telstar 1, 75
  video neighbourhoods, 78–9

consolidation, 4, 6, 16, 24, 29–31, 102, 128
  and global suppliers, 153
  and media delivery, 130
  and scale, 111
  and TV production sector, 105–9, 111,
    118, 151
content creators. *See* TV producers *and*
    YouTubers
content delivery networks (CDNs)
  definition, 85
  providers, 87, 136–40
  and streaming delivery, 87
content market, 42, 116, 118, 147
Contractor, Farok J., 31
convergence, 29
  device, 25
  industrial, 25
cosmopolitanism, 14, 160–1
  and streaming platforms, 160–1
Craig, David, 27–8, 156
creative destruction, 143–4, 153
crunchyroll, 83
cultural imperialism thesis, 11–13
Cunningham, Stuart, 13, 27–8, 156

dailymotion, 71, 83
Dancing with the Stars, 46–8, 106
data centres, 85, 97–8, 140
  and AI/ML, 142
  and Netflix, 141
  and sustainability, 99
  and tech giants, 98
  and YouTube, 161
  hyperscalers, 97
DAZN, 73
Defoe, Daniel, 74
deterritorialisation, 13
  and the cloud, 87
Deutsche Telekom, 26
de-verticalisation. *See* vertical disintegration
Dicken, Peter, 23, 74
digital economy, 1, 4, 10, 25, 64, 189
digital video recorders (DVRs), 123

digitisation, 1, 4, 24–9, 50, 79–80, 190
direct to home (DTH) satellites, 76–9
Discovery, 30, 49–50, 52, 54, 61, 63, 110
  and the cloud, 88, 140
Discovery+, 73
Disney. *See* Walt Disney
Disney+, 30, 42, 61, 66–7, 69–70, 101, 160
  and content delivery networks (CDNs),
    137
  content investment, 62
Disney+ Hotstar, 60
Distraction Formats, 112
Dorfman, Ariel, 11
downloading, 83
  and streaming, 80
DramaFever, 72
Dyke, Greg, 128

economic upgrading, 20, 175, 180
Eisenstein, Elizabeth, 74
Endemol, 105, 108, 110, 172, 185
Endemol Shine, 108, 113, 179
equipment manufacturers, 104
Ericsson, 128
  acquisitions, 130–1
ESPN+, 72–3
European Commission
  digital strategy, 156
European Space Agency, 76
European Union (EU), 39, 175
Eutelsat, 76–8, 134–6

Facebook, 27, 30, 100–1, 155
  advertising revenue, 155
  and undersea cable networks, 95
Facebook Watch, 71
Fernandez-Stark, Karina, 19–20
fibre optic cables, 94–6, 98, *See also*
    undersea cable networks
filière approach, 21
filmstruck, 72
Flash Player, 82
flex, 134

Flynn, David, 111, 145–6
Fort Boyard, 113
free video on demand (FVoD), 3
Freeman, Christopher, 74
Fremantle, 46, 111, 179
FremantleMedia, 106
Frot-Coutaz, Cécile, 2, 162
fuboTV, 64

García Canclini, Néstor, 12–13
García Márquez, Gabriel, 12
Garvie, Wayne, 42
Gawer, Annabelle, 64–6
Gereffi, Gary, 9, 18–21, 180, 184
Ghoshal, Sumantra, 169
Glaser, Rob, 81
Global
    definition, 9
global commodity chain (GCC) analysis,
    17–18
global integration, 1, 7, 14, 33, 36, 56, 59,
    143, 146, 153, 157
global production network (GPN) analysis,
    22–3
global suppliers. *See* suppliers
global supply base. *See* shared supply base
Global TV industry, 2, 4, 15, 92, 169, 174,
    See also global TV system *and* TV
    industry
    and China, 8
    and GVC-oriented policy, 175, 180
    social and political values, 175–9
Global TV studios, 6, 106, 108–11, 119,
    189
    organisational configuration, 173
Global TV system, 4–5, 7, 37, 158, 179,
    190
global value chain (GVC) framework, 1, 4,
    10, 14–15, 157, 190–1
    dimensions, 21
    and GPN analysis, 22–3
    and Michael Porter, 22
    origins, 19

global value chains (GVCs)
    digital, 1
    and GVC-oriented policy, 179–80
    polarity, 153
    types of governance, 19–20
globalisation, 1–2, 7, 13–15, 24, 48, 157
    and the cloud, 87, 89
    and standards, 90
goldmines, 164
Goodson, Marc, 44–5
Google, 27–8, 101, 178
    advertising revenue, 155
    DeepMind, 142
    Google Cloud, 86, 141–2
    Google Cloud CDN, 138
    and undersea cable networks, 95
Google Video, 83
Got Talent, 46–7, 106, 160
Graz, Jean-Christophe, 91
Green, Joshua, 2
Green, Lucas, 111, 113
Greenaway, Sinead, 120, 129
Grey, Vince, 90
Griffiths, Ian, 43
Grundy, 105

Hastings, Reed, 28, 61, 144
Havens, Tim, 37
Hayu, 73
HBO, 52, 54, 60
HBO Max, 63, 66, 69
Herman, Edward S., 11
Hindhaugh, Jamie, 129, 152
Hopkins, Terence K., 17–18
Hulu, 63, 66, 69, 83
    Hulu Live, 64
hypertext transfer protocol (HTTP), 83–4

IBM, 98, 131, 141
Idols, 46–7, 106
IMDb TV, 71, 155
import substitution industrialisation (ISI)
    strategy, 184

industry co-evolution, 153
infrastructure, 5, 99, 120, 189
  broadcasting, 126, 129
  cable networks, 93–7
  cloud, the, 141
  content delivery networks (CDNs), 137
  data centres, 97–8
  definition, 93
  sustainability, 98–9
  YouTube, 161
Instagram, 71
Intelsat, 76, 79, 134–6
interdisciplinarity. *See* methodology
international
  definition, 8
international communication, 4, 10, 14–15, 23
  and free flow of communication, 11, 176–7
  history, 10–14
  methodology, 14–16
International Organization for Standardization (ISO), 90
International Telecommunication Union (ITU), 77
  and standards, 90–1
  World Conference on International Telecommunications (WCIT), 177
Internet Engineering Task Force (IETF), 91–2
internet protocol (IP) delivery, 1, 123, 126, 130–1, 170
  and globalisation, 174
  streaming, 80
internet protocol television (IPTV), 3–4, 25–6
Internet, the, 25, 32, 60, 74, 80, 122, 136
  and application traffic share, 99–100
  bubble, 82, 144
  and CDNs, 85
  and China, 179
  and data centres, 97

  and data infrastructure, 98
  and ITU, 177
  shutdowns, 178
  and standards, 92
iPlayer. *See* BBC iPlayer
Irokotv, 73
Irvine, Duncan, 183
Israel
  media policy, 184
  and the TV format trade, 185
  TV producers, 184
ITV, 38, 43–4, 49, 66, 73, 106, 122, 149, 182
  broadcast engineering, 122
  ITV Studios, 46, 107, 111, 113, 115
  media delivery outsourcing, 127, 129

Jacka, Elizabeth, 13
Japan, 38, 184
  TV format exports, 49
  and TV format trade, 185
Jin, Dal Yong, 30

Keane, Michael, 178
Kilpatrick, George, 169
Kirch group, 38
Kirch, Leo, 78
Kirpatrick, Jeane, 177
Korea
  TV exports, 39
  TV format exports, 49
Küng, Lucy, 22
Kyncl, Robert, 161

lead firms, 6, 36, 115, 142, 145–6, 151, 157, 189
  and global integration, 7, 56
  and GVC-oriented policy, 180, 182–3, 188
  and methodology, 15, 34
  organisational configuration, 170–2
  and outsourcing, 157
  revenue and market capitalisation, 149

lead firms (cont.)
  and suppliers, 19–20, 143, 151, 190
  and tech giants, 152–4
  and TV GVC, 189
Lee, Ji-Ren, 152
Lerner, Daniel, 11
Li and Fung, 133
Limelight Networks, 138
Lobato, Ramon, 61

MacBride, Seán, 12, 176–7
macromedia, 82
Mattelart, Armand, 11
McChesney, Robert W., 11
media delivery, 6, 189
  definition, 120
  and organisational configuration, 169–70
  publication, 123–4
  reception, 125
  suppliers, 151–2
  transmission, 124–5
mergers and acquisitions (M&As), 29–31,
    116, 145, 189
  and global TV studios, 108, 119
  and media tech, 130, 153
Meta. See Facebook
methodology, 8
  global communication approach, 14–16
Microsoft, 82, 86, 155
  Microsoft Azure, 87, 140–2
  Microsoft Azure CDN, 138
  and undersea cable networks, 95
Middle East, 178
  content market, 183
  media policy, 183–4
  transnational TV networks, 51
  TV producers, 183–4
Milberg, William, 31–2, 184, 188
minimum efficient scale
  and the CDN industry, 139
Mitele Plus Internacional, 73
Mittel, Jason, 2
modernisation theory, 11

Morley, David, 13
Mosaic, 81
Moving Picture Experts Group (MPEG),
    81
  and standards, 92
MTV Networks, 49–50, 52, 54, 159
  MTV Play, 73
  organisational configuration, 170–2
  and reality TV, 171
multinational companies
  digital multinational enterprises
    (MNEs), 25
  and open societies, 176
  organisational configurations, 167–9
Murdoch, Rupert, 78, 178
music festivals
  and communication satellites, 80

National Aeronautics and Space
    Administration (NASA), 75
NBCUniversal, 27, 63, 72, 106, 116
  NBCUniversal International Studios,
    111
Nederveen Pieterse, Jan, 13
NENT Studios, 111
NetAid, 82
Netflix, 27, 30, 43, 57, 60–1, 66–7, 83, 101,
    116, 145, 149
  and Blockbuster, 144
  and the cloud, 88, 140
  and the content market, 116
  content investment, 61
  and data centres, 141
  distribution at scale, 61
  localisation, 161
  and microservices architecture, 88
  and Open Connect, 137
  recommendation system and
    personalisation algorithms, 116–18
  and TV producers, 150
network theory. See also Castells, Manuel
New World Information and
    Communication Order, 12

New World Information and Communication
    Order (NWICO), 176–7
News Corp, 178
NextUp, 73
Nollywood, 187
non-rival consumption, 58

open societies, 175–6
    and market economy, 176
organisational configuration, 7, 158,
    167–74
outsourcing, 33
    and the CDN industry, 137
    definition, 31
    and media delivery, 120, 127–30

Page, Larry, 28, 178
Pager, Sean, 187
Paramount+, 67
Pawley, Edward, 122
Payne, Cathy, 111, 113–14
pay-TV, 61
    and direct to home (DTH) market, 78–9
    and streaming services, 56–7
Peacock, 63, 66, 72, 170
Pearson, 105–6
Picard, Robert, 22
Pietrobelli, Carlo, 180
platforms. *See also* streaming platforms
    industry, 65
    internal, 64
    multi-sided, 65
    network effects, 65–6
    streaming business models, 66–7
    supply chain, 65
    transaction, 65
    types, 64–6
Pluto TV, 71
policy, 7, 175
    GVC-oriented, 175, 180–8
Ponte, Stefano, 153
pop stars, 47
Porter, Michael, 21–2, 146

ports events
    and communication satellites, 79
post-production, 103–4
power asymmetries, 7, 19–20, 112, 143,
    182, 184
    and the TV GVC, 144–51
procurement, 151
Progressive Networks. *See* RealNetworks
ProSiebenSat.1, 149

Rabellotti, Roberta, 180
Randolph, Marc, 28, 61, 144
Rapid Blue (South Africa), 183
Rayburn, Dan, 82
reality TV, 106
    and MTV Networks, 171
    and post-production, 103
    and TV production companies, 106
RealNetworks, 81–2
RealVideo, 81
Red Arrow Entertainment, 106–7, 111
Red Bee Media, 127–8, 169–70
Redstone, Sumner, 178
research companies, 104
Robins, Kevin, 13
Rochet, Jean-Charles, 65
Rodrigue, Michel, 48
Roku, 64
RTL Group, 38, 106, 110, 149
    RTL channels, 53
Russia
    and the Internet, 178
    Sputnik, 75
Rysman, Marc, 65

Salto, 66
'SatCab' EU Directive, 50
scalability, 71
scale, 28
    and the CDN industry, 137–40
    and the cloud, 88
    and the digital economy, 189
    and global suppliers, 133

scale (cont.)
and streaming, 59–64
and TV production, 111–13
Scannell, Paddy, 74
Schiller, Herbert, 11
Schmidt, Eric, 28
Schramm, Wilbur, 11
Schumpeter, Joseph, 144, 153
Schumpter, Joseph, 143–4
Scott, Allen, 31
segmentation, 4, 6, 31, *See also* vertical
disintegration
and firm behaviour, 33
and vertical integration, 102, 118–19
Shahid, 73
shared supply base, 131, 153–4
Shifman, Limor, 162
Shine, 106, 108, 172
Shomi, 72
Shudder, 73
Shultz, George P., 177
Sinclair, John, 13
Sky, 27, 30, 38, 51, 57, 60–1, 63, 78, 123,
127, 142, 170
Sky Go, 64
SkyShowtime, 63
Snapchat, 71
Société Européenne des Satellites (SES),
77–9, 127, 134–6
Society of Motion Picture and Television
Engineers (SMPTE), 91
Sony, 131
SET India, 164
Sony Pictures Entertainment, 106
Sony Pictures Network India, 54
Sony Pictures Television, 106
Sony Pictures Television International
production, 111
Sputnik, 75
standards, 152, 154
and globalisation, 90
and GVCs, 89
and streaming delivery, 92
Stankey, John, 30

Star, 54, 63
Startlight Networks, 81
StarWorks, 81
Starz Play, 73
Stinehour, Josh, 121
Stocker, Volker, 139
streaming, 5, 56, 92, 148, 157, 160, *See also*
and creative destruction, 143–6
and the digital shift, 1
and downloading, 80
growth, 56–7
and history of screen entertainment, 57–9
and internet traffic share, 99–100
live, 126
origins, 80–2
and scale, 59
streaming delivery and streaming platforms
and broadcasting, 1, 3–4, 59, 72, 99, 161,
190
and video on demand (VoD), 80
streaming delivery
adaptive streaming, 83–4
codecs, 84
coding formats, 84–5
definition, 80
history, 80–2
and standards, 92
streaming platforms, 5, 66–73, 140, 160
and cosmopolitanism, 160–1
and drama, 38
internationalisation, 62–3
launch dates, 83
and tech giants, 155
and TV rights, 42–3, 114
and video consumption, 99
Sturen, Olle, 90
Sturgeon, Timothy J., 25, 152–3, 180, 184
subscription video on demand (SVoD), 3,
43, 60–1, 66
and content market, 42
and cosmopolitanism, 160–1
and pay-TV, 56–7
and streaming platforms, 67–70
UK viewing figures, 155

Sundance Now, 73
super-aggregators, 69
super-indies (UK), 106
suppliers, 6, 143, 157, 189
  global, 6, 120, 152–4, 157
  and global integration, 7
  internationalisation, 146–7
  and knowledge transfers, 134
  media delivery, 151–2
  and methodology, 15
  multi-sectoral, 120, 133–4, 152
  sector-specific, 120, 145–7, 157
  and TV GVC, 189
  TV production, 147–51
  turnkey, 133
Survivor, 47
Susen, Simon, 12

T Series, 164
Target Entertainment, 112
tech firms, 27–9
tech giants, 6, 131, 152
  and data centres, 98
  and sustainability, 99
  and TV industry, 154–6
  and undersea cable networks, 95
technology, 5, 24, 27, 74–89, 92–3, 99,
    104, 120, 129, 189
  AI/ML, 142
  and GVCs, 181
  and infrastructure, 93
telecom companies (telcos), 25–7, 30, 63
telefónica, 26, 30, 137
television. *See also* broadcasting *and*
    streaming
  definition, 154–6
  and tech giants, 154–6
  and video ecosystem, 99
Television without Frontiers EU Directive,
    50–1
Thompson, Mark, 128
TikTok, 27, 66, 71, 100–1, 186
Time Warner, 27, 30, *See also* WarnerMedia
Tirole, Jean, 65

Tobagi, Fouad A., 80–1
Todou, 83
Tomlinson, John, 12–13
trade publishers, 104
transactional video on demand, 3
transnational, 158
  definition, 8–9
  media firm, 173
  organisational configuration, 168–72
transnational TV networks, 158–9
transnationalism
  and YouTube, 161–7
transnationalisation, 7, 13
  and the cloud, 87
  and the global shift, 174
Tubi, 71
Tucker, Shane, 128
Turkey
  TV exports, 39
TV distribution
  definition, 113
  and TV rights, 114
TV formats, 160
  definition, 44
  game shows, 45
  and GVC-oriented policy, 184–6
  reality TV, 45
TV GVC, 4–5, 8, 24, 33–4, 36, 146, 157,
    179, 187, 189
  and connected value chains, 104
  content production, 102–19
  country participation, 180–9
  and creative destruction, 143–6
  and GVC-oriented policy, 175
  media delivery, 120–42
  modes of governance, 147–52
  organisational configurations, 169
  polarity, 153
TV industry, 1, 4–6, 14, 29, 33, 99, 101,
    120, 143, 146, 156, 189, *See also* global
    TV industry
  digitisation, 25
  global integration, 34, 37, 55, 146
  and global suppliers, 131

TV industry (cont.)
  globalisation, 157
  and satellite operators, 136
  streaming platforms, 56, 64–71
  and tech giants, 154–6
  and video ecosystem, 2
TV producers
  Africa, 40, 183, 187
  developing countries, 186
  Israel, 184
  and lead firms, 147–51
  Middle East, 183–4
  and scale, 119
  and streaming market, 145
  and the streaming market, 157
  as suppliers, 147–51
  and TV formats, 45
TV production, 102–13
  and British policy, 181–3
  central hub, 113
  creativity, 172
  and organisational configuration, 172–3
  sector, 105–11, 118, 150, 175, 181–4,
    186, 188
  and the TV GVC, 151
TV rights, 41–3, 63, 114
  and transnational TV networks, 50
  and UK GVC-oriented policy, 182
TV series
  and deficit funding, 114
  trade, 37–41
  TV rights, 41–3
TV studios, 103
  Elstree Studios, 103
  Pinewood Group, 103
TV trade
  polycentrism, 40, 48, 55
  TV formats, 44–9
  TV series, 37–41
Twitch, 66, 71, 73, 155

UK
  Broadcasting Act 1990, 182
  Broadcasting Act 1996, 182

Communications Act 2003, 182–3
  foreign-language TV series, 40
  and GVC-oriented policy, 181–3
  media delivery case study, 121
  TV exports, 38
  TV format exports, 49
  and TV production sector, 150
  TV production sector, 105–6, 181–3
undersea cable networks. See also fibre optic
    cables
  and tech giants, 95
  and the Open Cables Working Group
    (OCWG), 95
  rates, 96
  telegraphic cables, 94, 96
UNESCO, 11–12
  and NWICO, 177
United Nations Conference on Trade and
    Development (UNCTAD), 21, 40–1,
    179–80, 187
upside flexibility, 139–40
USA
  antitrust inquiries, 156
  and communications satellites, 75
  Federal Communications Commission,
    122
  Financial Interest and Syndication Rules,
    105
  First Amendment, 175
  and the global TV system, 190
  and NWICO, 177
  Office of the United States Trade
    Representative, 188
  transnational TV network brands, 52
  TV exports, 38
  TV format exports, 49
  TV production sector, 105

van Bavel, Bas, 176
Verizon Digital Media Services, 138
vertical disintegration, 4, 24, 31, 156
  and GVCs, 31–3
vertical integration, 6, 30, 102, 108, 115,
    118–19, 131, 147

Vertue, Beryl, 41
Viacom, 178
ViacomCBS, 63
  and the cloud, 88
  content investment, 61
video codecs. *See* codecs
video ecosystem, 2, 80, 99–100, 118, 123
video neighbourhoods, 136
video on demand (VoD), 4, 123
video sharing, 3, 66
  and streaming platforms, 62
videocassette recorders (VCRs), 123
Viki, 40, 71, 73, 161
Vimeo, 83
virtual multichannel video programming
  distributors (vMVPDs), 64
von der Leyen, Ursula, 156

Wallerstein, Immanuel, 16–18, 144
Walt Disney, 30, 51–2, 62–3, 70, 73, 116,
  131, 149, 169
  content investment, 61
  organisational configuration, 170
  and video monetization, 69–70
Walter Presents, 40, 73, 161
Warner Bros., 106, 114
  Warner Bros. International Television
    Production, 111
Warner Bros. Discovery, 61, 63
WarnerMedia, 30, 63, 116
  content investment, 61
Wavve, 73
Who Wants to Be a Millionaire?, 46–7,
  106
Winkler, Deborah, 32
World Administrative Radio Conferences
  (WARC), 77
  and standards, 91

World Wide Web Consortium (W3C),
  91–2

Yeung, Henry Wai-Chung, 22–3
Youku, 83
Youngest Media, 111, 145–6
YouTube, 2, 27–8, 66, 71, 83, 100–1,
  155
  advertising revenue, 155
  Alexander, Jess, 164–5
  and content rights holders, 165–7
  Baby Shark Dance, 163
  channels, 163
  creators. *See* YouTubers
  Despacito, 162
  Edwards, Jamal, 164
  Free Documentary, 166
  Gangnam Style, 162
  The Great War, 164–5
  India's top channels, 164
  infrastructure, 161
  memes, 162–3
  monetisation, 66
  organisational configuration, 171–2
  Quintus Media, 166
  SBTV Music, 164
  scale, 62
  Sheeran, Ed, 164
  and sports leagues, 165–7
  transnationalism, 161–7
  viral videos, 162
  Wittig, Florian, 164–5
  YouTube TV, 64
  YouTubers, 62, 162–7, 172

Zee Entertainment, 51, 139, 164
Zein, Andy, 114
Zhang, Joy Danjing, 178

Printed in the United States
by Baker & Taylor Publisher Services

Printed in the United States
by Baker & Taylor Publisher Services